CW01430470

Fighting the Bolsheviks

WINDSOR CASTLE.

Soldiers of the United States, the people of the British Isles welcome you on your way to take your stand beside the Armies of many Nations now fighting in the Old World the great battle for human freedom.

The Allies will gain new heart & spirit in your company.

I wish that I could shake the hand of each one of you & bid you God speed on your mission.

George R.I.

April 1918.

Donald Eugene Carey

Upon arriving in Liverpool, England, on 3 August 1918 each man of the 339th Infantry was presented an envelope imprinted with: "A Message to You from His Majesty King George Vth." It contained a folded card on Windsor Castle stationery with the words of welcome shown above. Carey, whose ancestors fought against King George III on American soil, was proud to received this form letter from King George V.

Fighting the
Bolsheviks

The Russian War Memoir of
Private First Class Donald E. Carey,
U.S. Army, 1918–1919

Edited by Neil G. Carey

★
PRESIDIO

To all those men and women who answered their country's call during war or peace throughout the history of the United States.

Copyright © 1997 by Neil G. Carey

Published by Presidio Press
505 B San Marin Drive, Suite 300
Novato, CA 94945-1340

Library of Congress Cataloging-in-Publication Data

Carey, Donald E.
    Fighting the Bolsheviks : the Russian war memoirs of Private First Class Donald E. Carey, U.S. Army, 1918–1919 / edited by Neil G. Carey.
        p.   cm.
    ISBN 0-89141-631-5
    1. Carey, Donald E. 2. Soviet Union—History—Allied intervention, 1918–1920. 3. Soviet Union—History—Revolution, 1917–1921—Personal narratives, American. 4. Soviet Union—History—Revolution, 1917–1921—Participation, American. 5. Soldiers—United States—Biography. I. Carey, Neil G. II. Title.
DK265.42.U5C37   1997
947.084'1—dc21   97-16772
                                                                        CIP

Printed in the United States of America

Contents

Foreword

This book will find favor with all types of readers, from the casual to the academic researcher of the World War I history, for it is the story of one of the many-faceted roles the United States played in that defining conflict.

It is the author's laconic depiction of a young rural farm-bred school teacher who was transformed by his experiences during the rigors of boot camp, a brief training stay in Great Britain, and nearly a year in the trackless forests of northern Russia facing the threat of death from Bolsheviks while enduring arctic cold.

It is not the story of an adventurous farm boy thrown in the cauldron of war and emerging a battle-hardened hero. Far from it—Donald E. Carey defines at the outset what he perceives as his contribution in obeying his country's call to the colors. He wants nothing more than to be a private in the U.S. Army, do what he is told and return as quickly as possible to civilian life.

Forces well beyond his control soon intrude upon him. His fellow conscripts, many with foreign-origin names, are young men drawn from the big cities of Michigan, Wisconsin, and Indiana. He eschews their company and he is content to remain in camp visiting canteens and YMCA centers rather than exploring life in the cities and towns where he is stationed.

After his brief training by British instructors, he spent nine months doing duty. He spent the next nine months soldiering against the Bolsheviks in practically every battle and skirmish in northern Russia. There he endured sickness caused by lack of sanitation and unpalatable (and sometimes nonexistent) army rations. Carey had a difficult time coming to terms with the vermin he and other soldiers encountered. This was perhaps the one greatest thing that prevented him from forming a closer bond with the Russian peasants encountered in this strange land.

viii   FIGHTING THE BOLSHEVIKS

American soldiers arrived in northern Russia in late summer of 1918, disembarking at Archangel. They were told they were there essentially to prevent Germans from establishing a submarine base at Murmansk and to guard the tons of war material sent to the Russian Army before the Tsar was overthrown in 1917.

The new government of Marxist revolutionaries signed a peace treaty with Germany and Austria-Hungary in March 1918, thus eliminating the Eastern Front. Another reason for Allied intervention was to try to prevent the transfer of German troops, including prisoners of war, to bolster the German army in the west.

Other unstated reasons were to help re-establish the Eastern Front, taking the pressure off the Allies in the west, overthrowing the defacto Bolshevik government and making the world safe for democracy.

All this was to be done with 5,000 British and 5,000 American soldiers and few other token allies, with the British in the lead. It mattered little to those in command for the safety of Archangel that the Bolsheviks had seized every scrap of war material before the arrival of Carey and company, and nary a German was seen or heard from.

Carey was brought up as a strict Christian and practiced what he had been taught. While guarding the precious American supplies he was exposed to the venality of his fellow soldiers in pilfering those supplies and selling them to the eager-to-buy Russians. He also succumbed to a little pilfering himself to augment his meager rations. Carey describes how he underwent combat at lonely, snow-covered forest outposts in temperatures of 40 plus degrees below zero, without reinforcements or proper communications from headquarters at Archangel, confronting with his fellow soldiers an overwhelming number of Bolshevik troops fighting for their own land against untested conscripts who had little understanding of why they were there. We share with him his realistic thoughts of why they were trying to kill the enemy—for the simple reason to keep from getting killed by them.

After the armistice of November 1918 it was difficult to justify the American presence. Morale sank and grumbling rose, as it did for the British and the few French, Canadian, and Italian soldiers who were also fighting and dying in Northern Russia.

The practical-minded Carey, however, accepted the reality that he was in the U.S. Army and must accept the discipline of that institution. That acceptance sustained him and his comrades until, mercifully, they were given orders to return to the America and resume the lives they dreamed of in that primitive, cold land.

One must express admiration for the author's son, Neil G. Carey. His diligence and devotion to his father's memory inspired him to spend many tedious hours transcribing notes in almost illegible penciled form of various sizes on poor quality paper that the author was probably lucky to obtain. The book is a labor of love by a patient and devoted son, and we are the beneficiaries of that filial devotion.

F. R. Carroll, Ph. D.
President, The Great War Society

Preface

"We will remember," Nikita Khrushchev said in 1959 while visiting Los Angeles, "the grim days when American soldiers went to our soil . . . to combat the new revolution."

While on a visit to the Soviet Union in May 1972, President Nixon delivered a "Message of Friendship" over Moscow television, saying: "Most important of all, we have never fought one another in war."

In his 1984 State of the Union address, President Reagan told the Soviet Union, "Our sons and daughters have never fought each other."

Most other Americans are equally unaware of that historic time when American soldiers and sailors fought Russians revolutionaries—Bolsheviks—in north Russia and Siberia.

But Khrushchev was, and many other Russians are, well aware of those grim days.

This is the daily record and recollections of Pfc. Donald E. Carey, E Company, 339th Infantry Regiment, 85th Division (detachment in north Russia), one of the 5,600 American soldiers who fought the Bolsheviks there during 1918 and 1919.

Commanded by British generals; usually fed strange-tasting, unflavored British rations of inferior quality and inadequate quantity; giving unconscionably poor medical treatment; encountering the class system of England, and being looked down on by some British as uncouth colonists; none of this improved the morale of these "forgotten" American soldiers whose major battles were fought after the Armistice of 11 November 1918.

"Why are we here?" these American soldiers asked. They never received adequate answers. What meager information their officers possessed was soon made obsolete by events on the Western Front.

Some of the acknowledged reasons causing President Wilson to order American troops to Russia and Siberia:

1. He wanted to maintain an Eastern Front. With the collapse of the Czar's government in 1917, the Germans were able to move more than forty divisions and great quantities of matériel westward. Even more German fighting forces could be deployed to the Western Front after the Treaty of Brest-Litovsk, signed on 3 March 1918 by Germany and the Russian revolutionaries. Transfer of these German troops from the Eastern Front to the Western Front was expected to prolong the war until 1919–20.

2. Collapse of the Eastern Front would permit the Central Powers to obtain food, oil, and natural resources from Russia; plus allow ships to bring in supplies via Murmansk and Archangel, presently denied to Germany by the Allied blockade.

3. He was hoping to deny German U-boats access to bases at Murmansk, Kola, and Archangel, while preventing Germans and Finns in Finland from advancing eastward and capturing the food and supplies already piled in these ports.

4. Since 1914, massive quantities of Allied matériel of war—ordered by the czarist and Kerensky governments—had been landed at Murmansk, Kola, Archangel, and Vladivostok. Bolsheviks might use, or sell and deliver, some of the three hundred thousand tons of coal and two hundred thousand tons of matériel to the Central Powers.

5. He planned to support the White Russians, who were expected to form a stable and more democratic government that would acknowledge Russia's debts and foreign loans; all repudiated by the revolutionaries in February 1918—a great loss to the Allies.

6. Thousands of trained and armed men of the Allied Czech Legion, plus Czechs and Slovaks living in Russia, and Czechs captured from the Austro-Hungarian army and formed into fighting units along the Eastern Front, were on their way via the Trans-Siberian Railroad to Vladivostok. The Allies expected to move some of these troops by rail into northern Russia, where they would be reequipped and reorganized to fight on the Eastern Front; the remaining Czechs would be transported by rail and sea to the Western Front.

7. The Allies desired not to abandon those White Russians who had requested Allied military aid, for they would be liable to reprisals if the Reds were allowed to win the revolution. Northern Russia had not surrendered to the Reds in early 1918. The state of Archangel was the largest section of the Russian empire to be relatively free of violence, oppression, and revolution. Founded in 1584, Archangel, about 740 miles northeast of Petrograd (Saint Petersburg), was the world's largest city so far north—two degrees (120 miles) from the Arctic Circle.

Once Allied troops were in Archangel, there was the difficulty of a winter withdrawal—the port was usually iced in for about six months. Thus, after the Armistice there was little chance of getting these soldiers out, other than by a roundabout single-track railroad that might be cut by the Bolsheviks, leaving the last men scheduled for withdrawal to the mercy of the Reds.

As early as I can recall, my father thrilled me with tales of his service as a member of E Company, 339th Infantry Regiment, American North Russian Expeditionary Force—"The Polar Bears"—part of the Allied intervention, fighting in the state of Archangel, Russia, from September 1918 to June 1919.

Evenings, weekends, and any moments he could snatch were spent writing his "War Diary," from notes kept daily while in service. It was a never-to-be-repeated record of experiences in the "war to end all wars."

Men of the 339th Infantry formed the largest contingent in this Allied force composed of British, Canadian, French, Italian, Polish, Lithuanian, Serbian, Czechoslovak, and White Russian soldiers. Their opponents were Red Russian revolutionary soldiers. They fought in the mud, snow, and ice of north Russia's vast, nearly flat forestlands and marshes: a harsh land of coniferous forest sliced by dark, serpentine, north-flowing rivers, and speckled with coffee-colored lakes.

Donald Eugene Carey was born in Detroit, Michigan, on 17 December 1892. The oldest of two sons and a daughter, he was raised on a farm in Eaton County, Michigan. In 1915 he graduated from

Olivet College, then taught school in Camden, Michigan, until called for induction in May 1918. At age twenty-five he was older than most soldiers.

In May 1917 Carey declined the opportunity to take ROTC training and later, the probability of a commission that his uncle—a lawyer with political ambitions—offered to obtain for him. "I didn't want to be even a corporal," he often told me. "I didn't want the responsibility for the lives of other men."

Donald E. Carey was the twelfth generation of Careys in America; the product of a Christian family, filled with the parochialism and prejudices found in a small farming community of central United States in the early years of this century. He was raised at a time when patriotism, love of country, pride in the United States and her achievements were taken for granted. So was faith and trust in elected officials, and the knowledge that the United States was right and would prevail "because God was on our side." An avid student of history, especially American, his concept was that if it was American, it was the best.

Serving in that fruitless far-off campaign in frigid North Russia in no way diminished his love for God, home, and country.

From his handwritten diary I have deleted many repetitive details, while leaving the picture of a citizen soldier's day-to-day existence in this little-known portion of World War I.

All times have been changed to the twenty-four-hour clock. Thus 8:00 A.M. is 0800; 3:30 P.M. is 1530.

Editor's notes, where appropriate to clarify, expand, or correct some point, are enclosed in parentheses.

Quotations from books or newspapers are inserted to amplify the overall view.

Neil G. Carey

Chronology of Important Events

1914

28 June: Archduke Francis Ferdinand is assassinated at Sarajevo.

30 July: General mobilization ordered in Russia.

26-31 August: Germans crush the Russian Second Army at Tannenberg.

1915

March to October: Allies fail to open the Dardanelles to supply Russian with weapons.

4 June: Russia begins an offensive in eastern Galicia and inflicts such heavy casualties to the Austrian army that Germany is forced to transfer thirty-five divisions from the Western to the Eastern Front.

17 November: HMS *Donegal* escorts convoy carrying arms and ammunition from France to Archangel. Construction of port facilities begun at ice-free Murmansk, Russia

1916

Massive military drives along all fronts. The naval Battle of Jutland. By the end of the year nearly all educated Russians opposed Czar Nicholas II.

1917

Early March: Russian people in Petrograd revolt; the army and aristocrats join the revolutionaries. Czar Nicholas II is forced to abdicate. A provisional government is formed and announces that Russia will continue to fight the Germans. Soviets of workers' and soldiers' deputies form throughout Russian as an unofficial partner of the provisional government. Soviets fail to win power and Lenin flees to Finland.

6 April: United States declares war on Germany.

26 June: American Expeditionary Forces begin landing in France.

1 July: The last Russian offensive of WWI is launched.

8 July: The provisional cabinet appoints Alexander F. Kerensky Prime Minister.

Lenin returns in October and by 7 November the Bolsheviks (from the Russian word *bolshinstvo,* meaning *majority*), overthrow Kerensky.

July: Britain and France consider sending troops as well as war matériel to Russia.

1918

3 March: Bolsheviks sign the Treaty of Brest-Litovsk with Germany.

6 March: Royal Marines land at Murmansk; the first allied troops on Russian soil.

21 March: Germany launches offensive along the Somme.

23 June: The Allies occupy Murmansk.

25 June: U.S. Marines capture Belleau Wood.

16 July: Nicholas II and his family murdered by Ekaterinburg Soviet.

8 August: British troops break the German line at Amiens.

5 September: E. Company, 339th Infantry Regiment arrives at Archangel.

26 September: Allies begin their final offensive on the Western Front.

11 November: Germany signs the armistice.

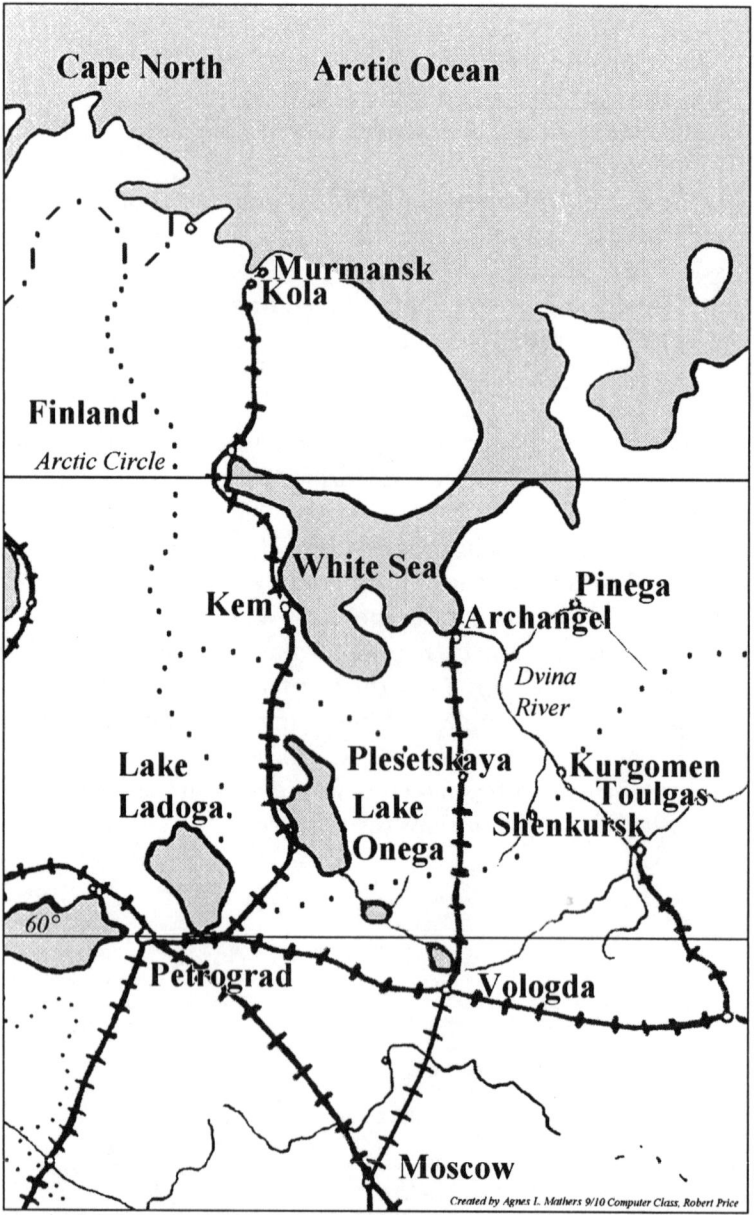

General Operation Area of the American
North Russian Expeditionary Force 1918-1919.

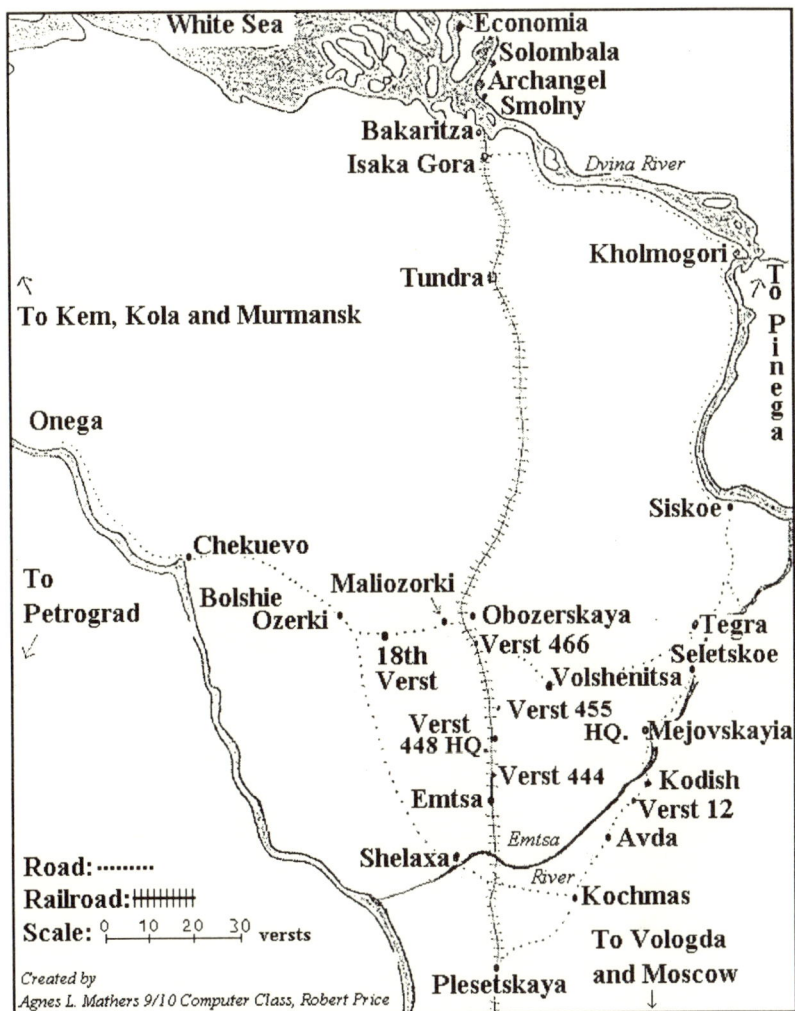

White Sea

Economia
Solombala
Archangel
Smolny
Bakaritza
Isaka Gora
Dvina River

Kholmogori

To Kem, Kola and Murmansk
Tundra

To
Pinega

Onega

Siskoe

To
Petrograd

Chekuevo
Maliozorki
Bolshie
Ozerki

Obozerskaya
Verst 466
18th
Verst

Tegra
Seletskoe
Volshenitsa

Verst 455
HQ.
Verst
448 HQ.

Mejovskayia

Verst 444

Kodish
Verst 12
Avda

Emtsa

Shelaxa
Emtsa River

Kochmas

Road: ········
Railroad: ╫╫╫╫╫╫╫
Scale: 0 10 20 30 versts

To Vologda
and Moscow

Created by
Agnes L. Mathers 9/10 Computer Class, Robert Price

Plesetskaya

Area of Operations American North Russian
Expeditionary Force 1918-1919.

Chapter 1
Greetings ... Uncle Sam Wants You!
10 January to 27 May 1918

My questionnaire from the War Department's Eaton County Local (Draft) Board arrived at noon Thursday, 10 January 1918. It was number 1,991 and mailed with the latest 100 notices from Charlotte, Michigan, our county seat. As I claimed no exemptions, filling it out was simple, and I did it at school.

Sixteen days later, despite an exceptionally hard snowstorm that raged all day and blocked the roads, I received a card from the Local Board informing me that I was placed in Class A1. Not until the first week in February did we have a break in the zero weather that had been plaguing us since the new year. It was a relief to all, especially those in cities where fuel could not be obtained. The war and abnormally severe winter weather caused much suffering in America.

On 11 February I was notified to appear before the Local Board for a physical exam on the 18th. I anticipated this, as it would afford me a brief vacation at home.

Father and I took the morning train to Charlotte. We visited Uncle John C. Nichols at his law office before Father went on to Hastings to attend a meeting of the Eaton and Barry County Insurance Company, where he was reelected a director.

At the Court House I filled out a form, witnessed by Sheriff Fuller. Then I stripped for the medical exam. My eyes and ears were tested. My weight was 125 pounds; height, five feet six inches. Finally, Dr. Bradley checked my heart and lungs. He told me that I had a slight

1

hernia. The exam was a farce, as practically all men passed. "Put on your clothes," Dr. Bradley said. "Go home, and get ready for the war." I'm glad I passed.

The following week Mother sent me a list of the 200 Eaton County men in Class A1 who passed their physical. Ten men made up the first draft. None were called for the second draft. There were only thirteen names after mine, so I did not expect to be called for some time.

Saturday evening, 30 March, I turned my watch and alarm clock ahead one hour following the new daylight saving bill passed by Congress.

Saturday, 6 April, was the first anniversary of America's entrance into the terrible European War. The training camps are in order, and we have troops holding the line in France. President Wilson had achieved an illustrious place among the leaders of the world, and for America, had practically secured the leadership of world affairs. Nevertheless, he was subjected to severe criticism. I was a firm supporter of the administration and believed winning the war would "Make the World Safe for Democracy." I believe Wilson is to this generation what Lincoln was to his.

Due to the severity of censorship, the letter from Dwight A. Davis, a Vermontville neighbor who had been in France for seven months, scarcely mentioned the war.

After studying and attending church on 14 April, I read the March issue of *The World's Work*. Articles of special interest were "Single Men in Barracks," "Fighting Germany's Spies," and "Health at Home to Help the Army. "

School was closed at noon, Friday, 26 April, by an Executive Proclamation setting apart the afternoon as Liberty Day.

Sunday I heard for the first time Victor Haughey (son of the couple who operated the rooming house where Carey stayed while teaching in Camden) sing, "Will the Angels Guard My Daddy Over There," a new war song.

During the first weekend in May I learned from the newspaper that 10,149 Michigan men would be called up beginning 25 May. I was sure my name would appear in that list.

Soon after school was called Friday, 17 May, a senior girl informed me that a telegram awaited me. Leaving Mr. Hettler in charge of the room, I went to the phone and received the message: "Name is on the list for twenty-fifth. Come home. Eugene Carey."

I'd planned to leave Camden and have a short stay at home before reporting at the training camp, but regretted leaving so near the end of the semester. Superintendent Hettler also received his call to service. After rhetoric and solid geometry classes I left to settle my financial affairs, receiving $56. 50 for the month's pay.

In the afternoon I spent enjoyable periods with my plane geometry and ancient history classes; of my six classes, I most enjoyed teaching those. Classes let out at 1500 so high school students and teachers might spend the rest of the warm afternoon on the lawn eating ice cream.

After parting with my pupils, I left school and hurried to pack my trunk. I enjoyed instructing, hated to leave, and greatly wanted to see the seniors graduate on 29 May. In the evening a farewell reception was tendered me.

I liked my pupils. Though some caused me trouble and were disciplined, I usually sympathized with them, regarding myself not merely as their instructor, but as an example. My conduct was the same as at home, and I was careful to do nothing that could possibly subject me to the slightest criticism.

Though anxious to get home, I regretted leaving the home of Mr. and Mrs. Haughey. These kind people did everything possible to make their home agreeable for me. I left Camden by auto, going to Montgomery where Mr. Hettler and family, and Superintendent Arink of Montgomery, met me at the depot. Before my train arrived, twenty coaches of troops from Camp Custer pulled into the city. They were a fine-looking group and seemed in the best of spirits.

Sunday afternoon Father and I drove to Charlotte to discuss my missing induction orders with Uncle John C. Nichols. Tuesday afternoon I walked the three miles from Vermontville to the farm, then drove to Charlotte to learn whether my induction orders had been sent to Camden. "You are not in the quota for 27 May," County Clerk Ford said, "and will not be called until June." I was chagrined to think that I'd left school before there was a need to do so.

Wednesday, Father and I went to the farm and I returned with a three-horse team. While dragging the five acres behind our town home, Mother attracted my attention by whistling and waving a large brown envelope: my orders to report for military service. Only after Uncle John called Mr. Ford's attention to his oversight were my orders sent. I had four days before my call to the colors.

I could not think of leaving home for what might be the last time without strolling over the farm with Max (younger brother) to once more see and photograph the scenes of our childhood.

In the evening I wrote to many of my pupils and sent them copies of pictures I'd taken, developed, and printed.

After dinner on Monday, 27 May, Father and I drove to Charlotte. Uncle John accompanied us to the Court House. When the Court House clock struck the hour of two, I told Father I was no longer a civilian. According to my war orders I was automatically inducted into the military service of the United States. For one who enjoyed reading military history I was not elated by this change, though I was proud to be a soldier.

Twenty-six young men assembled in the office of County Clerk Ford. Among them were James Sanders, Howard DePue, Elmer Ottney, Leo Baker, Rocco Latorre, Ivan Hahn, George Benson, Everett Roe, Leonard Morey, Andrew Crisher, Otto Federan, Ernest Olmstead, Forrest Helms, and Milford Thompson. I knew Ottney by sight since taking our physical exam.

No ceremony marked our induction. We were formed into a haphazard line and the roll was twice called. The first, to ascertain if all were present, and the second, I presume, to accustom us to the inefficiency so characteristic of the army.

We were grouped on the Court House steps and photographed. The picture included Father standing in the doorway witnessing the scene. I was at the extreme left of the rear row.

After being dismissed we drove home and I spent the evening writing friends.

Chapter 2
So This Is the Army
28 May to 13 July 1918

At 0900 I reported at the Court House, where we were formed into a double rank by James Sanders, appointed our temporary captain to conduct us to Camp Custer. A prayer was offered. Satin badges with EATON COUNTY in red were pinned to our left shoulders before we fell out.

After a lunch of coffee, doughnuts, and sandwiches, we were presented with small flags, then marched behind the city fire department and a fife and drum corps to the Grand Trunk depot.

I bid my people farewell and boarded the train: a sad, tearful occasion and I was astonished to see Father and Max break down. At this, I almost lost control of my emotions.

On the train were a large quota of drafted men from Livingston County. We arrived at Camp Custer in midafternoon. Long, irregular rows of unpainted buildings sat on barren sand. That monotonous scene was broken by a green-painted YMCA hut and a Knights of Columbus building. Our awkward group, in the varied dress of civilians, entered this new career amidst the confusing bustle of uniformed men and huge army trucks.

We were vaccinated within a half hour of detraining, though nothing could prevent the devastation later wrought in our cantonments by Spanish influenza.

Amid shouts of "Where are you from, boys?" or "Wait till you get *that* shot!" and other good-natured railleries from passing soldiers—

most clad in blue denim fatigues—we were finally taken to barracks 474 and placed in quarantine for ten days: "Longer upon the advent of contagion."

Barracks 474, situated directly in front of Regimental Headquarters, was a long, unpainted, two-story structure, typical of those hastily constructed buildings. At the rear was a combination latrine and washhouse with showers. Outside were long tables and benches where we ate. If the day was windy, our food was spiced with genuine Camp Custer sand. On rainy days we ate inside. There were no shade trees around that raw, new barracks; even the slightest vestige of grass had been removed. Barrenness, with the glare of hot sun reflected from the sand, was characteristic of the camp, except around Headquarters and officers' quarters, where lawns were kept green and neat by fatigue parties.

Barracks floors were bare. Light and ventilation were obtained through many windows. Electric lights were little used, and all were extinguished at 2200. Much of the space was occupied by individual steel bunks. Steam radiators served only as dust collectors to be cleaned before every inspection of quarters.

Our Eaton County group was assigned the same barracks. We endeavored to stay together and occupied two rows of bunks on the second floor. I selected a bunk between Sanders and DePue, with its head next to a window. The heads and feet of our bunks were alternated. At my right was a rack for rifles.

Other Michigan men were in our room. Among them were Earl Metcalf, John Doherty, Henry Bok, Joseph Brieve, Joseph Noble, Leon Bell, Edward Timm, and Charles Beyerle. There were also many men of foreign birth or extraction from Hamtramck, a Detroit suburb. Most were Poles or Russians. Though some were American-born, they were little different than those from Europe, due to their segregated life in Hamtramck. Clinging to a harsh, unintelligible jargon, they could scarcely speak understandable English and constantly talked their "Wop lingo" despite numerous commands to "Talk United States!" They were a bit of Old Europe set down in the United States and turned me from a believer in immigration to an opponent. Though slow to learn, they were willing workers and as a rule made good soldiers.

By no means did I dislike all of them, even at first. Later, I learned to respect many. Philip Burlak, a quiet and nice-looking young man, appeared different. Born in Odessa, Russia, he'd been in the United States for six or eight years and spoke fairly good English. He was intelligent and polite and became a valuable interpreter.

Before the end of the day we received our first military equipment: two woolen O.D. (olive drab color) blankets, a poncho, and a mess kit. We put the mess kits to active service when chow was served, lining up and each prospective soldier awaiting the supplying of his mess kit with food. On the whole, the meals were good; much better than I expected. Judging by the way the immigrants plunged in, it was better than they were accustomed to.

We were required to sign our war risk insurance policy. The usual amount of each was $10,000. For this, $6.60 was deducted from my monthly pay. Though I'd been evading a life insurance agent for a couple years, I promptly signed the government policy, naming Father and Muriel (sister) as beneficiaries.

I found our address posted on the barracks bulletin board. On a YMCA postcard I wrote to Mother requesting writing paper, envelopes, and stamps, giving my address: Pvt. Donald E. Carey, 12th Co., 3rd Batt., 160th Depot Brigade, Bldg. 474, Camp Custer, Michigan.

After forming a double file, one of our noncoms stuttered and stumbled through our names when we stood retreat at the close of our first day in camp.

The various scenes and events of that first day: hurrying men and officers; the occasional salute; marching troops; incoming recruits; noisy motorcycles and trucks; and numerous unidentified bugle calls. All of these formed a lasting but confused impression that clung to my subconscious mind, refusing to be banished even by the sleep that came with exhaustion—only to be disturbed by the clear bugle notes of reveille.

Rain cut short our morning drill, so the lieutenant—a fine young man with a wide mouth, keen sense of humor, and an easy smile—took us to the barracks, where we were issued uniforms, but not permitted to wear them until passing another physical examination.

In the afternoon we were mustered into service, and from 2000 to 2200 (8:00 to 10:00 P.M.) I was on quarantine guard. During this time my thoughts reverted to Camden, where the commencement exercises were taking place. I regretted not being there.

At 0200 I again went on guard till 0400. It began to rain soon after I took my post, and in spite of my new poncho I got wet. Then I slept till 0545.

After breakfast we went to another barracks and were examined. After stripping, all marks, pits, scars, and birthmarks were recorded; fingerprints taken; teeth, ears, eyes, feet, general condition, and reflexes tested. It was a thorough exam, but I passed. I had no hernia, as the Local Board had pronounced, but a relaxed something on my right side. My heart was too rapid, but not so recorded, though the doctors were slow to decide. My lungs were normal. We were shot for typhoid and I had a sore arm for a day or so.

Camp Custer, 30 May 1918

Dear Folks,

Our hilarious bunch reached camp as hungry as wolves and, as we expected, didn't get anything till evening. The food is OK. We wash our dishes in the same tub, but no one cares, or at least I don't. A great bunch of men are here. Hundreds have come in the last few days. Everything is on the move.

I have not forgotten that this is not only Decoration Day, but also Mother's birthday. I wish you many more.

Send writing pad for my diary. Write.

Love, Donald

We drilled all day. In the afternoon I saw three-inch shells burst atop a hill about two miles away. The gun was a mile from us. Near the woods a machine gun and some infantry were firing. It was like a miniature battle.

"When I get to the real thing," I told DePue, "I suppose my hair will stand up and I'll shiver like a poplar leaf in a hurricane."

While we watched the shells burst I asked the lieutenant if allotments were "made solely to dependents?"

"Yes," he replied. "She'll have to wait."

I laughed, as did all who heard him, and said, "I wasn't thinking of that."

Before leaving the field we had a parade for the colonel.

We spent Saturday forenoon at drill. Before being dismissed, a number, including myself, were notified that we had been accepted for service and told to put on our uniforms. First, I got a regulation haircut. My shoes were large, but comfortable.

I spent most of Sunday in the barracks writing letters. I received a package of envelopes and writing paper from home, my first mail as a soldier. One of the YMCA men addressed us in the evening.

> *Camp Custer, 2 June 1918*
>
> *Dear Folks at home,*
>
> *Life here in quarantine is not so disagreeable as you might imagine. This week has gone fast. The faster it goes the sooner I'll see Europe.*
>
> *Drills are OK but the physical exercise gets me across the back. There are some disagreeable things, but they are trifles compared with the trenches. Come down when you can. I can see you and visit, but cannot leave the grounds.*
>
> *Love, Donald*

We were called from drill to list our preferences of service and other statistical info. I put in for light or field artillery. In the evening I did my washing and saw in the *Charlotte Republican* the photo taken of us on 27 May.

We drilled after breakfast until the lieutenant was reminded that 5 June was a holiday—due to the registration of all young men who became of age since a year ago. I spent the rest of the day sleeping and writing.

> *Camp Custer, 5 June 1918*
>
> *Dear Folks,*
>
> *Just a year ago I registered for the draft, thought it would catch me sooner.*
>
> *You should have heard the lieutenant bawl out a couple of the Wops in our company. He talks two languages: English and profane. I like him and try to do my best. It's a darned shame I didn't take the reserve officers' training last year. I could do it, but I'd hate*

*the responsibility. I'm sure there are few men in our barracks better
educated than I.*

*Come over whenever you can and stay around till you find me.
Love, Donald*

A different lieutenant drilled us before we were called to write a
simple psychological test. He put us through the paces in the afternoon till a thundershower sent us to the barracks. He was severe, and
had little sense of humor and less patience.

We arose at 0445, an hour earlier than usual, and spent the day
in hard drill. In the forenoon Maj. Gen. Chase W. Kennedy, the
camp commander, was pointed out to us. In the afternoon Sergeant
Fergerson drilled us for a short time. He was a tall, handsome, soldierly man with a great store of command and self-confidence. Before leaving the field we took a hike of over two miles. It was strenuous, and being somewhat ill—possibly my vaccination—I suffered
considerably.

I was quite dispirited after drill, but letters from Mother and
friends in Camden have an encouraging effect. I read them twice.

We lined up in front of the barracks for drill, but the lieutenant
was more interested in seeing the Saturday review, so we were dismissed. I didn't feel well so did little. I got an idea of the great number of men here when many of the twenty-two thousand participating troops marched past our barracks.

In the afternoon we were each issued two circular aluminum iden-
tification tags. Mine are stamped Donald E. Carey 2051687.

While eating supper I saw the eclipse of the sun. The lower left
portion was invisible. In parts of the U.S. the eclipse was total.

From 1800 to 2000 I was on fire guard and policed the barracks
and latrines.

Our schedule required eight hours of work daily excepting Sundays. Wednesday and Saturday afternoons, unless detailed for guard
or fatigue duty, we were left to the enjoyment of a few leisure hours.
But theory and practice didn't always cooperate. Drill periods were
often broken by rain, by orders to draw clothing or equipment, or
by orders to report at the infirmary for shots.

We had to be in our bunks by 2300, but the lights went out at 2100. We got up on weekdays at 0545 and on Sundays at 0615. I got more sleep than ever before, as I usually retired at 2100.

There are some disagreeable things about army life: cleaning cuspidors; sweeping barracks; scrubbing tables; making my bunk; and washing my mess kit in the same water with others.

About 1015 Sunday, Father, Muriel, Albert, and Mr. Thompson (Albert's father) came. We visited till 1200 when I had mess, then went on guard. I hated to see them leave. Father took my civilian clothes home.

In the afternoon we were called to state whether or not we were U.S. citizens.

On Monday afternoon we were released from quarantine and taken to another barracks and issued rifles, bayonets, and cartridge belts. The rifles were saturated in grease and required considerable work to clean. Mine was number 211398.

After training in the manual of arms we prepared for retreat in front of barracks 446. Beginning with supper, we ate our meals in the mess hall. After supper considerable time was spent inspecting Company E men for venereal diseases.

We drilled with rifles, and then returned to our barracks for a second shot in the arm. Mine was slightly sore for a day or so. I cleaned my rifle till called to the mess hall, where we first donned the gas mask and then were instructed in its use. It is disagreeable to wear. After another gas drill we learned to sight our rifles. Then a third gas drill. After supper I went to the canteen for the first time.

There was much talk about camp that we would leave by early July and be sent to Italy.

Camp Custer, 12 June 1918

Dear Folks,

After being released from quarantine we were transferred to Company E, 339th Infantry. So I'm a foot soldier. That satisfies me. I never hoped to be an officer. I'll be content if I make a good soldier.

I'm not going to try to get away next Saturday. I'll try later. We're going to the rifle range in a few days and I can't afford to miss the

*training. It may mean saving my life after I get to Europe. I'll have
to get busy cleaning my rifle, it requires considerable work.*
    Keep well and come down Sunday.
    Love, Donald

Tear gas drill in the morning. After early dinner we marched to
the rifle range where I fired ten shots. I made 33 out of a possible
50 points at 100 yards in the prone position with the bayonet fixed.
It was my first experience at firing and made me nervous.

On Friday we left for the range after an early breakfast. I shot at
200 and 300 yards and did "Damned poor!" Then I went to the butts
where I flagged targets after the bullets passed over.

After the weekly inspection we drilled. Then to the rifle range. I
fired forty shots, the first ten standing at 100 yards, and made two
bull's-eyes, scoring 42 out of 50. At 200 yards I knelt and my first shot
was a bull's-eye: I scored 30. At 300 yards I scored 34 in the prone
position. I made one hit out of a possible ten in rapid fire at 100
yards. I thoroughly enjoyed it.

After supper we were issued leggings. DePue and I cleaned our
rifles and then went to the Liberty Club.

Reveille at 0500. Then to a building near the rifle range where we
were gassed with chlorine—with our masks on.

Upon returning I found Father and Max awaiting me. After
changing my clothes we met Mother, Doris, and Caryl (wife and
daughter of Max) at the YMCA. We ate dinner together, then went
to the rifle range and had a long visit. It was good to see them. They
left after 1500.

The barracks was exceedingly hot, and after supper I did my washing, though I hated to do it on Sunday.

Monday forenoon at the range I fired fifty shots in different positions with all kinds of results—including one bull's-eye. After dinner I went to the range and finished my target practice. At the 500-
yard range I saw a machine gun fired. Though often hearing this
quick-firing implement of war, I'd never before seen one.

At reveille I was ordered to report for kitchen police duty. KP in-
cludes everything tiresome and disagreeable connected with a

kitchen. I worked from 0500 to 2015 without rest, so retired as early as possible.

Friday, at dinnertime, while I was still working in the kitchen, Albert and Muriel arrived, and I got them an army dinner. They visited the range and artillery, while I continued my KP, and left about 1600. Just before supper I was told that I was entitled to a pass home. Without taking time for supper I hurried to get ready by 1900, when the passes were issued. DePue and I took the trolley to Battle Creek, where we boarded the train for Charlotte. I phoned Father from the depot and he picked me up at midnight.

Twenty-third of June was Muriel's twentieth birthday. I arose early on that beautiful Sunday and posted photos in my album. Albert took me to Charlotte on his motorcycle to pick up proofs of my photos taken Saturday.

After supper Father and I drove to Camp Custer. I hated to leave home. Father cried when he left, just as had Mother. I felt sorry for them. I did not expect to see them again until this fiendish war is over.

I little thought when I graduated from the university on 24 June 1915 that just three years later I'd be wearing khaki.

Monday forenoon we were reviewed by Maj. J. Brooks Nichols and given our first bayonet drill. We were inspected for venereal diseases and taught to make up our heavy packs.

Camp Custer, 25 June 1918

Dear Folks,

I've been here four weeks this afternoon. I'm satisfied we'll not be here another four. Every indication points to a speedy departure. The canteen closed last night; trains are loaded and coaches awaiting someone—probably our division. I believe we will leave within ten days.

Many men arrived here today. They'll soon be enjoying the pleasures of army life. I don't mind it so much when I feel OK, unless it's some dirty work like KP or guard duty. Don't worry about me. Look at it with pride and think of it as a great experience. It is hell, but I can't help feeling proud that I'm in the service of the U.S. and in the greatest war of all history. I expect to survive and tell you about it.

Love, Donald

Detroit Free Press **26 June 1918**

Ex-Czar Slain by Red Guard. Troops Break into Residence of Former Ruler, Murder Him, Is Report from Ekaterinburg. Romanoff Exile City.

Washington, 26 June

YANKS IN FRANCE ONE YEAR TODAY

In the forenoon we were reviewed by 1st Lt. John J. Baker, and then given skirmish line deployment. After noon we again drilled with our heavy packs.

Before supper I was elected secretary of the YMCA Bible class for Company E.

As we passed through the mess hall each man received a lunch preparatory to a regimental hike. I saw the headline of a paper held by Lieutenant Dressing stating: RUSSIAN PEOPLE SHOOT EX-CZAR.

Our 339th Regiment, commanded by Major Nichols, hiked to the edge of Galesburg. After eating in the field, we commenced the return. That nearly bushed me. It was terribly hot and I suffered for water. We marched about twenty miles.

After supper instead of resting we mopped and cleaned the barracks as well as cleaning our rifles. There were few days when I was so exhausted.

Monday morning I went to the rifle range as a scorer for the new men of our company, many still in civilian clothes. These men were never quarantined, just issued rifles and sent to the range.

Camp Custer, 2 July 1918

Dear Mother,

. . . I've been deployed as a skirmisher and had some bayonet practice. The latter is a tiresome drill and staged with an effort to bring out the brutality in a man. Doesn't it seem strange to think that perhaps I'll have to wipe something redder from my bayonet than the oil in which it was packed? It is not a pleasant conception. This whole business is far from being one of my choice and is by no means in accord with my bringing up or education.

Thursday we were deployed as on a battlefield. It was great sport and I enjoyed the running and dropping till a heavy shower soaked

*me. An aeroplane, the only one I've seen since at Ann Arbor in
1916, soared above us. All we needed was more noise and death to
make the whole affair quite realistic.*

*Every afternoon we make up our heavy packs and drill. Usually
I'm so tired I can hardly put one foot before the other. Also, we're not
getting the food we need. I can't work on an empty stomach. This afternoon is the first time I've felt half-decent since last Friday's twenty-
mile hike.*

*I have one task that haunts me more than all the Huns in Eu-
rope; that's keeping my rifle clean. Even keeps me from getting home-
sick. Ever since it was issued I've petted it with an oily rag till it
howls with delight. It was closely inspected last Saturday and passed
OK, but some were dirty and their neglectful owners have spent time
in the kitchen for being so careless.*

Love, Donald

I never spent the Glorious Fourth in such a useless, dissatisfied
manner. There was no drill or celebration, and few visitors, for many
soldiers were given passes, so I remained on my bunk most of the
day and wrote letters. I did not get a pass, as I preferred mine for
Sunday. After a rotten dinner I read the 6 July issue of *Colliers*.

With heavy packs weighing at least forty pounds our regiment left
the barracks at 0700 on Friday for a twelve-mile hike. It was not so
difficult as the hike of a week ago. We marched over some fine
shaded roads, returning about 1130.

A regular field inspection of all our issued stuff and rifles was held
Saturday forenoon. My rifle and bayonet passed.

After dinner I received a pass and took the train from Battle Creek
to Charlotte, where I telephoned Mother to have Father come after
me. While waiting I bought the sheet music for "Will the Angels
Guard My Daddy Over There" and enjoyed two chocolate sundaes.
On the way home we stopped to visit with Max, who was getting up
hay in the south flats.

Muriel and I played the new music and "Aloha Oe." Albert, Max,
Doris, and Caryl were there in the evening. It was great to get home.

After drilling on Monday morning we returned to the barracks at
1100 for a venereal inspection. Retreat was held in the field for the

first time and all of the 339th Infantry Regiment was out. Another
first: I saw the colors hauled down.

After a late supper I received $26.40, my first army pay. I now had
over $50.

Ottney returned from the hospital after his bout with pneumonia.

SPECIAL DELIVERY

8 July 1918

Dear Folks,
The captain informed us after retreat tonight that the camp will
be closed at 0500 tomorrow (Tuesday). Also no more passes will be
issued. Send my washing at once.
Also watch.
With love, Donald

Detroit Free Press 8 July 1918
BOLSHEVIK DOOM BELIEVED SEALED; MOSCOW IN PERIL
Units of Army, Navy can move in two weeks.
Entire division to go, already chosen, officials hint.

Washington, 7 July
Tentative preparations for placing a strong military force in
Siberia went forward rapidly today. Orders to army and navy
units were dispatched and concrete instructions for members
of the economic mission were formulated.

The belief is widely held here that a pronouncement of the
attitude of this country and of steps which are to be taken to
safeguard interests of the United States in Siberia will be made
by President Wilson within a few days.

Officials, although declining to discuss terms of the expected statement from the White House, state the American
public should be prepared for a positive declaration marking
a new epoch in the participation of the United States in the
war.

In diplomatic circles it is believed an announcement by the
United States of its desire to aid the law-abiding people of

Siberia will result in a reaction against Germany in Russia. It is predicted by officials who have recently returned from Moscow (that) strong measures by the United States at this time will hurl the Bolshevik party from control.

Copenhagen 7 July
The entire population of the Murman coast (on the Kola peninsula, bordering the White Sea and the Arctic) has broken with Russia and joined the Entente (Allies), according to a dispatch from Vardoe, Norway, to the Christiana Tidens Ten.

(This was the first public notice that U.S. troops might be sent to Siberia and Russia.)

We drilled and had physical exercise until 1030. Then 2d Lt. Carl Berger explained the operation of the Browning automatic rifle (BAR) to us. Later we stood venereal inspection.

One of our Eaton County men, Everett Roe, either deserted or took French leave (AWOL). After ten days it will be desertion. I rather liked the guy and felt sorry for him.

Detroit Free Press 10 July 1918

KAISER DEMANDS PETROGRAD, WITH MOSCOW, REPORT. SEEKING REVENGE FOR ASSASSINATION OF ENVOY.

Allies to aid, U.S. in Russia. Peaceful penetration is President's proposal.

Washington, 8 July
Viscount Ishii, Japanese ambassador, has been invited to an interview with President Wilson. Urgent representations have been made to this government on behalf of Czecho-Slovak troops in Russia, who are declared to be threatened with extermination.

It was surmised in diplomatic quarters President Wilson requested Ambassador Ishii to acquaint his government with the fact the United States favors the principal of military assistance to Russia and to obtain the Japanese government's views of the immediate military action practicable by Japan, the number of troops which might be engaged in an expedition, the distance it might penetrate, extent of Chinese co-operation and what collaboration by the American government is desirable.

By Arno Dosch-Fleurot, Copyright 1918 by *New York World,* by cable to *Detroit Free Press.* Archangel, Russia, 4 July

(Delayed) I find here, as in Murmansk, Russians and Allies agree American aid should be equal to that of other Allies. It will be necessary to have help of a united Allied character. The situation here is entirely different from that in Murmansk, where the local Soviet has invited help of the Allies. The Soviet here formerly sided with the Allies but control is now in Moscow, making the extension of Allied help for Russia difficult in this region, though it is welcome in Murmansk.

Paris, 9 July

The Bolshevist government at Moscow, according to reliable dispatches tonight, is threatening to conclude an alliance with Germany and mobilize Russia's manpower against the Entente.

As a result of the assassination of the German ambassador to Russia, Count von Mirbach, Germany, it is reported, will demand passage for her troops by way of Petrograd (Saint Petersburg) to the Murman coast, the inhabitants of which the Bolsheviki are denouncing as friendly to the Allies.

Germany, it is said, will further demand control of Petrograd and Moscow.

London, 9 July

Prominent Russian residents in London consider the Czecho-Slovak movement in Siberia as the only reliable basis for a struggle against Bolshevikism and the restoration of order in Russia.

Camp Custer, 11 July 1918

Dear Folks,
I'm writing what I believe will be my last letter from this delightful camp. I don't know when we leave, and couldn't inform you if I

did—we were ordered not to tell—but if you receive no letter dated 12 July, you'll know we left on that date.

A heavy rain late this afternoon drove us from the drill field, so we listened to two one-hour lectures by two of our lieutenants. Every day this week we have stood venereal inspection. That never worries me.

Last night we were taken to the Liberty Theater, where Mr. Hooper of the Michigan Bar Association addressed us on the legal rights of soldiers.

Hundreds of rail cars have been awaiting the departure of our division. Many trains have already gone. Keep this strictly to yourself, it is not to be published to a soul. It is said we will be the fourteenth train to leave tomorrow, and that one leaves every hour. If so, we'll leave in the evening. Now don't tell this to anyone, as it may cause trouble: Our major has already left.

I hope I never see (front line) service, though I don't object to a voyage to Europe. However, the sooner I'm in civilian duds, the more satisfied I'll be.

With love to all, Donald

Camp Custer, 12 July 1918

Dear Folks,

We drilled all day. At retreat we were ordered to take everything that we will not immediately need from our heavy packs and put it into our barracks bags. The bags leave at 0930 tomorrow. This means we will leave sometime tomorrow—probably in the afternoon. Hundreds have already left and the drill fields looked pretty deserted this forenoon. Brigadier General Penn addressed us this afternoon for the first time.

I'm anxious to get started to see the country. I'd like to remain here for just one reason—to get home once in a while, but I guess the next time you see me I'll be a veteran of the most fiendish war ever fought. Don't worry.

With Love, Donald

Camp Custer, 13 July 1918

Dear Folks,

We leave for Camp Mills, Long Island, N.Y., tomorrow forenoon.

Our barracks bags left this morning. We sleep in our duds tonight on bare bunks, as our heavy packs are already made. Last night I slept with no straw in my bed tick. We did practically nothing today. You'll get all of my recent letters in a bunch, as they've been held up. Mail addressed as usual will follow me.

Love, Donald

Chapter 3
To Camp Mills
14 July to 20 July 1918

We fell into line about 1100 and quietly marched to a train of eleven coaches and two baggage cars. We were seated three to a double seat, so one of every group of three rode backward. I sat next to the aisle, facing forward. I would rather have been by the window to see more during this trip nearly halfway across the continent. With us were our rifles and heavy packs, making our positions crowded, uncomfortable, and difficult to sleep.

Our important sergeants ordered us to keep our heads and hands within the windows. The sash effectively cut off the view, for the windows were not to be raised over nine inches. We were not to leave the car. To enforce this, a guard with bayoneted rifle was stationed at each end of every coach.

Sergeant McCormick was especially irritating when he assumed the air of a cocksure lieutenant and told one of my comrades not to say "Yes, sir" to him, as he wasn't an officer and it was unforgivable to say "sir" to anyone not an officer.

At 1300 in the heat and quiet of this July Sunday, our train pulled out of Camp Custer. I suspected that in leaving we were leaping from the frying pan to a position nearer the fire, but I hailed our departure with delight as a break in the monotony of army life and as an escape from the sandy, uninteresting, and disagreeable camp.

There was nothing spectacular about our departure, no waving flags, cheering crowds, martial music, or tearful farewells. Only quiet and order.

We passed through Olivet, my alma mater. It was good to see it once more. Our train, with its burden of human freight so needed to help in the terrible struggle in Europe, rushed along the track cleared of all traffic. Three hours after leaving Camp Custer we stopped in Detroit.

The Detroit Red Cross were on hand to feed us milk, orange juice, chocolate bars, and sandwiches. Best, to me, was the privilege granted to drop a line to the dear ones left at home. In great haste I wrote that we were "on way east."

Our stay in Detroit was short. Passing through the tunnel under the Detroit River, we entered Canada. This was the third time I'd been out of Michigan, and the first I'd been out of the U.S.

Stopping at Windsor, we were given an official welcome by a Canadian who said, "Damned glad to see you. I know what you will do and how you'll do it. So just do it quickly."

Before the end of our brief stop I mailed to Father a stamped card presented to me by the Committee of Welcome.

I made the most of this opportunity to see southern Ontario. We met with considerable cheering along the route. Individuals and groups greeted us with a cordial word, waved flags, and one woman waved a dish towel—that recalled my recent experiences on KP.

It was too dark to see Niagara Falls, America's greatest scenic spectacle. After a five-hour ride through Canada, we crossed the suspension bridge into Niagara, New York, where a civilian mailed a letter for me.

At noon we stopped at West Point, the only place along our route announced to us. Woods so encircled the view that only a few buildings could be partly seen. Some men were shooting at targets. During the twenty-minute layover we had dinner.

After twenty-five hours in the coaches we detrained at Hoboken, New Jersey. We halted in a dirty section of the city, boarded a harbor craft, then waited two hours before leaving the dock. A camouflaged transport loaded with khaki-clad troops slowly moved out. A slate-colored battleship—the first I'd seen—entered the harbor.

Before our craft left the dock we were warned not to rush from one side to the other, for fear of swamping it. During this one-hour ride I gazed at the harbor front with the avidity of a twelve-year-old.

Greatest was the Statue of Liberty, though it was not so large as I'd imagined. Ellis Island and the Immigration Station were pointed out.

We disembarked on Long Island, where we were given a light meal before boarding the train for Camp Mills. Upon detraining we were assigned to canvas tents, each designed for a squad. There were only seven of us that first night, as there was a blank file in our squad. I could scarcely believe I was on the Atlantic coast, so far from home, but I finally crawled onto my canvas cot.

It was about 0200 before we could get to sleep. Sunrise and reveille parade found E Company resting from its exhausting experience of the past two days. My first impression of Camp Mills was not favorable, and as the day advanced things did not improve. The accommodations and conveniences of Camp Custer were appreciated as never before.

Cavalry tents and canvas cots cannot compare for comfort with the barracks and steel bunks of Custer. The latrines were low, poorly constructed, and had an evil odor. Above all, the drinking water was warm with an insipid, rotten, mineral taste.

There was one thing I never lost interest in: the aeroplanes. I frequently saw three or four at a time, and once I saw thirteen. The hum of their motors was a familiar part of life at Camp Mills.

After breakfast we prepared for inspection, displaying all of our possessions upon the dirty, though often policed, company street.

The morning paper of 18 July announced the death of Quentin Roosevelt. We were on the same island as his illustrious father (ex-President Theodore Roosevelt).

We received an issue of clothing that included two O.D. blouses. Later we were given puttees—long, narrow, khaki-colored rags to wrap around our legs in a special manner. This put an end to wearing canvas leggings, forcing some to get up earlier than usual to dress, or receive extra duty for tardiness at morning formation.

While in our tent the peculiar whistling of an aeroplane attracted my attention; upon stepping out I saw my first large triplane.

During the hot Saturday forenoon we packed our barracks bags and carried them to a freight train a short distance from our tent: conclusive evidence that we had been ordered to move. It is taken for granted that Europe will be our destination.

At noon one hundred of us marched to the camp prison. It consisted of many tents surrounded by barbed wire and accommodated a motley group. The reason is apparent: Camp Mills is near the port of embarkation for overseas duty—duty many unscrupulous men seek to avoid.

We were formed into a single line and each given three cartridges. Then an officer of powerful build with a deep, resounding voice informed us of the seriousness of our duty. "You are to guard and work these prisoners. Some are desperate characters, susceptible to making an unannounced departure," he said. "If you can't bring them back, leave them where the Military Police can get them." I determined to kill any assigned to my care if they attempted to escape—for escape would necessitate my serving the remainder of the prisoner's time.

I looked after three fellows, one a fairly good-looking American and two surly men of foreign extraction. I secured them from the pen, and with a rake and two hoes they followed the detail, with me packing a bayoneted and loaded rifle over my shoulder.

I was strict. They ridiculed me, saying that clowns like me were too green to see that they had nothing to gain by attempting to skedaddle, for in a few days they would sail for Europe and be released. This did not diminish my vigilance while they killed time pulling weeds and raking near the camp. I spent four hours working harder and under greater strain than they to keep them busy. I violated most of the officer's orders by letting them smoke, go to the latrine, and talk to me.

Before turning them over to the company guarding the entire prison, they were given a bath. One Jew in civilian clothes, who had been arrested for overcharging soldiers, found it difficult to keep up, and on the way from the bathhouse was so stubborn that Joe Nobel gave him a brutal punch in the rear with his bayonet.

Chapter 4
Europe, Here We Come
21 July to 2 August 1918

I arose at 0530 on Sunday, 21 July, and with my comrades spent the forenoon making up our heavy packs and policing our section of camp. At 1230, after a tedious wait in company formation, and wearing woolen blouses, we made a short, uncomfortably hot march and boarded a train.

Just a week after leaving Camp Custer, we pulled out of Camp Mills. I was pleased to leave Custer, and doubly so to leave Mills.

Upon detraining we marched aboard a ferry that took us to Hoboken, N.J., our port of embarkation. In company formation we entered a large structure where Red Cross personnel gave us colored brick ice cream; much appreciated, as the day was hot. They also gave each man a card. I addressed mine to Father. After signing it and adding my organization, it read:

> The ship on which I sailed has arrived overseas.
> Pvt. Donald E. Carey
> Co. E. 339th Infantry
> American Expeditionary Forces

Finally, after some wait, we mounted the gangplank in single file and boarded HMT (His Majesty's Transport) *Northumberland*, a large British merchant vessel. As we were about to step upon the gangplank, an officer called each man by his surname to which he responded with his given name and initial. Rumor says we are bound for England. I hope so.

We were immediately assigned quarters in the hold where stationary tables and benches had been fitted. While the officers enjoyed comfortable quarters, the men grumbled about being crowded into the hot, foul-smelling, unventilated hold like cattle. We lay at anchor in Hoboken overnight and slept in canvas hammocks suspended over our mess tables. The discomforts of such contrivances can be imagined better than described.

After a fair night's rest I arose at 0530 and idly awaited our departure at 0930. As the ship began to leave, all men were ordered into the hold. We were disappointed and angered at not being permitted to see the wonders of New York Harbor. However, we were permitted on deck before clearing port. As we turned seaward and the land receded, I could not restrain a few tears at leaving the finest country on the globe, to meet a fate that God alone could discern.

In case our vessel should be torpedoed, we were ordered to wear life preservers. These reminded me of the old New England pillories. They were pulled over the head and tied about the waist in such a manner that a pillow rested upon the chest and back. They added to our discomfort, made our meager quarters more crowded, our movements clumsy, and were hot in warm weather. Orders to wear them day and night were often disregarded after dark, as it was impossible to sleep comfortably in them. They were frequently used as pillows.

During the day I watched the seventeen ships of our convoy and escorts, all armed I believe, and most daubed with various designs of camouflage. Most, like *Northumberland,* had been commercial ships. For escorts we had a battleship or cruiser and some destroyers. A dirigible—the first I saw—hung over the convoy for a short time. The ships were in formation around *Northumberland.* It was pleasing to see them plow through the calm, dark blue sea on a zigzag course.

Except for a slight rocking one would scarcely realize the ship was moving. However, this slight sway made me light-headed, but never did I feed the fish, though some did. This I couldn't afford, for we were poorly fed. The steam-cooked, unseasoned stuff—rice, meal, potatoes, and tripe—prepared by English cooks in their native manner was so unpalatable and sickening that I ate little during the voyage. Oatmeal without sugar and milk seemed to so mix with the foul stench of the hold that it was particularly nauseating. I did enjoy bully beef (canned corned beef) and cauliflower pickles. The men justifiably cursed the rotten food, so unappetizing that many left the tables hungry and all lost weight during the crossing.

I spent most of the forenoon of our first full day at sea on the crowded deck visiting with Ottney, DePue, and Walter Franklin of Chattanooga, Tennessee, who entertained me with accounts of the South. A bulletin was posted giving the basketball scores, and of greater interest to me, it stated that the enemy was slowly being forced back.

In the afternoon fire and submarine drills were conducted. Men were selected to throw over rafts and every soldier was assigned to a raft. The drills were again practiced in the evening and on each day at sea. I had no particular fear of submarines and could not believe my fate was close at hand. I worried about my food, pack, and rest.

Had Robert Louis Stevenson met *Northumberland*'s crew he might have selected them as characters for *Treasure Island*. With one exception their cadaverous, dirty faces, unkempt clothes, and rough language brought visions of a gang of pirates. They succeeded in taking most of the cash from those of our outfit reckless enough to gamble.

I spent my second day at sea as a kitchen flunky. We were required to work only a couple hours at each meal: getting the food—such as it was—and cleaning dishes. An easy task compared to work at Camp Custer.

Wind rocked the ship and many were seasick. Though I felt lightheaded I managed to retain what little I found appetizing enough to eat. I took a saltwater bath, which was not altogether satisfying.

Rain added to the continued disagreeable weather. I read *The Foreigner*, by Ralph Connor, and during the evening wrote my people.

The letter was censored by First Lieutenant Phillips, who did so poor a job with an indelible pencil that every marked section was legible.

> *Dear Folks,*
> *I suppose you worried upon hearing of the sinking of the Jamaica. I was not aboard. We received news of it by wireless, and news from the Western Front is reported to us.*
> *Have you received any papers concerning my insurance? Don't worry about me. My motto is, "I'm coming back safe, sound, and sane."*
> *With love to all, Donald*

During the day I found the canteen and bought chocolate and candy. A number of men, including Sergeant Kennedy, resold articles procured at the canteen for a profit. When caught they were assigned to shovel coal for the engine rooms. Each day they returned covered with coal dust.

The ship's roll awoke me at 0200. Though sick, I did not vomit, but ate little during the day. It was disagreeably cold on the upper deck as I watched the vessels dip and roll. The decks were so crowded that it was difficult to find a sheltered nook with more than standing room. Usually there were such gobs of spit and phlegm and cigarette butts that I preferred to stand.

The tobacco supply ran short. Slaves to this habit begged for the butt, often before the cigarette was lighted. They shamelessly asked for and received a tow—or suck—from another's cigarette. Regardless of the possibility of disease, they stuck the foul, spit-covered cigarette in their mouth and returned it to the owner. Butts were picked up from the deck and relighted.

After breakfast on the first day of August, the battleship escorting us turned about and left for home. We were not long without an escort. Soon seven British destroyers approached at great speed from our rear. With three on each side of the convoy and one in its lead they escorted us to England. I never tired of watching them.

During the night we entered the Irish Sea through the North Channel—between Ireland and Scotland. The sea calmed and the day warmed. Before noon a dirigible met our convoy and was pulled down to one of the ships. Soon I saw the coast of England, a welcome sight.

At 2230 I commenced two hours of guard duty on an upper deck in the forepart of the vessel watching for submarines, mines, or anything suspicious. With only a raincoat for extra warmth, my greatest difficulty was keeping warm, for a cold, raw wind blew furiously.

Chapter 5
Interlude in England
3 August to 25 August 1918

Excited voices awoke me at 0500 on 3 August. Hurrying on deck I found we were slowly ascending the Mersey River to the docks of Liverpool. Fog and clouds shrouded the buildings. Vast numbers of large seagulls hovered. Mowed lawns, neat yards, and buildings evidenced that England's greatest port was well cared for.

We remained aboard until late afternoon, viewing the area and ruminating on what England had in store for us. One good feature of traveling à la military was that I need not inquire concerning baggage and how to get to where I am going. I never knew my destination. But I could speculate as to whether I would escape cleaning the quarters or unloading barracks bags, or get a good meal or a night's rest.

After debarking at the Riverside Railway station we were given small cakes by the American Red Cross. Then we marched with heavy packs at a rapid pace over the rough cobblestone streets lined with cheering crowds; many of us found it a footsore experience.

We entrained at the Great Central Railway depot, and crowded eight to a compartment in a coach entered from the side. Soon each soldier was presented with a letter, the envelope imprinted: "A Message to You from His Majesty King George Vth." The King's words of welcome, though perfectly legible, were written in a scribble that would have disgraced a sixth-grade pupil. I added my name and addressed the envelope to Father, who received it on 2 September, a souvenir of my first day in the Old World.

Some men left their compartments to visit with the English girls lining the depot area.

Our train pulled out of Liverpool and I viewed the beautiful rural scenery. Brick buildings roofed with tile gave it a picturesqueness. The barns, for the most part small thatched structures, were evidence of a lack of wealth and progress so characteristic in America.

England—the source of our Puritan ancestors, our language, our constitutional government and law. Above all, the land that for four years had aided in holding at bay the most damnable autocracy of modern times. One appreciating the history of this nation, its greatness as a defender of liberal ideas and government, and its noble work in this greatest of wars, could not help thrilling at being there.

At midnight, after a ride of three and a half hours, we detrained for a short time at Derby, where each man was given a cup of coffee. Finally, through sheer exhaustion, I fell asleep in a sitting position. From time to time I awoke to feel the train rushing through the night.

It was daylight when Lieutenant Baker's authoritative voice routed us out. In the cold and gloom of a foggy Sunday morning—the fourth anniversary of England's declaration of war against Germany—we detrained at Brookwood, in southern England.

Forming up, we marched about one and a half miles along a beautiful winding road to Camp Stoney Castle, Aldershot, southwest of London. Our small section of camp consisted of only enough white canvas tents for E and H companies, a washhouse, latrines, and kitchen. This was the estate of the famous African explorer Sir Henry M. Stanley. On one side of the camp, otherwise surrounded by woods, small trains of the Great Central Railway often sped past.

Though depressed and tired upon arrival, I soon appreciated the natural beauty of the place with its grass, excellent drinking water, and rolling country.

For the most part I spent the day in idleness; saw a few aeroplanes and listened to one of the Laddies of Hell excitedly relate in his Scots dialect how the "bloody shells would blow up great embankments and buildings." Particularly interesting was his uniform—kilts—and he revealed that no underclothing was worn. He and other Scots and English soldiers were encamped near us awaiting transfer to France.

It was some time before we were fed, and having eaten only corned beef and hardtack since leaving the ship, I was hungry. My chow of brown bread and greasy mutton stew was interrupted to aid a detail distributing rubber ground sheets and small tubs to the tents of our company. Upon returning, I found the soggy potatoes frozen in my stew by a coat of tallow fully a quarter-inch thick.

Late in the afternoon I made the mistake of leaving my tent to get near the head of the chow line—just in time to be caught by First Sergeant Comstock, who ordered me to eat at once, then aid a number of our men under an English sergeant preparing to feed more of our regiment not yet arrived. From 1730 to midnight we washed potatoes on a cement platform, boiled them, and cut up mutton for stew. It gave me considerable insight into field cooking. As we worked I watched the searchlights of London playing upon the sky, searching for Zeppelins. After helping to feed 1,300 men, and fully satisfying our appetites for the first time since leaving the States, we were dismissed.

I hurried to my tent to get as much rest as possible. The ground was our bed. A rubber sheet kept the dampness from penetrating our blankets from beneath.

Reveille sounded long before I was ready for it. I did not enjoy being routed out to dress in the chill of a foggy morning, so characteristic of England during our three weeks here.

In the afternoon we were called out for our first drill since leaving Camp Mills. It was good to get down to our regular work, and recalled better days at Camp Custer.

The next day, despite clouds and rain, we were given physical exercise and drilled. At 1400 we left with rifles and light packs for a pleasant two-and-a-half-hour hike over winding roads, past vine-covered brick houses and fields of partly harvested grain. This was my first encounter with the English custom of passing on the right.

Inevitably our midday chow was mutton stew—quite acceptable when I broke bread in it.

After supper, while in the tent reading the first twelve chapters of my pocket New Testament, the music of our band raised memories of Chautauqua days back home.

The following afternoon we hiked with light packs to another part of this beautiful country of winding roads, lovely hills, and strange buildings. After cleaning my rifle, I read the report in an English newspaper of Lloyd George's speech in Parliament recounting Great Britain's remarkable record during the four years of war.

Then Lieutenant Jeffers called me and inquired if I had any telegraphic experience or if I'd like that work. "No, sir, and I've not thought about it."

"I think I'll put you in anyway," he said. I was quite satisfied to remain an infantryman.

> *Somewhere in England, Sunday, 11 August 1918*
>
> *Dear Max,*
>
> *As yet I've received but two letters since I left Camp Custer. I expect a mailbag full some of these sweet days.*
>
> *We have in our company a full-blooded Chippewa Indian named Aaron Shaw from Saginaw County. He's quite an agreeable fellow.*
>
> *More sheep are said to be kept here than cattle and this is manifest about twice a day in our mutton stew. I like it, but many do not. Our bread is brown, but good, and we often get jam with it. Practically all my spending money goes for sugarless cakes, as candy and chocolate are hard to get at the canteen. It's a puzzle making the change from U.S. money into English, but I'm getting onto it.*
>
> *Do the folks worry about me? I don't want them to. Wait till I worry, then you people may.*
>
> *With love, Donald*

> *Somewhere in England, 11 August 1918*
>
> *Dear Folks,*
>
> *Our company is going to get passes to London in a couple days, but I'm not going because the time is too short. The band is out and it recalls the Chautauqua season. Wish I could have been there with you. I suppose Albert dodged around in my place. Has he been reclassified? How is his affair with Muriel developing? He's OK. The more I see of other fellows, the better I think he is.*
>
> *I'm watching the Allied successes with much interest. I hope to see the whole enemy line collapse before I get into it.*
>
> *With love, Donald*

We drilled in the morning, then struck our tents to ventilate and dry the ground sheets and blankets upon which we slept. In the afternoon, while those not sent to signal school enjoyed the tortures of a hot hike with heavy packs, I accompanied a group, including Aaron Shaw, Leonard Morey, Elmer Conwell, and others to a place away from camp where we were initiated into the secrets and duties of the wigwag and semaphore codes.

Though we were not informed, we were gradually being equipped and prepared for service decidedly different from going to France. After a short drill we were dismissed and issued a distinctive type of rifle. It was longer, slenderer, lighter, and less substantial than the U.S. rifles we turned in. Its thin, triangular, screwdriver type of bayonet did not present so formidable an appearance as our stocky, knife-type bayonet received at Camp Custer.

It was a Russian rifle! No wonder they lost the war. What was the object of equipping American troops with such a rifle? Were we to fight alongside the Russians against the Huns on the broken-down Eastern Front? Certainly no troops would go to France with this worthless weapon.

After returning from signal school at 1600, I was issued a first-aid kit, sweater, steel helmet, and gas mask.

The next forenoon was spent drilling, with emphasis on the manual of arms. We felt quite proficient in this—until the unwieldy Russian rifles were awkwardly whipped around in each other's faces in a manner disgraceful to raw recruits. The vigor with which we were accustomed to handling our rifles only succeeded in throwing them into positions unworthy of us.

We were ordered to turn in the gas masks issued the day before. Within hours military inefficiency manifested itself when we were called out to receive new masks. Then Sergeant Kennedy took part of the company to a gas house where we were subjected to tear and chlorine gas as we tested our masks. Guarded German prisoners were working in fields along the roadside.

After gas mask inspection, I attended signal school. I never appreciated the work more, for while we leisurely studied signals, the rest of our company—because a few failed to get out in time for inspection—spent three hours hiking with heavy packs, suffering company punishment.

For some reason—probably an officer discovered a dirty man—all E Company men were ordered to bathe before retiring.

Everything in our tent was taken out for Saturday morning inspection. This was always a tiresome bore, because no two sergeants could give similar instructions concerning how our equipment should be laid out.

With others, I was assigned to guard our camp. The guardhouse was a large tent near the entrance. Second Lieutenant Carl Berger, the officer of the guard, required us to learn the general orders. He gave considerable advice and instruction concerning the formalities and practical features of guard duty, including the necessity of using one's ears as well as eyes.

John Beyer fell asleep on duty and was caught by Lieutenant Berger, who did not report him, but punished Beyer with considerable extra guard duty.

At reveille our company appeared for the first time in overseas caps. I had slipped on my old campaign hat, but hurriedly changed when I learned it was no longer in vogue. The cocked hat excited our amusement. With no forepiece and worn at a decided tilt, it afforded no relief from the sun and permitted rain to dribble down the face.

The officers inspected us as we stood with our military possessions laid out on the ground before us and with one sock on the left hand and its mate laid across the forearm. This was followed by inspection of barracks bags. Then our assignments were changed. I was put in the fourth squad, fourth platoon, under Cpl. Mark Van Keuren. My new companions were not so agreeable as those in the old squad.

After a poor supper I turned in my service hat, some summer sock, and light underwear. The supply department's issuing, recalling, and reissuing clothing created considerable disgust and ridicule.

Later, when needing a good night's rest, we were compelled to remain up half the night to be paid. It was 2230 when I was given an English five-pound note, two shillings, and sixpence. We were paid alphabetically, so I can imagine when those at the end of the line were paid.

While on a long hike to the rifle range Aaron Leventhal of Charlotte failed to keep in step, and after being corrected twice, First Sergeant Comstock stepped into the file behind Leventhal and

wickedly kicked his legs when he got out of step. It angered and disappointed me that Comstock, whom I regarded as one of the most
agreeable top kicks, should do this.

At the range we acquainted ourselves with the firing peculiarities
of our Russian rifles and concluded they were poor weapons. All were
inaccurately sighted, yet we were not permitted to make adjustments.
My first shots went wild, but by aiming at the lower left corner of the
target I hit the bull's-eye. Others found their rifles equally faulty. All
of us regarded them with disfavor.

I can only condemn the idiotic policy of furnishing troops with
such flimsy, inaccurate weapons. Considering that vast quantities of
ammunition for these rifles was already in the area we were to go,
the reason is explicable. Nothing eliminates the fact that the better
equipped we were, the better would be the results of our expedition—and the better our chances of surviving.

After being paid I tried in vain to change my five-pound note at
the canteen. Since I never left camp, I decided to let Sergeant
Marten, who was taking notes for other men, break mine when he
left on a pass. I considered the possibility of a breach of trust, but
thought it unlikely due to our rigid discipline.

Marten returned after three or four days—short of funds. Corporal Mylon threatened him with a walloping—and was paid the five
pounds due him, but for the rest of us only a pound apiece appeared.
Some took the matter to Lieutenant Baker, but received no satisfaction. I blamed only myself—a wiser fool.

The last afternoon in Camp Stoney Castle was my most enjoyable
in England. After dinner I sprawled out on a blanket near my tent
and napped in the hot sun. I read more of the New Testament and
invested in a number of sandwiches at the canteen. The roll was
called at retreat, indicating something unusual, and all were prepared to move in the morning.

One of the army's peculiarities are the persistent latrine rumors.
We were to go to Russia; our rifles and heavy clothing tended to confirm this. Others said we were bound for Italy. Some stated we were
to go to Siberia, via either the U.S. or the Mediterranean–Suez–
Indian Ocean route. It was even voiced that we were to return home
to aid in ending the war said to be recently declared between our

country and Mexico. Most rumors were preposterous and took little common sense to eliminate. As for Russia, it looked quite likely, and when Corporal Sanders told me we were going to Archangel to aid the Kerensky government, I felt he knew more than he was telling.

On our last Saturday in England I arose before 0400 and in the moonlight made up my heavy pack for marching. After a light breakfast of bread, jam, and coffee, then a general policing of camp, we formed into line. With mingled feelings of regret and anticipation we left in excellent marching order and swung down the winding road to Brookwood.

Our train pulled out on the London and South Western Railway at 0815 and arrived in North London at 1030. We soon boarded another train for the ten-hour ride to Newcastle. That trip was the greatest treat I enjoyed in England. Crops were being harvested. People waved. They cheered. Many saluted us with flags. Only boys and old men were to be seen. The young men were on the continent rolling back the "impregnable" Hindenburg line.

Amid the chiming of innumerable bells, we detrained at Newcastle, formed into heavy marching order, and hiked the short distance to the dock. Along our way was a large crowd of schoolchildren and civilians. The children begged for souvenir coins and sang many popular American songs.

After considerable tiresome waiting and confusion, we boarded HMT *Nagoya*, formerly a merchant ship plying between England and India. We were assigned quarters in the hold and given a good supper, keenly relished, as our dinner had consisted of only bully beef and hardtack. Instead of sleeping in a hammock I made my bunk on the floor, as did many others. I slept soundly.

Chapter 6
Newcastle to Archangel
26 August to 4 September 1918

On Monday, 26 August, I went on deck before breakfast and found we were still moored in the Tyne River. Alongside was another British transport, the *Czar*, loaded with Italian troops. Our Italian-speaking soldiers were conversing with them and many tossed coins in the hope of receiving souvenir coins in exchange. I threw three halfpennies, but my comrades beat me to all coins from the *Czar*.

The Italians were a fine-looking group. All were stalwart, and many, with black hair, ruddy complexions, and well-shaped features, were handsome. Their uniforms fit well and were neat and clean; more than could be said of ours.

Late in the afternoon, on the incoming tide, we left port and entered the North Sea; colder than the Atlantic. Fog soon enveloped us.

Our American Expeditionary Force consisted of the 339th Infantry Regiment; 1st Battalion, 310th Engineers; 337th Ambulance Company; and 337th Field Hospital Company, all under Col. George E. Stewart, U.S. Army, commanding officer of the 339th Infantry. This force of 4,477 men of all ranks, detached from the 85th Division, were aboard three camouflaged British transports: *Nagoya, Somali,* and *Tydeus*. The *Czar,* the fourth transport, was not camouflaged. The convoy was escorted by four or five small British vessels. A zigzag course was followed across the North Sea.

The canteen was opened and I purchased chocolate and other sweets after standing in a long line.

Our first throat inspection was held on Tuesday.

Assigned to KP duty, I helped bring the food and clean the dishes. After noon, for two hours, I guarded a water faucet to prevent waste of the ship's drinking water. While I was in the hold, a guard from another company slipped at the head of our narrow, wet stairs. His rifle slid across the floor and struck one leg of a stationary table. Instead of helping the soldier, who lay dazed, one of those knowing, cockeyed birds wearing a bar on his shoulder grabbed up the precious rifle, and with a "Good God!" bawled out the man, who soon succeeded in getting to his feet. I'd liked to have cracked open the officer's skull and made a microscopic examination for brains.

Much of our time was spent on deck viewing the sea. For the first time we were given physical exercise—double timing about the deck. This continued each forenoon for the next five days.

30 August 1918

Dear Folks at home,

I'm again sailing the high seas, bound for someplace in Russia. I'm sure you never dreamed of me departing for the scene of Napoleon's great Russian defeat. We left our delightful English camp after being there three weeks. I scarcely took my eyes from the window while we rode the train for ten hours. The roadside and fields are kept in better condition than in the U.S., but there is a sameness about the towns and farm buildings, making it rather monotonous.

The voyage—this is our fourth day at sea—has been uneventful. I've not been sick and have been eating all I want. If we keep traveling, we may not only be called "The Traveling Regiment," but we'll be home for July Fourth. Just think of me as enjoying myself and riding around in a sled pulled by the great Russian bear. I expect to return quite able to eat whale blubber and jabber in Russian.

It scarcely seems possible that summer is nearly gone. No vacation at home, and so much cool weather at sea and in England makes me feel that I have had no summer at all.

With love, Donald

I regret that I never knew exactly where we were. Our route was, of course, through the North Sea, Norwegian Sea, and around Norway's North Cape, through Barents Sea, and into the White Sea. We were too far offshore to see the Norwegian coast. It was our fortune—or misfortune—to be nearer the North Pole than most American citizens ever get to be. I did not see the midnight sun, though it was exceptionally light when I went on deck to the toilet at midnight to relieve a severe attack of biliousness.

I did not feel well throughout the day, though I wandered about the deck and read a considerable amount of the New Testament. The sea was calm. At about 2000, five torpedo boat chasers joined us, escorts for the remainder of our voyage. Before retiring I bought sandwiches at the canteen.

Orders given to roll our heavy packs were countermanded. During the night the *Czar* headed for Murmansk.

After physical exercise I was on guard in a lower hold where many of the troops were ill. Most of them moped about their tables or bunks. An epidemic of Spanish influenza had struck. One officer remarked that E Company did not have so many ill men as his company. The statement about E Company was true, but soon more of our men were sick. Medical facilities were inadequate. Only cathartic pills (also called number nines) were available. How those in authority expected to cure each and every ailment solely with cathartic pills would stagger anyone.

The decks were disagreeably chilly after dinner. Cold soon penetrated the hold. It was unpleasant to be routed out at 0500 to stand guard for two hours in that evil-smelling, influenza-saturated hold.

In the morning I saw the east coast of the Kola Peninsula, the first land since leaving Newcastle. It was a welcome sight, though the dark, barren shore, blotched with snow, was not inviting.

I awoke during the night of 4 September to find I had a Spanish souvenir—the flu. Was weak and ill all day. Despite this I had to help clean our quarters. At the infirmary I was given a cathartic. Instead of sleeping on the floor as I'd done throughout the voyage, I crawled into a hammock.

Chapter 7
So This Is Russia!

5 September to 19 September 1918

Our voyage through the White Sea, across Dvina Bay, and up the Dvina River would have been of great interest, but I was too ill and weak to go on deck sightseeing. Consequently I saw little except a few houses clustered into villages and an occasional flour mill; in my ignorance I thought these were windmills constructed after Dutch models.

Early in the morning of 5 September I went on deck and nearly fainted while waiting to use the toilet. I did see the southern part of Archangel with its varicolored structures of wood and masonry along the dirty waterfront. The many gilt onion domes of cathedrals were more picturesque than anything seen in England.

Nagoya slowly passed Archangel, and at about 1000 stopped along the east bank of the Dvina River at Smolny, a small suburb south of Archangel. We rolled our packs and waited to disembark. Though very ill, I sat at a table listening to the discussions common among soldiers.

A sergeant inquired as to who were too ill to carry their equipment. I added my name to the list, but at 1600 had to shoulder my pack and rifle and march on deck with the rest of E Company. Down the gangplank we went and I stepped on the blood-cursed soil of the despotic czars.

After the usual delay we marched across the rotten planks of a vast wharf dotted with large warehouses, arriving at a gate where a dingy Russian soldier stood guard. The gate was swung open. If I had stepped on Russian soil upon leaving the *Nagoya,* I now wallowed in it. The mile or less of cobblestone street along our route was covered with six to eight inches of dark, sloppy mud.

At last we arrived at a large wooden structure—the barracks for E Company. As I stepped into the building, Charles Hayward fell onto a bunk and, gazing at me with a look of mingled amusement and disgust, yelled in his decisive way, "Some shit!"

This was Russia. Mud, filth, and dark skies were our welcome. We were disappointed, disgusted, and disheartened. Our welcome was unpleasant. Our prospects, gloomy.

The barracks, long and capable of accommodating the entire company, excepting the officers—who always reserved the best quarters for themselves—was characteristic of the rude architecture of northern Russia. It was dirty, poorly lighted, inefficiently heated by three large, tall, cylindrical steel stoves, and overrun with cockroaches. We entered in formation and were assigned bunks so that our squad was together. The bunks were long platforms about fourteen feet wide, partitioned lengthwise through the middle, and about three feet above the floor. On each side of the lengthwise partition men slept side by side. Thoroughly exhausted, I rolled out my blankets on one of these hard, uncomfortable racks and attempted to rest and await recovery from the flu.

Our camp was on the east side of Troitsky Prospect (street), Smolny's main thoroughfare. Running north and south, the street separated us from the wharf area. Though Russia was backward, there were signs of progress: Archangel was lit by electricity and had streetcars; one line passed our camp. I was surprised to see women operating streetcars here, though in Hoboken I first saw women conductors. Later, these Russian women went on strike and were replaced by American troops.

Numerous troops were stationed in Smolny in early September, for other barracks were occupied, probably by units too shattered by the flu to do any active duty along the river or railroad. These various barracks, battalion headquarters, officers' quarters, mess halls, washrooms, kitchen, filthy latrines, and mud-covered areas constituted our unpleasant camp. The drinking water had a sickening taste. We settled down to make the best of a depressing situation.

Not all of the 339th Infantry landed at Smolny. The 3d Battalion, Maj. J. Brooks Nichols commanding, hurriedly debarked at Bakaritza—a small town farther upstream and on the west side of the Dvina River—and were soon fighting. While our men lay dying from flu in Archangel, they were dying of bullets and making history along the railroad. Other forces also hurried up the river to engage the Bolos. (The soldiers' term for the Bolsheviki or Reds.)

Our guard duty in Russia now appeared to be a genuine military expedition. What was the object of sending us to this strange country? This was the farthest north any military force of the United States had ever been sent to fight on foreign soil. Throughout the winter I heard this question discussed in every possible light. To me, the administration, unless decidedly hoodwinked, had some purpose it was not publicizing any more than its war plans in France.

Like many E Company men, I retired that first night in Russia unfit for service, and so dispirited by my surroundings that it mattered little what occurred. While my parents were rejoicing that I'd left the cantonments at home in time to escape this terrible epidemic killing thousands of young men, I lay ill with the same dread disease amid conditions far worse than anything in the sanitary, well-provisioned camps in the States.

Believing my condition justified my not falling out for reveille, I made no effort to get up until ordered to do so by Captain Heil. Telling him, "I'm too ill," elicited an unsympathetic, "That makes no difference. Get up!"

Shivering in the cold of a damp and gloomy Russian morning, I stood my first reveille in this godforsaken land. With others I went on sick report. This necessitated a hike of over a half mile to the infirmary, where the inside of my throat was swabbed with iodine and I was given cathartic pills. As a climax to this poor treatment we were ordered to be exercised twice a day. Wading through mud and breathing the cold, damp air in our debilitated condition, it was a miracle that many more of us didn't die.

The medical department lacked supplies. It was their duty to ensure that they were properly supplied before we left England. None of us in the infantry sailed without his rifle and the means to fight. In Michigan, after the war, I again suffered—though less severely—

from this similar epidemic. My civilian doctor, a veteran of the Civil War, did not order me to exercise twice daily in a muddy field enveloped in cold fog or rain.

Our barracks was the stage for many distressing scenes that first week. Men became thin from the flu and unappetizing food. Many just moped about. Others, unable to leave their bunks, agonized and came close to death. Two men near my bunk suffered intensely. Their moans and paroxysms of coughing indicated their serious condition. Somehow they survived. Others did not. The horror of this barracks of sick men was extremely depressing.

My condition slowly improved due to my own resources, for at the first indication of the flu I had greased my nose, throat, and chest with a salve brought from home.

Since becoming ill I had eaten little. My appetite and the British rations were equally poor. Their rations lacked quality and quantity. There were a few items—English hardtack, tea, jam, and a dried vegetable compound—that I can't forget. Who could? The hardtack may have had nutritive qualities compacted into its 5 x 3 x .5 inches, and was aptly named. Some men cracked or broke teeth on it. The tea was vile, but good compared to the tasteless dried vegetables so resembling grass that this epithet was applied. Only the jam was appetizing. A small amount twice a day was virtually all I ate for my first two days in Russia. At a ridiculously high price I purchased a few chocolate bars from another soldier.

I appealed to Lieutenant Baker to be relieved when I saw my name among the guard detail. He denied it, saying that I was in better condition than many others; the flu had greatly reduced the company's number of functional men.

After being inspected, we made a long, rapid, tiresome march to a guardhouse in Archangel. At midnight, with eight others, I stood guard for nearly five hours around the residence of Ambassador Francis, who had quit Petrograd (Saint Petersburg). Some of the men rested in the ambassador's large auto.

Joseph Brieve of Holland, Michigan, was E Company's first casualty. He died due to the flu on 7 September.

I went on fatigue detail with a small group under Sergeant Marten. We cleaned—for the officers—a number of dirty rooms overrun by cockroaches. Weak from the flu, I asked to be relieved at 1000. This granted, I lay on my bunk until time to mount guard at 1600. I walked a post along the busy Troitsky Prospect. The wooden walk was free from mud. I saw many civilians.

The Russians' proverbial size was no greater than that of our troops and like most races varied considerably. Their coarse, heavy features were invariably accentuated by a great mass of unkempt hair, heavy beard, and mustache having a tinge of red. A sallow complexion and wrinkled skin gave the impression of dissipation. No doubt they led a hard life in a hard land made doubly harsh by war, revolution, and the Bolshevik regime.

Clothing was of every type from old-fashioned black suits to those made of burlap or flour sacking. Headdress ranged from derbies or caps to tall woolen or fur hats of the cossack style. Boots of soft leather or felt were worn by both sexes. Women were no better dressed than men, but displayed a greater variety of colors, usually covering their heads with some varicolored rag. I associated with these people as little as possible, therefore am not so competent to describe them as some of my comrades who always referred to them as "lousy and dirty." I was struck by the beauty of some of the children. Their light hair, blue eyes, and ruddy complexions contrasted with their elders'.

We were relieved of guard duty by another company. Learning that mail would leave in the morning, I hurriedly wrote my first letter sent from Russia. After supper I helped carry logs to our barracks, already being remodeled with bunks of a different type.

Archangel, Russia, 10 September 1918

Dear Folks at home,

I've been on guard for twenty-four hours and am frightfully tired.

Can you see the icebergs and the thermometer at sixty below? Don't imagine too much. We went above Iceland and even higher than nearly all of Alaska. We saw no ice but had cold, disagreeable weather towards the end of the journey. Along the shores of Lapland we saw snow. We arrived here the (censored), and got off the following afternoon.

We are living in barracks heated by three large Russian stoves.

They are more comfortable than our old tents. I imagine we're here for some time.

While on the ship I captured the Spanish influenza and was quite sick, but have been on the job since Sunday. I'm too tired to write much. I hope this finds you all well. By all means don't worry about me. Let me know how things are at home. I've had no mail from the U.S. since leaving. I'll try to write more later.

With love, Donald

During the next two days E Company lost two more men: Harold Maybaum of Ainsworth, Indiana, died 9 September, and John Bigelow of Copenish, Michigan, died on the tenth.

I was one of the large force of E Company men at the funeral of these soldiers and those of other companies who had died of the flu or been killed at the front. We marched a short distance to a large masonry building used as a hospital. In tents beside the hospital the dead lay in coffins of new, unpainted pine boards. We rested on the damp ground until two coffins were placed on a truck, then followed them to the main dock where other dead were brought by barge from the front. After considerable delay these were loaded onto various contrivances, including a macabre gilt-covered, horse-drawn Russian hearse.

We finally began one hell of a march. I thought it would never end. With the caskets in the lead, followed by the regimental band, we traversed the length of Archangel. Far to the north of the city we entered a cemetery where Maybaum and Bigelow of E Company, and seven other American soldiers, were buried with full military honors.

A Catholic chaplain conducted the rites. As we stood at salute I wondered how many more of us would be buried in this dark, muck-like foreign soil so far from home and those we love. I was glad to get into my bunk and rest after the exhausting return march.

Thursday was another day of drill in the forenoon and funeral detail in the afternoon. How often would we repeat this experience? We marched to the dock where we waited for some time, viewing numerous small tugs and fishing boats. In midstream two battleships lay at anchor, the larger having five funnels. A number of dead were brought ashore from a small river tug. At least one casket was wrapped in the Union Jack; so the British were also losing men. Instead of marching to the cemetery we were ordered back to Smolny.

We had about twenty Bolshevik prisoners of war cleaning the filthy latrines and kitchen slops. This unkempt group was assigned tasks none could relish.

We were officially designated the American North Russian Expeditionary Force—the ANREF.

Our company assumed guard of the camp at 1600. I walked my post, a lonely stretch of mud along the camp's south side. As I slowly paced my beat, I dreamt of home and books and memorized the dates of the presidential administrations. I also prayed that this cursed war might soon end and that we be safely returned to those we loved.

After chow I was ambitious enough to accompany Sergeant Kennedy to a haystack in the cemetery near Smolny, where many of us filled our bunk ticks with hay, making them quite comfortable. After I left Smolny, some of the men remaining there had to pay for this hay stolen from an old widow who needed it for her cow, her only means of livelihood.

Our food was absolutely vile when we arrived. Soon it greatly improved. Sunday noon we were given potatoes for the first time since arriving in Russia. Breakfast consisted of stew, tea, jam, and hardtack. The stew was probably beef, though I am not positive that horse meat was never substituted. A Russian slaughterhouse was not far from camp and I often saw the poorest old horses in Archangel stagger past; soon drawn back, cut up, and ready for the city's restaurants. For dinner we received tea, rice, meat, potatoes, gravy, and hardtack. Supper was a stew of meat, beans, potatoes, tea, and hardtack. I ate all the hardtack I could obtain. Once we were issued bread. It was hailed as a delicacy.

When three men failed to appear on time for reveille, the entire company was double-timed about a half mile through the mud of Troitsky Prospect. It was a good breakfast appetizer but did not add to my love for Lieutenant Baker.

I felt better than at anytime since arriving. With physical betterment, my spirits also rose.

While I was on guard a young Russian stepped up to a telephone post like a dog to relieve himself, regardless of passersby. I fiercely bawled him out but did not scare him till I brought my bayoneted rifle into a threatening position.

After supper the company was assembled and Captain Heil called for volunteers to go down the railroad with him. Few responded. I followed the personal advice of a Civil War veteran to do no volunteering. The captain selected 110 men, among whom were DePue, Sanders, Franklin, Leo Baker, Leventhal, and Hayward. There was considerable speculation as to the purpose of this division of E Company.

Early on the morning of 18 September, E Company was astir to see Captain Heil and his force depart. Those of us not making the trip were detailed to carry barracks bags to the Smolny quay. A river tug manned by Russians finally steamed to the dock. Major Nichols arrived and asked Captain Heil if he was sure the craft was going to Bakaritza. "No, sir," he replied.

The major ordered an interpreter to ascertain the tug's destination. This was the craft sent to take Captain Heil's force to the other side, so loading continued and the men departed—uninformed as to their prospective duties. Landing at Bakaritza, they entrained for Isaka Gora, where they held the line of communications until 8 November.

Those of us remaining at Smolny were now under the command of 1st Lt. John J. Baker, who had a free hand. First Sergeant Comstock was nearly dead with pneumonia, so Sgt. Harold Laird was the acting top kick. This division of E Company ended my service in Corporal Van Keuren's squad, and I was assigned to Cpl. Robert Burton. The worst of this was having to sleep in the same bunk beside a disagreeable, stupid, ill-tempered, bowlegged Russian from Detroit.

Archangel, Russia, 18 September 1918

Dear Folks at home,
I drew my third weekly allowance of cigarettes tonight. Doesn't that sound bad? I get away with them exactly as I did at home. (Carey never smoked, but sold, traded, or gave away his allowance.) I've developed another terrible habit—I eat butter whenever we have it.

*Of course you want to know what kind of a place Archangel is.
Being the second worst venereal disease city in the world, it must
be—unlike its name—far from angelic. The streets of cobblestone
and mud are extremely hard to march along. They are like the gutters
of one of our dirty towns magnified a few dozen times. There are electric lights and streetcars.*

*The people of Russia are a fine-looking bunch. They appear to be
quite shy of the barber, and I have a suspicion about their cleaning
up very often. They seem to have an oversupply of horses, for they
butcher them for meat. A good horse sausage would be about as appetizing as anything one can conceive. I'll not indulge unless they begin to feed the U.S. Army, and I guess there's no danger of that. The
Russian language is very musical; a conglomeration of z's, x's, and
v's that would drive one insane eventually.*

*We've remodeled the interior of our bunkhouse and have a num-
ber of bunks. Ottney and I are together. We have our separate beds
but they are in the same bunk. DePue is still the same good scout,
and I have a couple other companions from Kentucky and Tennessee.
I like to hear them tell about the South.*

*It is now 7:45 P.M. and too dark to write more. When in England
it was still light at nine o'clock.*

With love, Donald

On 19 September the ground was covered with our first frost. As
there had been considerable stealing, a company inspection of all
personal property and equipment, except our rifle, bayonet, and bed
tick was held during the forenoon in an open shed on the wharf. A
few things may have been returned to their rightful owners, but if E
Company contained any petty thieves they were not all left at Smolny
when the company was divided. One man was held to ridicule when
Lieutenant Baker spied half a life preserver stolen from HMT *Nagoya*
and used for a pillow. It was cold and I stood with my back to the
wind and my hands in my pockets as Lieutenant Baker inspected my
equipment. He saw two pairs of O.D. gloves; one should have been
canvas. When questioned, I forgot to remove my hands from my
pockets. Calmly, though authoritatively, Lieutenant Baker said, "Take
your hands out of your pockets when you talk to *me!*"

I jerked them out with a "Yessir!" and explained that both pairs of gloves had been issued.

While on guard that stormy evening I saw the recently arrived *Rhodesian Transport*.

Upon returning to the guardhouse we were told orders had been received for us to leave Smolny the following morning. G Company, aroused from a prospective night's rest, grouchily relieved us. In a state of nervous expectancy I retired at 2300.

Charlotte Leader 19 September 1918 (Charlotte, Michigan)

The War Department announced that Americans have been landed in Archangel to take part with other Allied forces there in fighting the Bolsheviki and reestablishing order in northern Russia. The troops are from some of our northern states and many of them speak Russian. Hitherto the only Americans were marines and sailors.

Chapter 8
Bakaritza

20 September to 23 October 1918

I crawled out of my bunk at 0500, and after packing my equipment, secured a good breakfast of rice, stew, bread and jam, and tea. Then 109 of us boarded a river tug. I regretted moving because we were now getting American rations. A few E Company men were left on the Archangel side of the river, as they had not recovered from the flu.

Our heavily loaded craft swung into the deep water of the Dvina River and I enthusiastically viewed the few buildings and mills for grinding grain along our route. We landed at Bakaritza, a small town on the west bank of the river, south of Archangel, through which a railroad passed. Like Smolny, this place had a large wharf area and was an important base on the line of communications.

Large transports and small tugs were at the wharf. Artillery pieces were being off-loaded from a ship onto freight cars. We marched to a barracks southwest of the wharf; our quarters until 24 October.

After a cold lunch we put our new abode in order. Late in the afternoon, while some men split wood, I huddled near a small fire and tried to keep warm. It was dusk by 1830.

I arose at 0600 and washed in a pond behind the barracks. The cold water was freshened during the night by a hard rain. It rained in this far northern country much oftener than at home. It would have been a fairly pleasant time of year if the sun had an opportunity to dry the soil and warm the air.

After a good breakfast—food and sleep were important factors in my army life—I accompanied Corporal Damagalski in search of branches to make into crude brooms similar to those used by the un-progressive natives.

The *Palm Branch,* an English ship, and two other vessels were moored at the wharf in the afternoon when the corporal and I wandered about, attempting to steal an empty wine cask to convert into a pair of tubs. A cantankerous French soldier effectively bawled us out, though we could not understand his excited lingo.

After supper the company barbers—working outside—found a few Russian boys and cut their hair in a ridiculous manner. Even Lieutenant Baker indulged in this horseplay by running the clippers lengthwise and crosswise on one youngster's head.

I changed my clothes for the first time since leaving England. Late at night, rumor—always rife—reported the Allies had captured Moscow, and that two million Japanese soldiers had landed on the Siberian coast. (Japanese and American troops were in Vladivostok, Siberia, but the total was less than a hundred thousand.)

There was no bridge across the wide Dvina River at Archangel. Our war with the Bolsheviki and expedition into the interior of the state of Archangel was conducted on both sides of the river, so Bakaritza, on the river's west bank, was an important base. Here necessities of war could be brought by water, unloaded, then shipped by rail to various points along the line of communications and to the front, where the enemy as being pushed into the interior.

Large ships unloaded their cargoes of food and munitions at Bakaritza, then loaded at Archangel with flax needed in British factories. Sizable open and enclosed sheds and warehouses, many filled before our arrival, were scattered on the old planked wharf; all surrounded by a high board fence and guarded gates, except on the river front.

Here were rifle and artillery ammunition, petrol, various other munitions, flour, sugar, and every type of canteen supply including soap, chocolate, apples, canned goods, peppermint candy, liquor, and tobacco. Because these supplies had been shipped to the Kerensky government—preceding the Lenin-Trotsky regime of disorder—our Allied force was equipped with Russian rifles to save the time and expense of transporting a vast supply of American and British rifle ammunition.

I believe most of these supplies were manufactured in England and America for the Czar's government. Some had been taken by the Bolsheviki. Later, our company captured great quantities of munitions, including one-pound shells bearing the inscription "Made in USA."

Guarding this stock at Bakaritza was a small force of English, Scots, Russians, French, and other American troops besides E Company. Supply company made its headquarters here. The Russians were supposedly—though not always—anti-Bolshevik, and known as the British Slavic Legion—B.S.L. They were fed, paid, and equipped by the British. I believe the British brought only officers, commissioned and noncommissioned, with the expectation of organizing and officering these simple people.

Many of our troops were unfair in their attitude toward the British, attributing evil to all their motives, while holding the French and Russians in high esteem. With my knowledge of British and European history I could better appreciate the greatest democracy on the eastern side of the Atlantic.

E Company's chief duty during our month in Bakaritza was to guard these supplies. Preparation for guard duty included a rifle free of rust, neat uniform, greased shoes, and a shave.

After dinner I was assigned a beat along the river side of a large, open warehouse filled with canteen supplies. Here were candies, cakes, chocolate, liquor, dried and canned fruit, canned vegetables, and beans—everything a hungry soldier fed a monotonous ration could desire.

While looking at the large transports anchored only fifty yards away I noticed a camouflaged floatplane, captured by our troops as they fought southward along the railroad.

During my evening shift the English major in charge of the warehouse treated me to two small, gnarly apples, for which he apologized. One was for the other guard. That only whetted my appetite, which was somewhat satisfied when Conwell broke into a box of dried apricots and a box of candy bars, which we avidly devoured. Of course, this was stealing. It was the first time I had done such, but I was not filled with remorse. I regarded it as justifiable, for such luxuries were unobtainable in any other manner. We all had a great craving for sweets, which the kitchen force could not, or at least did not, satisfy. This was a campaign of great thievery by our troops at Bakaritza. While Captain Heil and his men were forcing down mutton stew at Isaka Gora, we were living on the fat of Allied supplies.

I never regretted not volunteering to accompany the captain—who wanted only brave men to follow him—to Isaka Gora, where they saw less military service than we.

While helping to get lumber for a washhouse to be built in the rear of our quarters, I saw four camouflaged three-inch artillery pieces west of our barracks. Looking through the telescope of one I saw a woman at work in a field over three-fourths of a mile distant. These guns, manned by Russians, were for protection of the camp and town.

In the afternoon Lieutenant Baker took three of us to the YMCA to pick up checkers, books, and a small phonograph. I retired early but awoke to hear the phonograph producing tunes that years later I occasionally catch myself whistling, reminding me of those evenings in my bunk in Bakaritza—the best place I found in gloomy Russia.

As we had no reveille and I was not listed for guard duty on 24 September, I arose later than usual. Upon going to the pond for my morning wash I found the ground covered with the second frost of the season. In the forenoon I worked on construction of the new washhouse.

After noon chow—including a jam tart—we drew two loads of lumber from a sawmill near the wharf. Instead of our officers drafting a few of the numerous Russian horses, we drew the wagon. "The American soldier makes a good jackass!" I told my companions. On the way to the barracks we met a large army truck driven by a thick-shouldered native who turned toward us and gave our wagon a severe jolt. Had I not jumped, I would have been seriously injured or killed.

After inspection, we marched to the wharf area for guard duty. Just within the stockade by the main gate was our guardhouse: a small, dirty structure. There was little opportunity to rest, for the room was so crowded with Russian soldiers that I could not lie down. Throughout the night they jabbered or sneezed out their inharmonious language, smoked evil-smelling cigarettes, and ate oily canned sardines, a delicacy they greatly prized.

During my shift from midnight till 0200 the aurora borealis was visible; its long, quivering streamers of white and yellow light reminded me of the London searchlights playing upon the sky. I expected them to be far more brilliant, but at no time in Russia did I see so colorful a display as seen in Michigan in March 1917.

Passes to Archangel were issued. I did not ask for one. Many men returned with tales of how easy and cheap it was to secure Russian girls. Those starving people would sell their souls for a cigarette, a half bar of chocolate, or even a hardtack. Often, for good measure, the girls gave assorted venereal diseases. The first case in our company soon appeared.

Dirty Archangel and her natives held no attraction for me. Also I had a severe migraine headache until 1500, when I succeeded in sleeping it off. Later, I wrote by the light of a candle stuck on a mess table—electric lights, first turned on the previous night, failed. By 1930 it was quite dark, notice of the approach of winter that no one anticipated with pleasure.

Four months earlier our gang had met at the Charlotte Court House to be inducted.

We were held in formation until the Russian force also guarding the area arrived. Amid confusion and orders of *Smyena* and *Valna* they were formed into a line for inspection. Then we were posted or marched to the guardhouse.

I was fortunate to be at a guardhouse where I could find room to lie on the floor and sleep between my two-hour shifts. Nightly the warehouse containing canteen supplies was being pilfered. I was at the petrol dump, a warehouse containing oils, gasoline, ammunition, and aeroplane bombs.

I took all the chocolate I could eat when men brought it to the guardhouse and shared their plunder. Occasionally a Christmas cake soaked in brandy was divided, or a large can of California peaches. Some men were wasteful, punching a hole in the can, drinking the juice, and throwing away the peaches.

I was alert as I paced through the building, for an attempt had been made by a Bolshevik spy to blow it up. Occasionally a shot was fired by some nervous soldier. One night the guard from another company, walking the post I was first assigned, shot and killed a drunken civilian who failed to stop when ordered to halt. The civilian would not have been injured had I been on duty. I was more afraid of being shot by some nerve-shattered man of our regiment, or the possible explosion of the dump accidently fired by a cigarette fiend disobeying the "no smoking" order in the wharf area.

Henry Bok and I worked all day in the kitchen, an opportune time, for the forenoon was cold and wet. We ate all we desired and, like good soldiers, did as little as possible. Mess Sergeant Graseck had a hen cooped in the kitchen. It was probably stolen and undoubtedly afforded a good meal for the sergeants or officers.

Everything was covered with frost the lovely first morning of October. With the new month came a great improvement in our rations—real American food: bacon, jam, coffee, and oatmeal for breakfast; hardtack, tea, beans, and pickles for dinner. Though varied somewhat, these constituted our diet for some time. The kitchen force bettered this when given stolen supplies—baking biscuits when provided with white flour.

Most men were too absorbed with securing liquor to waste time in genuine foraging. As for punishment from our officers, we knew there was little to fear, for Lieutenant Baker had said: "Steal all you can. The best soldier is the one who gets away with the most. *But don't get caught.*"

I did little entering and taking, not because it was beneath me nor that I did not want the supplies, but because I did not know how far one could go without punishment, and I did not care to serve a term in Leavenworth, Kansas, after the war. Often when guarding a warehouse I let others get what they wished, and often shared in the booty. Though I had fifty dollars there was no army canteen. When a canteen did open, a limited allowance was sold per man. Fruit was unobtainable in the dirty stores of Archangel. No wonder many of us stooped to pilfering what we craved.

I drew the line on selling stolen supplies. I believed the rumor that men of Supply Company sold food and clothing and had thousands of dollars in Russian money, readily exchanged for U.S. dollars before we left Europe. Many E Company men sold stolen material to Russian civilians. Probably some slipped through the loose Allied lines to be resold to the enemy. One morning a man inducted with me in Charlotte asked me to carry his blanket roll as we left the guardhouse so he could pass the gate guards with five thousand American cigarettes wrapped in his shelter half. This he did at least another time, availing himself of passes and selling the cigarettes to Russian civilians. Others did similar feats. Little wonder gamblers could display Russian notes worth hundreds of American dollars.

The appetite for liquor was strong; worse, some got drunk on duty. Private Nugent, among the first to be caught, was sent to the guardhouse and later court-martialed. American troops were not the only ones obtaining liquor. The corporal of the guard had me help bring a drunken civilian, discovered in another shed, to the guardhouse. The unkempt fellow of about thirty-five was so drunk he could scarcely walk as we led him reeling between us. I slugged him on the right shoulder when he fell against me. At the guardhouse I saw a U.S. private from Headquarters Company brought in by a British officer for stealing two cans of jam.

Apparently I ate too many chocolate bars while in the guardhouse, for I was too ill with a migraine headache to eat breakfast. I slept the remainder of the day.

The first snow of the season fell during the morning of 3 October, melting as soon as it touched the wet ground. The natives claimed the season was unusually mild.

Mail finally arrived and was welcomed with much shouting. I'd received no mail since 19 July and was anxious to learn of events at home. I received six letters and two cards, the latest dated 26 July. Part of the letters I read at noon, the rest at night. All were reread. Our electric lights were again functioning.

After supper John Beyer and I visited a Russian bathhouse and I took my first bath since leaving England 43 days earlier. The steaming, crowded place reeked with the sweat of bathing soldiers and civilians. I did not indulge in the Turkish steam bath so prized by the Russians, but thoroughly bathed with soap and washcloth and a pan of hot water.

On Sunday I was assigned to the small, overcrowded guardhouse near the main gate. With me was Private Gessinsess, a disagreeable Russian Jew from Cincinnati, Ohio, whose tongue could rattle half-understandable English faster than any American with English ancestors. We guarded two large enclosed warehouses near the gate. Leisurely strolling our beat we described a figure eight around the buildings.

I saw a captured hydroplane in flight. Its shrill motor reminded me of the triplane seen at Camp Mills.

While I was on post in the evening sergeants Laird and Masterson, and Corporal Burton, all of E Company, appeared. Pulling the hasp and lock from a warehouse door, they entered. I was more responsible than Gessinsess for permitting this and spent a nervous forty-five minutes while they noisily rifled the shed for liquor. I resolved that no man would again illegitimately enter my post. If they had used good judgment and quietly secured what they were after, I should not have minded, but the breaking of boxes was plainly audible outside—so much so that Gessinsess would have turned them over to the corporal of the guard had I not persuaded him to keep quiet. We warned them to make less noise and rush their dastardly business. Finally, each drunk and reeling with a crate of booze on his shoulder, they left and somehow succeeded in getting past the guards at the gate.

Men from the 337th and 338th Infantry arrived from France. During lunch I visited with a large fellow, Clyde Miller, of Monroe, Michigan (referred to hereafter as Clyde Miller #1). He was one of seven men from B Company, 338th Infantry, sent to Russia to replace casualties suffered by the 339th.

Due to a defect in the kitchen chimney we did not get breakfast until 0800. Later, Lieutenant Baker took us to the sawmill for sawdust to fill the space between the outer and inner siding of the washhouse nearing completion. He secured a truck after deciding it was impossible to carry all we required in a large canvas. Then, instead of the usual fatigue duty that regularly followed our guard duty, we drilled for the first time since leaving Smolny.

After dinner Lieutenant Berger took command of the drill. Finding the plank flooring too easy for marching, he incurred my lasting hatred by taking us to a cow pasture covered with mud and manure, where we made up for the lack of drill since reaching Bakaritza.

Little time was wasted at rest. Usually the men could smoke most of a cigarette. This time they barely had time to take a couple puffs before commanded to fall in. When the lieutenant became tired the sergeants took over; when they were exhausted he put the corporals in command. Not only did he drill us severely, but he kept us long after we normally ended the day's duty.

Feeling that some spiteful motive animated this, I was angered and felt little pity when I saw him mortally wounded at Kodish.

Though stealing among the troops was not unusual, it was unusual for troops to administer punishment. Some of the liquor and cigarettes stolen from the warehouses was again stolen from men in our barracks. Not long after I lay down, scuffling attracted my attention. Peeking over the edge of my bunk, I saw six or seven men roughly handling Tarnacki, one of our stolid Polish soldiers. Bromley repeatedly slugged him in the face. Then they hustled him outside and I heard a faint splash. Looking out the window, I saw a series of ripples pass over the stagnant pond in front of the barracks.

For two weeks we had not assembled at reveille. Some men abused this and did not get up when the bugle sounded. Then First Sergeant Comstock, whom we left nearly dead of pneumonia in Archangel, rejoined us and we were routed out to go through the usual formalities.

One day I guarded a vast quantity of hardtack packed in waterproof tin boxes.

Our men often criticized the English for, among other things, their refusal to salute Americans. Orders required the formal halting of everyone after dark. On two occasions I halted English officers on the wharf, compelling them to come through the mud abounding between the plank road and me to be recognized. This done, I saluted with the customary present arms and always received a return salute, usually some remark about the weather, and the officer departed with a "Good night, sentry."

I thought we were treated with more consideration by English officers than by our own, who were formal and terse. If some of the incidents I heard related were true, it was the English who had cause to complain. One corporal told me that, when asked by an English officer why he did not salute, he said: "We quit doing that in 1776!"

I arose at 0600 on Friday 11 October and read until called for fatigue duty in the new washhouse. After supper I received a letter from

Father and Mother dated 19 August with a photograph of Muriel, who graduated from high school in June. It also told of Uncle John Cary's death from cancer. (The other four Cary brothers Americanized their names by inserting the *e* shortly after the Civil War.)

A newly constructed U.S. canteen opened and before dinner I stood in line with French, English, Americans, and Russians to purchase a can of milk and peach jam. The allowance sold each person was disappointingly limited.

We drilled in the afternoon. In ridicule of the British, whose commands were different from ours, Sergeant Fergerson, of Kentucky, sternly ordered—in the presence of a group of British and American officers—"Left . . . Wheel!" just as the head of the column was ready to pass through the main entrance. Despite the foreign command and amid considerable suppressed amusement, we rounded the turn.

> *Somewhere in northern Russia, 12 October 1918*
>
> *Dear Muriel,*
>
> *Your photograph arrived last night and I was pleased to get it. It is an excellent likeness. You have one of me in uniform, haven't you?*
>
> *The letter from home was dated 19 August, and it reads as though you and Albert are married. Apparently another letter, not yet received, contains all information about the event. Though I've not been officially notified, I'll send my congratulations to Albert, and wish you much joy. . . .*
>
> *Don't let work prevent keeping up with your music. I expect to hear those old selections and some new ones when I return. They always recall pleasant memories of home; mainly, I suppose, because I only heard them while enjoying my vacations there.*
>
> *I trust this finds you both well and happy. Give Albert my best wishes. Write and tell me about the great day. I wish I could have been there.*
>
> *With love, Private Donald E. Carey*

On Sunday a YMCA officer was supervising civilians loading supplies from the shed onto one-horse Russian wagons, then aboard a barge delivering them to soldiers fighting upriver.

While I was on guard, Corporal Damagalski told me a wireless was received stating the war had ended. Though fervently hoping this was true, I doubted it. However, it brought about celebrations in camp that soon became carousals instead of dignified offerings of thanksgiving.

Officers and men spent the night in a drunken spree. The Officer of the Day did not make his nocturnal rounds until after daybreak. One of our privates appeared at the guardhouse drunk. The usual forenoon inspection of the guard dismount did not take place because the new Officer of the Day failed to appear.

After some wait we took it upon ourselves to dismount without being inspected, and in a drizzling rain marched to the barracks, where I cleaned my rifle.

Sometime during the night I awoke. The barracks was in an uproar. Men were singing, yelling, talking—all raising hell. Three or four blue-coated Frenchmen entered, and as I peeked over my bunk at the scene below, Noone gaily stumbled around with one of their dark blue caps jauntily tilted over one ear.

Later, I was awakened by a thud. I awoke Burnham with a couple vigorous kicks and asked if Bromley, who slept at the edge of the platform, was there. "No!" Caring little whether he was hurt or not, I had a couple fellows attend to him before I fell back asleep. In the morning he came to and wondered why he had a sprained wrist. As it was a drop of at least twelve feet, he might better have wondered why he hadn't broken his neck. During our stay in Bakaritza I saw more drunks than ever in my twenty-five years.

Many, including myself, were given a scare by the rumor that English officers would search the barracks for stolen goods. After eating all the chocolate I could and hiding the rest, and sinking a bar of English toilet soap in the wash pond, I awaited the ordeal. It proved to be a venereal inspection. That never worried me, but scared one of our sergeants into making a hurried exit just before Lieutenant Baker ordered a guard posted at the door.

The remainder of the afternoon was spent in drill. I felt fine, and when such was the case, I enjoyed drilling. At retreat Sergeant Comstock advised the men against their drunken tendencies, warning them of possible courts-martial, especially if found drunk on duty.

Some, when supposed to be on post, had spent the time dead drunk in the guardhouse while others stood double or triple shifts.

Paul Stanicki, one of our Poles, fired his rifle during the customary inspection of arms before being dismissed after twenty-four hours of guard duty. Forgetting to unload the rifle was not soothing to Lieutenant Baker. All passes were discontinued. In the afternoon the men were given a hike with heavy packs through crotch-deep mud and water. The lieutenant accompanied the men and waded with them.

During my shift from 0430 to 0630 there was a fire in a village west of Bakaritza. A confusion of bells was heard for a half hour. Judging by the sound, more persons were ringing bells than fighting the fire.

Again the Officer of the Day did not appear to inspect us prior to guard dismount, so the sergeant ordered us back to the barracks. Lieutenant Baker learned of this and angrily sent us back to the wharf where, after a long wait, the officer appeared. To his regular duties he added inspecting our canteens for whisky. Mine had contained lime juice and washing did not eliminate the odor.

"What do I smell in your canteen?"

"Lime juice, sir," I replied, to his satisfaction.

We were ordered to roll our heavy packs after noon chow and Lieutenant Berger hiked us south of Bakaritza along the railroad to the wireless station about halfway to Isaka Gora. Though we were not required to wade any water, we did not escape the mud.

After dinner I visited with Walter Franklin, who came from Isaka Gora on a pass. He told me DePue was serving a term in the guardhouse. He and Charles Benjamin were caught foraging on the wharf at Bakaritza, each with a jug of lime juice they mistook for rum. These unlike liquids were in similar jugs bearing confusing labels such as "2a." The pair, being about the same stature, were given the sobriquet, "The Lime Juice Twins."

In the evening it snowed considerably, and before I retired, a winter scene of great beauty was visible in the Arctic twilight. And Father and Mother ask how it is in sunny France. If they could only see this region.

Early in the morning I was told our company had been ordered to the front. The arrival during the forenoon of the flu convalescents left at Smolny, and distribution in the afternoon of overshoes and rubber capes tended to confirm this. There was considerable speculation concerning our move until the order was countermanded.

The decision to keep us at Bakaritza was satisfactory to me, though the fact that we had been ordered to the front left me with an instinctive feeling that our stay here would be short.

About 1630, as I was waiting in line at the barracks for my overshoes and cape, a loud rifle report rang out amid the noise from the barracks. "More company punishment," I said to myself.

There was considerable confusion near the barracks' front door. Then Corporal Kooyers and another man came out, their hands covered with blood. Others followed, carrying Cpl. Martin Campbell of Portland, Michigan, to the medical station, where he died within a half hour. Campbell was one of our convalescents arriving from Smolny that morning.

Henry Jones of Trail City, South Dakota, was responsible. I was not acquainted with this young man, though his bunk on the upper tier was less than ten feet from mine. Apparently Jones had had to sell—at considerable sacrifice—a ranch when he entered the army. He decided to end it all by suicide on his bunk while most, if not all, of the men were below. The trigger of his rifle was placed on a nail. It fired before he raised the muzzle to his head or chest. The bullet passed through his sleeve and bunk before hitting Campbell in the abdomen as he slept on a lower bunk. This cast a depressing gloom over the men, for Campbell was a capable and popular man.

Jones was arrested, court-martialed, and convicted of murder in the first degree.

The next morning I was posted with orders to guard the lard shed, an open structure near the guardhouse and the river. Unlike most of the well-filled sheds, this one held only a big pile of boxes in one corner containing chocolate, cigarettes, and probably lard. Two Englishmen were supervising Russian men and women loading some of this onto droshkies—crude, one-horse wagons. At the other end was an assortment of large boxes, machinery, ropes, and harnesses, where a party of Englishmen were working.

A number of railroad switch tracks were along both sides of the shed. Between the river and the shed were scattered many kegs of fish from Norway, apparently undisturbed since being rolled off the ship.

About noon the shed was deserted except for four English privates. As I leisurely approached, a red-faced, middle-aged English sergeant ordered them to move some of the kegs so a locomotive and cars could pass. One man, standing apart from the others, started to obey at the second command, but stopped when one of his comrades said they were working within the shed and not required to work outside. The sergeant threatened to show them what British soldiers would or would not do. Reluctantly, they obeyed. I thought they were displaying more nerve than judgment, but said nothing, concluding that royal armies also had men who did not enjoy fatigue duty.

After their task was finished, I met the sergeant and a British lieutenant. I presented arms, received prompt recognition, and started on just as the sergeant said, "And by the way, sentry, I don't want you to interfere when I give orders to my men."

I immediately faced him and emphatically denied having interfered or having said anything. His, "I heard what you said" was a deliberate lie. Regardless of the lieutenant—a silent spectator—I closed the argument by pointing at him and angrily saying: "Moreover, I take my orders from American officers only!"

I was told—another latrine rumor—that two thousand U.S. regulars had landed at Archangel and would soon leave for the front.

Upon returning to the barracks after guard dismount we were ordered to pack our bags immediately. We carried these and other company equipment to the wharf in the afternoon. This naturally led to much speculation: some saying to Onega; others, to the front. Even to Mexico.

After a supper so unsatisfying that "rotten" would not adequately describe it, I accompanied a couple men to the British YMCA. Many soldiers, British and American, were enjoying its comforts. Maps, magazines, bulletins, and phonographs were in use. I studied a large wall map of Russia—to no advantage, for all names were printed in Cyrillic.

Rumors were so untrustworthy and news at such a premium that I had no opportunity to discover what was occurring in either France or Russia.

Chapter 9
Return to Smolny

24 October to 29 October 1918

The usual cheerfulness of our Bakaritza barracks departed with our barracks bags and equipment. I disliked leaving. Apprehensive as to the comforts of our next abode, I rolled my pack of three blankets, two towels, and a bar of soap.

After the usual delay—fatigue duty and policing up—so characteristic of a military move, we formed up and departed, leaving our comfortable quarters to an English force whose officers were already inspecting it. Some men complained that just as we got a place satisfactorily arranged, an English outfit always took it. We had just obtained a large supply of firewood and nearly completed a new washhouse—as yet unused.

A large warehouse caught fire as we marched across the wharf to the dock. Thick black smoke rapidly rose. We did not stop, but boarded a small tug and made an enjoyable river voyage of six miles downstream and across to Smolny.

Three large American transports, including the *Aniwa*, were anchored there. Instead of bringing the rumored force of two thousand regulars, they brought supplies.

We carried our bags to the barracks we'd used upon arriving in Russia. Some of the bags were heavy with bottles of liquor. Until I found mine when we rested along the way, I dropped the one I carried, hoping to lighten the load. We settled in and spent the evening talking.

Shortly after breakfast our fourth batch of mail was distributed. I received nineteen letters, all dated between 21 July and 13 September. It took exactly six weeks for the most recent to reach us. Seven were from Mother, my best and most regular correspondent. Others, too, received much mail: one man getting seventeen letters; another, thirty-four. Little wonder our postal service was slow and congested. One letter notified me that Muriel and Albert were married 21 August. I am the only unmarried one of our family.

My letter reading was interrupted by the bugle call to fatigue duty. With Aaron Shaw and a couple others under Corporal Haynes, I was detailed to take two Lewis guns and mail to Captain Heil's force at Isaka Gora. With our load we made the long hike to the dock—where the funeral details had assembled in September. Among other craft at the dock were HMS *Monitor 23* and two subchasers. These had been Russian but were now manned by British sailors.

At Bakaritza we boarded a jerky, wheezing train crowded with sailors and rode a few versts southward to Isaka Gora. (A verst is a Russian measure of length equal to 0.6628 miles, or 1.067 kilometers.) As could be expected of an unprogressive, revolution-torn country, the transportation system had broken down and required much repair. New rolling stock was needed. The country was fully thirty, if not fifty, years behind. With the Baltic and Black seas blockaded, Kola, Murmansk, and Archangel assumed great importance as inlets for war supplies.

For efficient transportation of military supplies when Archangel was in a death grapple with Germany on the Eastern Front—before the Brest-Litovsk Treaty—this single track system entering Archangel was inadequate. With the defense of the country in view, foresight would have required additional rail lines.

The trains were relics. If not manufactured in America, they were modeled after trains of our country. The small locomotive traveled at a moderate speed, burned the abundant wood, and was picturesquely adorned with a funnel-like smokestack characteristic of our Civil War era. Its whistle sounded familiar; those in England did not. The red-painted wooden freight cars, though smaller, resembled those at home. There were at least two types of passenger coaches. We entered one with a number of compartments.

Isaka Gora was a fair-size town similar to others of this region. After delivering the guns and mail we visited a number of our comrades. Anxious to see DePue, I located the guarded quarters of the

Lime Juice Twins—a boxcar on one of the sidings. They were in good spirits and appeared indifferent to their punishment. Their social life was supplied by five natives whom neither could understand, and whose racial characteristics were so Oriental that I thought these Mongolians were Japanese.

Our guardhouse, a large residence constructed of hewn logs and more imposing than the average Russian dwelling, was pleasant and comfortable. We occupied two adjoining rooms, each furnished with a table and chairs, which were well lit and overlooked the Dvina River. Characteristic of northern Russian homes, its unsanitary, odiferous open toilet was in a small room near the front door.

After being relieved at 1100 I wrote my people, attempting, lest it be my last opportunity, to express my love for them and my appreciation of what they had done for me. Not that I feared danger for myself, but I fully realized that Death stalked here as well as in war-riven Europe. How I longed to tell them everything that had occurred, and how I hated the army with its immoral, drinking, smoking men. What a satisfaction it would have been to know that at some later date I could tell them all. With pity for them and none for fate, I wrote with tears in my eyes, caring not for the censor.

During retreat it snowed so hard, I thought the officer could sensibly cancel the tiresome ceremony. However, once indoors and satisfied with an exceptionally good supper of stew, coffee, white bread, jam, and pie, I felt better.

Archangel, Russia, 26 October 1918

Dear Folks at home,

With the dirty Russian mud frozen solid it will be healthier here as well as more agreeable for us.

One of your letters stated Muriel was married 21 August. Both are to be congratulated. . . . Albert is a fine young man. I know of no better fellow among all the men with whom I've associated, and am pleased to have him for a brother-in-law.

So the government is taking drastic measures toward Sunday pleasure drivers. I have learned the saloons are to close 1 December for the duration, if the war doesn't end before then. I hope they will never be opened.

What has happened in the realm of politics? I'm sorry Uncle John (Nichols) failed to secure the nomination. He would have made an excellent representative.

I know you dread my being in Russia. I'm sure there is an ever-guiding Power that knows what is best. I'm glad you have been look-ing to Him for my safety, and I've been doing the same morning and night, sometimes oftener for all of you.

I often dream as I work of home scenes, and I'm sure you know that I fully appreciate home and all that you have done for me. Often when standing retreat or in parades . . . or when the band played, I've thought how badly Father felt when he left me last, and I couldn't restrain the tears myself. I'll never forget how the tears rolled down Max's face . . . I felt bad, too, but kept a stiff upper lip.

With love to all, Donald

I arose early and with a detail of forty-nine men hiked to the Smolny quay, where we boarded a vessel taking us to Bakaritza. There we moved a few pieces of artillery and other heavy equipment from one shed to another.

The day's outstanding feature was Sunday dinner with Supply Company. It was the best meal we had in Russia: beef, gravy, mashed potatoes, hardtack, coffee, tomato juice, and three helpings of chocolate pudding.

My night's rest was disturbed by a dream that Cuba and the U.S. were at war and the president called for one million volunteers.

Late Monday afternoon Lieutenant Baker sent me to Bakaritza for a roll of sheet music and some checkers. Supplied with a pass I hurried to the Archangel dock and caught a tug crossing the river. I returned on the boat at 1800. Upon boarding a streetcar I was nearly put off when I offered the lady conductor an English coin instead of paper rubles. A Russian-speaking American came to my rescue.

The company was issued winter clothing. Turning in my O.D. over-coat, I received a heavy reddish-brown greatcoat lined with goatskin, and a black fur hat that when untied at the top and turned down was white.

Archangel, Russia, 28 October 1918

Dear Max,

You implied that you dreaded to see me come here. I trust it is more because of the weather than the Bolsheviks. Others have survived the polar regions, so I don't see why I can't do so. The weather is like that at home in December; cold, ground slightly frozen, and covered with snow. As for the Bolsheviks, they are a nervous gang.

I suppose all types of farmwork will be revolutionized by the time I return. That will be my permanent occupation. I'm going to raise pigs. Haven't heard any squeal for so long that their bursts will sound like music. The nearest to a pig I've seen in Russia is a billion or so slabs of greasy bacon.

So far I've seen nothing in which the U.S. doesn't excel. Old Europe is properly designated. She is slow, dirty, unprogressive, and after the war will be weak as a kitten.

With love to all, Donald

Early in the forenoon I was ordered to Bakaritza for the third time in as many days. I was in charge of Burlak and Bladowski. Each of us carried an issue of winter clothing for men of our outfit in the hospital's venereal ward. While crossing the river I enjoyed a visit with an intelligent middle-aged British civilian. At the hospital many men occupied bunks in a large room. My loathing for the diseases acquired by their folly impelled me not to linger.

Each man was issued a heavy knife having a large blade, a can opener, and a sharp, round, slightly curved prong designed for cleaning horses' hooves. It could be attached to the belt by a ring. Because of the can opener it became indispensable.

My name was among those listed for promotion to private first class. This meant a slight increase in pay and perhaps less fatigue work and more guard duty.

After supper, a group of us, including Ottney, was detailed for provost guard duty in Archangel. Before leaving, Lieutenant Baker addressed us, supplementing his advice at Bakaritza to steal, telling us if any got in trouble, "whether right or wrong," to notify him, and military lawyers would be secured to acquit them. Though his code was neither moral or honorable, it was intended to help his men, in whom he took considerable pride.

Believing this concluded our duties for the day, a number of us retired after 2000. Our rest was short. We were routed out to roll our heavy packs. While lined up in the barracks I noticed Waterstreet, one of the replacements. This neat, fine-looking man was being subjected to the lieutenant's method of teaching how to make up a pack. Finally, about fifteen of us left, burdened with rifles, heavy packs, and barracks bags to trudge the uneven, rotten sidewalk lining Archangel's poorly lighted streets. After a long, weary hike we arrived at a massive structure of solid masonry—once a prison. We used one large room as a guardhouse. Having no idea when I would be called for duty, I curled on the floor beside my barracks bag and slept until 0400.

Chapter 10
Archangel Provost Guard
30 October to 7 November 1918

For nine days our small force of E Company men were part of Archangel's international provost guard composed of English, French, Russian, and American troops. Our duties varied from guarding officers' quarters and public buildings to patrolling streets and preserving order. The duty was not dangerous, but it could become so for individual guards in isolated quarters of the city in case of riot or an organized uprising of Bolshevik sympathizers.

The guardhouse was only ten yards from the Dvina River, and our comfortable, well-lit room overlooked that largest of north Russian rivers. The bank was high, steep, and lined with rocks upon which I usually stood when performing my morning toilet.

The electric-lit room had a high ceiling and high windows on the river side. Doors opened into the sergeant of the guard's room and the kitchen. Lengthwise through the room's center were two rows of double-deck bunks; on one of the uppers I made my bed. A table and a few chairs completed the furnishings.

We stood guard daily, each man having two shifts of four hours. My hours from four to eight, morning and evening, could not have been more satisfactory, as they afforded eight hours off duty both day and night.

My first shift began at 0345, when I was awakened from my sleep on the floor and, with the relief, crossed the city to a point east of the main street. With William Proper of Cadillac, Michigan, I was assigned a long beat around two blocks. It was moonlight and we had

71

no difficulty in slowly pacing along the dilapidated, uneven sidewalks.

Our orders required the halting of everyone who approached while it was dark. With the first stir of human life our sharp "*Stoi-ie!*" always brought the person addressed to a standstill and invariably led to a reply that was accepted as an adequate explanation, though neither of us could comprehend a word. Women always gave long explanations.

About 1700 there was a great uproar of whistles when a boat burned along the shore.

The mild, cloudy weather of October's last day melted the snow.

Opposite my beat in the business section was a large building displaying the American flag and occupied by officers. Diagonally across the main street was an open square and an imposing cathedral with religious scenes painted in many colors just below the towers. Along the square was the invariable array of one-horse droshkies and their drivers: the Russian equivalent of U.S. cabbies.

I was impressed by the throngs on the streets during the evening shift, and was astonished at the activity in a city so far north. Every description of civilian, regardless of age, sex, and circumstances, was hurrying as though some business required immediate attention. Mingled with the crowd were soldiers—so common they attracted little attention—and a few sailors. Allied military and naval officers in gold braid, red-banded caps, or other insignia denoting rank or special service branch were numerous and added color to this motley crowd. With loaded and bayoneted rifle on my shoulder, I paced my beat in the midst of this gay, hurrying throng, halting time without number to present arms in salute to officer after officer.

Two bright youngsters of about twelve passed. First in English and then in German, I said, "Are you going to school?"

Neither understood me. Pointing to the small pack one carried that appeared to hold a book, I repeated *school* and *schula* a few times until one said something ending with *gymnasium,* pronounced as in German. I told them I was a teacher. They laughed and hurried on.

One morning, before many people appeared on the streets, I was talking with Hess Snyder, the guard whose beat intersected mine at a corner, when two tall, heavy girls approached us. Before they reached the corner I started along my beat, and upon returning found them attempting to talk with Snyder. I said something to kid him and both girls immediately came toward me, stopping in my path. I halted to learn their intentions, raising my rifle to port arms, and one girl grasped it in a playful manner. I swore and ordered her to release it as I whirled it till I broke her strong grasp. Snyder laughed as I strode off. When I returned Snyder told me they were streetcar conductors on their way to work.

Accounts by our men of the immorality of the Russian girls were startling and disgusting. Unlike many men, I avoided the Russian females. I was determined to go through the war untouched by any girl and was afraid of venereal diseases. Our company had its share of VD before winter passed. Lieutenant McClung had read an order aboard the *Nagoya* naming Archangel "the second worst venereal city in the world." If others were as strict as I, there would have been no VD cases, no forfeited pay, fewer courts-martial, and fewer guardhouse prisoners.

Winter's approach was obvious as I watched the season's first choppy ice floating down the Dvina on its way to the White Sea. The water's chill was especially noticeable when I washed at the river's edge on the second of November.

In the afternoon, while I lay on my bunk reading, I saw a British transport slowly pass up the river on its way to Archangel. As I left for my post a large American Red Cross transport (hospital ship) slowly came in. Later, it lay at anchor in midstream beautifully lit with red and green lights as though decorated for some festivity, a reminder that our government had not totally forgotten us. It remained there, frozen in the ice all winter, and departed in June (1919).

About a half hour before I left for my evening shift the sergeant of the guard called for volunteers for a firing squad. Getting none, he drafted six men including Henry Bok of Hudsonville, Michigan. I was among the first the sergeant questioned concerning their hours of duty. Later, Bok told me they were taken to a large masonry building where six Russians, who had killed two Scots guards at Bakaritza, were brought forth three at a time and executed by twenty-four soldiers. Four squads of six each represented the British, French, Russian, and American forces.

The English officer in charge furnished the cartridges for executing the first three. The men drew cartridges from their belts for executing the second group. Bok kept the shells he used for a souvenir. The Russians were smoking, laying their cigarettes aside while laughing and calmly shaking hands before being lined up and shot. All contrary to my statement to Max that the Bolsheviks "are a nervous gang." I had underestimated their courage.

On the way to the guardhouse after four cold hours, I watched another small transport come in. A French man-of-war and the cruiser USS *Olympia* were anchored in the river. (*Olympia* was Admiral Dewey's flagship during the battle of Manila Bay in 1898, and in 1921 she transported the body of the Unknown Soldier from France to the United States.)

Provost duty was agreeable, considering I found army life exceedingly irksome. In one respect it was totally unsatisfactory: We were not given sufficient food. I am convinced this was caused by two kitchen flunkies from another company who cared less for our welfare than for lining their pockets with rubles by selling part of our food to the locals. Our ration of jam—always meager—was seldom issued. The E Company men who brought our rations to the kitchen said we should have had more than average—if they had been issued.

My meals were had at 0830, 1130, and 1530. The interval between supper and breakfast being seventeen hours, I was always ravenously hungry before leaving my post in the morning. Supposedly, we are about to leave for the front—wherever that is. At noon we were ordered to pack our barracks bags. We departed in time to arrive at Smolny barracks for a fine supper, with half a pie thrown in for good measure.

On Monday afternoon, 27 May 1918, at Charlotte, Michigan, these twenty-six men, on the steps of the Eaton County Court House, were inducted into the U.S. Army. Donald E. Carey is on the right end of the back row. His father is observing from the open doorway.

Men of the American North Russian Expeditionary Force (ANREF) debarking from His Majesty's Transport *Somali* on 5 September 1918. Most of the 339th Infantry proceeded to barracks at Smolny. Many men of the 339th suffered with Spanish influenza, and some died from it.

Offloading American ambulances in North Russia, 1918.

Offloading supplies from a British ship onto Russian droshkies. A Russian steam tug, used by Allied forces for river transport, lies alongside the pier.

Land transport, Russian style, fall, 1918. In November 1918, drosky wheels cut up the ungraveled trail to Seletskoe. Soldiers following marched and slipped in the mud on their way to the front.

Land transport, Russian style, winter, 1918-1919. Equipment, and sometimes men, of the ANREF were transported through narrow Forest Trails and across Frozen lakes and rivers on these wooden sleds driven by Russian civilians, some of uncertain loyalty.

H.M.T. *Czar* anchored in the Dvina River. In August and September 1918, this ship carried Italian troops to Murmansk, while the rest of the convoy proceeded to Archangel. In June 1919 it carried the men of E Company and other elements of the 339th Infantry from Economia, Russia, to Brest, France.

American troops debarking in North Russia. American and British officers confer in the foreground.

Flag-draped coffins of American soldiers ride in a gilt Russian hearse over Archangel's cobblestone and mud streets. American and French members of the allied forces march to cemetery outside Archangel. Some of the bodies were returned to the United States as late as November 1929.

Verst 454, on the line of communication, and near headquarters of the Railroad Front at Verst 455. Much of the vast, forested lands of North Russia are flat and often boggy. Two trains are on the sidings in the background.

Russian trains and crews at a fuel and water stop south of Bakaritza.

An armored train pushes a sandbagged flatcar manned by Allied troops—American, British, French, and Russians of the British Slavic Legion—between Obozerskaya and the front near Verst 444. One such steel flatcar mounted a naval rifle capable of firing more than thirteen miles.

Troops of the American North Russian Expeditionary Force construct a "strong point" along the front south of Archangel in the spring of 1919.

ANREF troops in winter garb beside a Russian wood-burning train and boxcars. The unheated boxcars were used for transporting troops and supplies to the front. A single track railroad and a dirt/snow road were the only year around line of communication between Murmansk and Bakaritza.

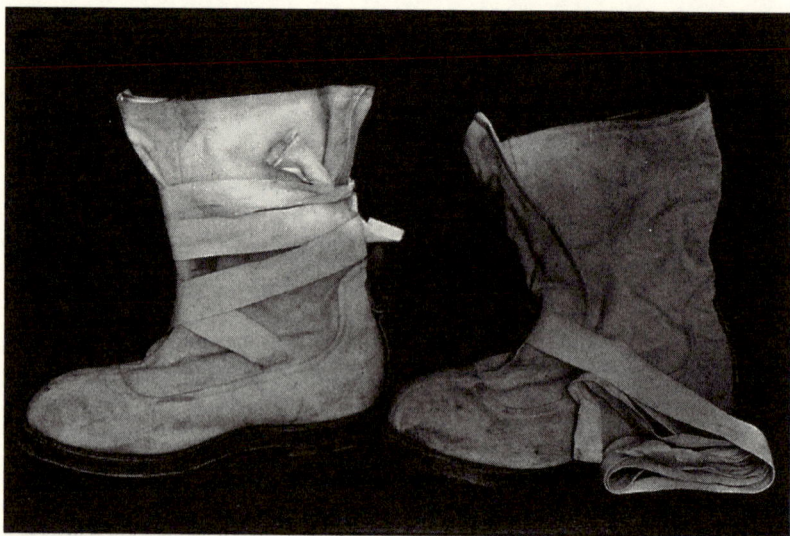

Shackleton boots. This British footgear, invented by Irish explorer Sir Ernest Shackleton for use in the Antarctic, was issued to ANREF troops for winter wear. Conditions were slippery and cold in the Russian north, and were, not surprisingly, abhorred by American troops.

Lapplander with his team of reindeer, sled, and ANREF passenger. The long pole is used for guiding the reindeer.

Scene along the Archangel waterfront.

Barracks under construction for the 339th Infantry, south of Archangel.

Archangel waterfront with firewood stacked along the shore of the Dvina River. The large building in the center is the Archangel headquarters of the 339th Infantry.

Signal Corps men of the ANREF with coils of wire and field telephone, in winter camp near the front lines. Fur hats, Shackleton boots, and cold tents were standard for these forgotten soldiers who engaged in their fiercest combat long after the Armistice.

Offloading supplies from British ship south of Archangel, Russia.

These British troopships, *Somali, Tydeus,* and *Nagoya* transported men of the 339th Infantry from Newcastle, England, to North Russia, arriving at Bakaritza and Smolny on 5 September 1918.

Waist deep snow, temperatures often dropping to forty or fifty degrees below zero, and brisk breezes combined to make North Russia a "frozen hell," for men of the ANREF, who earned the appellation: "The Polar Bears."

North Russian railyard with vast quantity of wood for use during the winter.

One of the numerous warehouses guarded by Allied troops.

Russians carrying sacks of grain into warehouse in North Russia.

Allied aviator showing depth and size of a shellhole amidst stumps along the North Russian railline.

Colonel George Stewart, U.S.A., commanding officer of the 339th Infantry Regiment, at his headquarters in Archangel, Russia. A Medal of Honor winner in the Philippine Campaign, Stewart was relieved by Brigadier General Wilds P. Richardson, U.S.A., in April 1919.

To the Front Line
8 November to 28 December 1918

After breakfast we carried our bags to the Smolny wharf and boarded a tug crossing the Dvina River to Bakaritza. A detail transferred our bags and company equipment, including a field cookstove, officers' baggage, food, and munitions, to the train.

Crossing the wharf to the Supply Company canteen, I bought two cans of salmon and a carton of gum, returning just as we were ordered to fall in. Unable to crowd these purchases into my pack, I gave Osborne a can of salmon, intending to split it with him later. That was the last I saw of it.

About noon we entrained in boxcars drawn by wood-burning, spark-spitting locomotives operated by Russians. Our route lay directly south of Bakaritza. We stopped at Isaka Gora, where we were joined by Captain Heil and the 110 men who left us at Smolny on 8 September. After a separation of nearly two months, E Company was again under the captain's command.

We continued southward into the state of Archangel, jolting over the rough track at moderate speed. This comparatively level area was forested with pine and spruce, interspersed with birch that relieved the monotony of coniferous trees.

The region was scarcely populated. We stopped at a few villages as large as Bakaritza. The only other signs of habitation were jerk-water towns, stations, or peasant cabins surrounded by small clearings where groups of natives in quaint costumes stood by the tracks to see us. This should have been interesting, but traveling with fifteen men in an unheated boxcar with no windows and only a door on each side was not conducive to sightseeing. Sitting on the floor, I caught glimpses when the door was occasionally opened. As the novelty of the trip wore off we settled down and made ourselves as comfortable as possible. It was too cool to travel far with the car doors open. As evening approached it became uncomfortably cold.

There was no stove. So we met the situation with Yankee ingenuity. At one of our stops we dumped sand in the middle of the car. On this a fire was built of wood foraged near the tracks. With the doors closed the car soon filled with smoke. A hole was cut in the roof, though it let in rain. Finally, I fell asleep, to be awakened often by the jerk of the train—then by a commotion. Our car was on fire! The fire had burned a large hole in the bottom of the car before it was discovered. The burning wood was kicked out and we continued our journey without heat.

Before daybreak, and some 115 versts south of Bakaritza, we were rolled out of our cold boxcars at Obozerskaya. This strategically important village along the Archangel-Vologda railroad was thirty versts north of the Railroad Sector Front. Roads to the east and west led to the front's right and left wings. The enemy appreciated the military importance of Obozerskaya, for in the spring, at terrible sacrifice, they had attempted to take the village.

After a good breakfast part of E Company was formed into two platoons: the first, under Second Lieutenant McClung; and the second, under Second Lieutenant O'Brien; with First Lieutenant Baker in command of both. There was considerable delay before our overcoats, groundsheets, and shelter halves—made into rolls—were loaded onto droshkies.

As we stood in line I heard Captain Heil tell Lieutenant Baker that Major Nichols ordered the packs carried by droshky. "My outfit," the lieutenant replied, "is soldierly enough to carry their own packs!" So we carried them halfway to Seletskoe, some sixty versts (forty miles) southeast of Obozerskaya.

At 0900 the order to leave was given. We followed the railroad a few rods south before turning east along the narrow, muddy wagon road. A dozen men constituted the point—to first encounter the enemy. They were followed by the first platoon, the wagon train, eight or ten cossacks, and the second platoon.

Though muddy, the road was in better condition than I anticipated. Being in the first platoon, ahead of the wagon train—which cut up the ungraveled trail—I found it easier marching than did those behind. I thought of the George Rogers Clark expedition as we splashed through mud and waded water, but the comparison was inapt, as our hardships were naught compared to those heroic Revolutionary War veterans.

The trees were cleared for fifteen to twenty feet on each side; beyond was dense, uninviting, never-ending forest. Just as along the railroad, every verst was marked by a verst pole—a cylindrical marker eight inches in diameter, about eight feet high, numbered, and painted spirally with alternating black and white stripes much like a barber's pole. At intervals there were survey lines—straight lanes cut through the forest. Our winding route occasionally crossed small streams; one was bridged by laying logs corduroy fashion. The Russian horses crossed this in leaps and bounds worthy of a circus troupe.

At noon we halted by the roadside and each man was given three hardtack and a half tin of bully beef; not enough for so strenuous a march.

We saw no sign of human life and only three long-deserted shacks. Darkness caught us still some distance from our objective, and I was not the only one extremely tired and weak from hunger. Less joking and more cursing proclaimed our jaded spirits. We staggered along hoping that every turn would reveal our stopping place. Finally we were halted.

About to make camp by the wet roadside, we were ordered forward. Soon we crossed a bridge spanning a tributary of the Emtsa River and on reaching the crest of a slight ascent found a small cluster of houses. Fires were quickly built. Though we huddled about them in close groups, they gave little comfort from the raw, cold wind.

A supper of bread, jam, beef, and hot cocoa was eaten with keen relish by the tired and hungry men. We were quartered in the houses. Guards were posted. I was detailed to guard the kitchen supplies and assigned a place on the floor to sleep.

I greatly needed rest after the wearisome march but was awakened at midnight for guard duty. The kitchen supplies were in droshkies in front of the house where I slept. It was a cool night and I consoled myself by eating dried apricots. Again from 0600 to 0800 I guarded these supplies. Near the kitchen fire, built by the preceding guard, I found bread and jam, eating all I desired while recalling our days of high living at Bakaritza.

To my surprise and approval, we were ordered to load our heavy packs upon droshkies and prepare for light marching order. This was quickly done and we resumed our march in the same order as the day before. It was less exhausting, although the road was muddier due to rain during the night. Crude jokes were indulged in. There was no sign of habitation along our way.

In the afternoon we met an empty wagon train. Our packs and equipment were loaded onto it and our original train turned around and gladly headed for Obozerskaya. We could have traveled faster but were slowed by the overloaded train. Throughout the march Lieutenant Baker energetically urged forward the drivers and horses with strong language and resounding blows. He was the spirit incarnate of energy and impatience.

About 1630 we crossed a medium-size river and immediately turned into the forest, where we made camp. The woods soon rang with the blows of axes as soldiers, and Russian drivers worked to build fires and cut pine boughs for bunks. It was a never-to-be-forgotten scene: trees falling; khaki-clad troops working and joking; easygoing Russians talking; small, wiry horses tied to crudely made droshkies; bright, crackling pine fires—all intermingled.

A few of us, including Leemaster, who marched at my right, occupied a spacious log structure near the road and river. Though it had no roof, only a dirt floor, and its sides were charred by fire, it afforded shelter from the cold night breeze. At the center we built a good fire that soon warmed our surroundings. With a short-handled ax borrowed from a Russian we secured pine boughs and made our beds beside the walls.

After a substantial supper we were content to talk and enjoy our cozy camp. While I was seated on a block of wood and writing in my diary, Lieutenant Baker and the sergeant entered. Baker said, "Is this the Bolshevik headquarters?" Noticing me with pen and pad, he asked if I was keeping a record, but said no more when I replied, "Yes, sir." After a few casual remarks he and the sergeant departed, and we turned in to test our beds and experience our first night of sleeping with the sky for a roof.

I was awakened at 0115 by a drizzling rain and got up to put more wood on the fire's embers. Pulling the shelter half over my head, I stayed dry. Some complained of sleeping in pools of water. My pine bough bed kept me from that.

About 0800 we were on the march. The road was increasingly difficult to travel due to pools of water and slippery mud.

While resting by the roadside on 11 November, I heard distant artillery fire on one of the fronts, my first time to hear it in combat.

Dusk was gathering when our column turned near a deserted shack and followed a winding route to the Kodish-Plesetskaya-Petrograd road. We plunged into the Tegra River's narrow valley. The river is much larger than those we had crossed. A few miles north it flows into the Emtsa River. We crossed the Tegra on a new bridge—covered with six inches of mud—built by a detachment of the 310th Engineers. The original bridge was burned when Captain Scott, a British officer commanding D Force, a unit including K Company, retreated northward in mid-September. At the same time the enemy fled southward and burned another bridge over the Emtsa north of Kodish.

At the south end of the bridge the road began a long, gradual ascent. Filled with mud a foot deep, it was difficult for us to travel and impossible for the light horses burdened with loaded droshkies. Reaching the top, many of us laid aside our equipment and spent an hour pushing, pulling, and lifting the train up the slope. Lieutenant Baker worked as hard as anyone, twice falling into the mud.

We arrived in Seletskoe at 1930 and were quartered in private homes. A large group of us occupied both floors of a spacious house. Selecting a bunking area on the floor of a warm upstairs room, I put down my rifle and pack and left to secure my roll. I was drafted by Lieutenant Baker to help unload kitchen supplies by lantern light. As I picked up a quarter of beef the lieutenant asked if I could carry it.

Upon returning to my quarters I was angered to find my rifle and pack—along with those of others—kicked into a corner, and my place occupied by Corporal Catellani.

"That son-of-a-bitch of a corporal kicked my equipment around the room!" Turning, I saw Lieutenant McClung. He appeared surprised. Neither of us said a word. I believe he sympathized with me. The room was crowded, so I went into another—smaller, unoccupied, and unheated. Later, a few men, including Franklin, also occupied this cold room.

At supper I shared my can of salmon carried from Obozerskaya. It and bread constituted most of my meal.

My puttees were covered with mud. I just unrolled them, waiting for the mud to dry, when it would come off easily.

Thus we spent Armistice Day, that day so gladly hailed by millions of war-weary people. We had marched to the Emtsa River Front ignorant of what was occurring on the Western Front. While death and danger ceased along the Allied line in France and Belgium, we were approaching the enemy lines to learn of hardship and horror. Rumors were so persistent that I gave no credence when told that hostilities had ceased in Western Europe. My first positive assurance was found in the 10 December copy of *The American Sentinel.*

Seletskoe, a long, narrow town of some five or six hundred persons with houses lining each side of the road, compared favorably with other towns I saw in north Russia. To the southeast was a cemetery. This was an agricultural community—as much as one could be so near the Arctic Circle. The land, cleared for a considerable distance and crudely fenced into fields, appeared to have been farmed for many years.

On the rolling hillside south of town, soldiers—either British or Russian—were digging a formidable line of zigzagging trenches.

Our two platoons needed rest. We were permitted to sleep later than usual and assigned no work. There was no announcement of this, so I spent the day not knowing when we might be called out to continue the march. I shaved, visited with Franklin, cleaned my rifle, and rested.

I retired early, expecting that tomorrow we would go to the front. Except for the possibility of disagreeable weather and exposure, I did not dread it. I had a firm belief that the enemy did not "have my number." I wished my people could know what I'd done and was doing. I prayed daily for them and that I might return safe, sound, and sane to all of them. They had my undying love and respect.

Our rest was broken the next day by two hours of extended drill in the meadows west of town. Probably our officers knew it would be the last opportunity before encountering the enemy.

The next morning we were fed earlier than usual and left Seletskoe, with our heavy equipment on a train of droshkies and carrying our "light packs and heavy rifles," as the men often called them. We hiked nineteen versts, or nearly thirteen miles, in a southwest direction on a winding road bordered by pine and spruce trees. Sometime after dusk we emerged from an area of dense undergrowth and arrived at Mejovskayia, a small settlement of about a dozen log houses situated near the west bank of the Emtsa River and closely surrounded by dense forest. In front was a deep ravine with a small creek flowing into the river.

Though there were sufficient quarters for our force, a group of us occupied a barn near the river. On bundles of rye straw I made my bunk and obtained a good rest.

It was late when the two platoons of E Company were routed out for a substantial breakfast of oatmeal. Afterward we marched six versts along the Seletskoe-Plesetskaya-Petrograd highway to "Headquarters," near the west bank of the Emtsa River, one of the large tributaries of the Dvina River. Headquarters was little more than a position about two versts north of the intersection of the road and river; a convenient place in the forest for the quarters of the officers and staff directly behind the front line of the Kodish-Seletskoe Sector.

To the right of the road was an unimposing structure of green pine logs occupied by those in command. Telephone communications, operated by corporals Sibley and Hittel, was maintained with Mejovskayia, Seletskoe, and Archangel. Pine trees protected Headquarters from aerial view. Nearby was the orderly room and another log building occupied by sergeants. Scattered on both sides of the road were many small pine bough shacks occupied by corporals and privates.

At Headquarters we halted and got our equipment from the droshkies. Then fifty of us were selected to leave for the front line. I wore an overcoat and steel helmet while carrying a gas mask, light pack, iron rations, two blankets, and a loaded and bayoneted rifle. We were equipped to meet the Red curse of north Russia.

Not in the darkness of night amid the thunder and flash of heavy artillery, the bursting of high-explosive shells, the plop of Very flares, the rat-tat-tat of machine guns, the screech of shells, and the zing of bullets, so characteristic of the Western Front, did we take over the front line.

On the contrary, it was about noon when we left Headquarters. After a short march our force was divided, and in single file we entered the forest on each side of the road. I was with Lieutenant McClung's group on the left. The poorly marked trail led through a swamp near the river. Here were brush shacks. We stopped at one of these about 1300, and I was posted nearer the river but not in view of it.

There was just as striking a contrast between our front and the Western Front as between our methods of relieving troops. No trench or rifle line marked our front. Only the deep, dark, gurgling waters of the forest-fringed Emtsa River marked the line between Bolsheviks and Americans.

Considering the American North Russian Expeditionary Force as a unit, the front line resembled a horseshoe with the left tip on the Pinega River, the right tip on the Onega River, and the opening to the north. It was not a continuous line. Between the left and right sectors were the Dvina, Emtsa, and railroad fronts, leaving the intervening area unoccupied. Considerable patrolling of the unoccupied areas kept the Allies informed of possible flanking movements, or wedges driven by the enemy between our various sectors.

I do not know the exact length of the front of the Seletskoe-Kodish Sector, or the Emtsa River Front, as it was more commonly called, but believe it was four or five miles. This front followed the river, with its left on the Artillery Position—though there was no artillery there. Its center, the Bridge Position, was at the intersection of the highway and the river. On the right was the Church Position, named for a small building on the enemy side of the river once used as a place of worship by Russian lumbermen. The line held at the right of the road was about twice as long as the left.

The Bridge Position was more carefully and heavily guarded with machine-gun emplacements—by the enemy and our forces—than any other point along the line. The 310th Engineers had erected this bridge to the right of the old one's charred piles—burned by the retreating Russians in mid-September.

Excepting the small clearing at the church and a section devastated by fire, the area on both sides of the river was heavily forested. Our side, uneven and cut by small creeks, was wet and marshy, except at the left where it was high above the water and gradually sloped to the river.

The stillness was disquieting. There was only the snap of a twig broken by a moving man, and the soughing of the breeze through the pines. We conversed in whispers. Orders were given in low tones. It was cold. Fires were not permitted lest the smoke attract artillery fire; or the blaze, the bullet of a watchful Bolo. The nervous attitude of the K Company men we relieved and their obvious joy in leaving compelled me to appreciate my proximity to the unseen foe. Units of L and Machine Gun companies remained with us.

K Company knew the enemy from personal contact and were justified in hastily departing. On 24 October K Company had crossed the river and, after severe fighting, taken Kodish, a small village about four versts southwest of the bridge, and advanced to verst 12. On 8 November they fought on the south side. The following morning, five days before our arrival, they evacuated Kodish and reformed along the north bank, where we relieved them. Later I, too, was glad to leave.

Nothing of interest occurred on my first post at the front. Upon my being relieved, the position was wisely changed to a site nearer the river, where any attempted crossing in that vicinity could be detected. Before dark I ate my none-too-satisfying meal of hardtack and a half tin of bully, then rolled out my blankets and slept on the floor of the cold, cheerless shack.

My second shift began after dark with Ray Jaunese, an eccentric chap whom I did not know well. Our post was farther downstream in a cluster of trees bordering the river. Though I had no experience in their use, I was given two Mills hand grenades and told to clasp down the handle, pull the safety pin, and toss them aboard any boat or raft the enemy might use to cross the river.

Jaunese, due to laziness or cowardice, lay on the ground, indifferent to our duty. Between our posts there was some distance where a stealthy enemy could easily pass, so I kept as keen an outlook on our rear and flanks as on the front.

About 2100 the stillness was broken by a loud voice some distance upstream. I was startled and thought a Red officer was giving orders to assault the bridge. Then I plainly heard him twice ask in excellent English, "Americans, do you hear me?" Receiving an affirmative reply, he proceeded in IWW (Industrial Workers of the World) style to harangue our outfit with Red propaganda. Though nearly a half mile away I distinctly heard nearly every word he said.

He asked why we were fighting them. Receiving no reply, he said, "You are here to help the English take our valuable timber region of northern Russia." It was the oft-attempted effort to break the alliance with our British cousins. "Poor Americans, dying in the swamps of Russia," was another of his sympathetic statements. Saying that he would appear again some night, he ceased his dramatic discourse.

I learned he had bravely appeared in view of our men near the bridge. I thought of him as a Russian Jew who had dwelt in America, learned English, and like Trotsky and Lenin, returned to aid in the destruction of his native land. His propaganda was wasted on our men, who regarded it only as something unusual to talk about.

My first night on front line duty was weird and fanciful. That I, a Michigan lad, reared amid the conveniences of an ordinary American home, should be standing in the shadows of a cluster of pines beside a large river sparkling with moonlight, listening to Red propaganda in this godforsaken country on such a hellish mission as war, far exceeded my wildest dreams.

Charlotte Leader 14 **November 1918 (Charlotte, Michigan)**
Monday: From the Adjutant General, Lansing
All calls for the army including individual inductions stand cancelled. Calls for the navy and marine corps still continue.

Instead of spending my third shift beside the river, I spent two hours with Corporal Buvo and Private Jaunese quietly wandering about in the dark woods attempting to find the post. The situation was amusing, vexatious, and bordered on the ludicrous when the overcautious NCO was afraid to utter any sound above a low hiss, and the men on duty made no noise to give him a cue to their position. So they stood four hours duty and then roundly berated the poor corporal for his inefficiency. We located them just as our reliefs appeared, so returned to the shack to sleep until morning.

When I arose at 0745 a thin coat of new snow bedecked the pine-needled carpet of the forest. After eating a cold breakfast, I was transferred to a post close to the water's edge amid dense clumps of pine trees riddled and splintered by bullets. I now appreciated the effectiveness of rifle and machine-gun fire.

At the end of our twenty-four hours of duty we were relieved by another detail from E Company and returned to Headquarters. After a warm meal, Franklin and I completed a half-constructed pine bough shack. With a roaring pine fire we warmed ourselves and dried our wet shoes and socks. After supper we talked and savored our cozy surroundings until retiring to enjoy a night of undisturbed rest. Franklin asked me, if anything should happen to him while here, to notify his wife that he had "always been true to her."

At Headquarters the cook's chow call brought us out at 0740. Two hours later, when the guard relief arrived from Mejovskayia, we left our sylvan camp. With our heavy equipment carried on four or five droshkies we rapidly marched the six versts to Mejovskayia.

Many of us made our quarters in an old barn. It was a raw, cold day. Fires were built and much of the afternoon spent seated about them.

While in search of water for shaving and washing I found the grandest view I beheld in Russia. Near our quarters the Emtsa River approached Mejovskayia from the south before curving gracefully northwest. The steep west bank rose a hundred feet above the dark water. On the opposite side the land sloped upward and was covered with a rank growth of underbrush. Otherwise both banks were covered with dense forest. Contrasting with the dark water and the deep green of the pines was a stretch of golden gravel gleaming in the bright sunshine.

Dinner was good and satisfying. Occasionally we heard the boom of enemy guns in back of Kodish as they shelled our front line. In the barn, Franklin and I made our bunks on the bundles of rye straw and retired early.

Franklin left for the front before I arose. I remained at Mejovskayia doing little besides sitting around the fire, cleaning my rifle, sewing on buttons, and similar odd tasks.

The next morning I left for the front, needlessly carrying my heavy pack, whereas a blanket or so was sufficient. We took over the front line at 1130, standing two hours on duty and four off.

All was quiet except for the artillery fire directed at our left and a few rifle shots which, judging by the yelping, were fired at a dog. The evening was moonlit and beautiful. As Private Hinkley jokingly prophesied, the Red propagandist appeared and delivered another discourse.

Relieved before noon, we returned to Headquarters. While seated on logs near the field kitchen and enjoying our noon meal, an aeroplane soared over from the south. Unable to identify it, we watched through the thin screen of trees covering us as it circled. Suddenly it fired four or five shots. Immediate confusion. Men scurried hither and thither. I dropped flat between two small trees. A man stumbled over me—without spilling his coffee. The plane turned and departed. We collected our composure and finished the meal amid outbursts of joking, though it had given us a good fright.

Sometime between Saturday noon and our return to Headquarters, two pieces of field artillery, manned by Canadian gunners (part of the brigade of Canadian Field Artillery composed of two six-gun batteries), were brought up and placed on each side of the road just north of the officers' quarters. Ultimately, log shelters were constructed over them and a couple log shacks erected for the crew, who were well liked by our men. This section of artillery quieted the enemy whenever he shelled our line.

Just before dusk, as DePue and I sat by the fire in front of our shack, the Canadian artillerymen notified the Bolos of their presence by firing three salvos in rapid succession.

This outdoor life among the pines soon developed in everyone a voracious appetite. My hunger was insatiable. Judging by the complaints most, if not all, of the men suffered the same hardship. Our rations at Mejovskayia and Headquarters were usually of sufficient variety, but invariably I could have eaten—with keen relish—fully twice as much. At the front our tin of corned beef and four hardtack lacked variety and plentifulness.

I resorted to strategy. By getting at the head of the chow line I obtained and ate my helping before all had received theirs. Then I fell in at the rear and secured seconds. Others also did this. Because men straggled in for breakfast, we could get away with this. Also, the cooks couldn't tell from the appearance of our mess kits whether we'd eaten or not, for facilities for cleaning them were so inconvenient or nonexistent that they were seldom washed.

The cooks were alert and more than once I was told that I'd been fed. "Like hell I have!" I'd brazenly reply and reluctantly be given seconds. I first did this when our breakfast of rice, bacon, jam, and tea was so good that I deemed a second course a virtual necessity.

At Mejovskayia, DePue and I made our quarters in the barn, but spent the cold, stormy afternoon around the campfire.

I arose early and after a vile breakfast—the oatmeal as tasteless and nauseating as it had been aboard the *Northumberland*—departed for the front. This promised to be more exciting than usual, for as we stood in front of Headquarters being casually scrutinized by Lieutenant Baker, who bawled out a couple men for not shaving, the enemy opened artillery fire on our right. Bursting shells showed that our sector was being bombarded. This unfriendly activity was disquieting. Tension increased when the fire was shifted left as we passed through the woods.

Progress was slow. Upon hearing the gun's boom we'd halt, listen for the shell to screech overhead, and await its explosion. Though outwardly calm, I suspected Lieutenant McClung did not enjoy the sensation. For the first time in nearly six months' service I was under enemy fire. The Canadians replied and quieted the Bolos.

We took over the line at 1130 and I went on duty, following the routine of two hours on and four off. Well behind our outposts and thoroughly screened by trees, a small fire was lit. It was cold and we huddled around the fire. Instead of unrolling my heavy pack and resting in one of the shacks, I kept close to the fire and did not sleep more than a dozen minutes during this twenty-four hours of duty.

All was quiet along our front on Friday, 22 November. Leaving before noon we returned to Headquarters where between dinner and dusk our time was devoted to obtaining a dry, dead pine tree for the campfire. These became scarce near camp, and we often had to go a considerable distance into the forest for them.

The day was cold and it snowed. I slept in a four-man shack a short distance from officers' quarters. With me were Franklin, Tubesing, and Clyde Miller #1, which constituted a Lewis gun crew. (There were two Clyde Millers in E Company.) With a roaring fire in front of our shack we were quite comfortable and made the best of this long winter evening by talking and joking.

It was soon evident to even the most casual observer that we followed a regular routine. Except for the first two times, the guards were notified the night before of their position on the front line. We breakfasted, received iron rations, and left Mejovskayia usually before daylight. Arriving at Headquarters we departed for the river outposts by way of three main trails to the right and left, and the one in front of the Canadian field pieces to the so-called Artillery Position. Relieved after twenty-four hours of duty, we returned to Headquarters, remaining in reserve overnight. In the morning, immediately upon arrival of the new guard, we hurriedly marched to Mejovskayia, returning to the front the following morning. Every day a few men were given an extra day off at Mejovskayia.

Need for our blankets at Mejovskayia and Headquarters necessitated the employment of native drivers with horses and droshkies—later sleds—to carry our equipment back and forth. They always accompanied the guard and remained overnight at first one place, then the other. At Headquarters with their poorly fed horses tied to the droshkies, they camped across the road from the officers' quarters. The next morning they hauled the equipment of the reserve force to Mejovskayia.

Two forces and two camps necessitated two kitchen crews. Both were in the open. At Mejovskayia the kitchen was first at the end of our barn, then moved to the creek. The kitchen at Headquarters was near the officers' quarters. Mess Sergeant Fletcher Atkins, better known by his English sobriquet, "Tommy Atkins," was ultimately replaced by his assistant, Edward Graseck, a short, fat chap from Detroit. Justly or not, Graseck was held responsible for our inadequate rations. This, and his supplying jam for the sergeants at the expense of the privates, made him unpopular with us.

Our force was increased by the arrival of Captain Heil and the two platoons we left at Obozerskaya, including my friend Ottney.

Though the day was cloudy and slightly warmer, there was need for a fire. We foraged poles from a Russian straight rail fence along the sides of the clearing by the barn where Ottney and I slept.

I arose at 0615 and obtained another two-course breakfast before leaving for the front. This time I went to the Church Position, an appropriate place to be on Sunday. It was a long and weary hike over uneven ground and across two creeks, one in a deep ravine that I crossed on a fallen tree. Fire-charred trees lined the ridge.

Snow fell gently all day. Back of the outposts and below the slight elevation between the enemy and us we built a small fire, huddling so close that our eyes were constantly filled with smoke. Later, while on post with Abraham Congress, a short, red-haired Russian Jew, my eyes were blurred and objects appeared indistinct. I thought I saw a head cautiously peep around the corner of the log church. Rubbing my eyes, I watched closely as it appeared and disappeared. I was tempted to risk a shot, but Congress saw nothing, so I concluded it was an illusion of my smoke-blinded eyes. The Canadians dropped a few shells into Bolo-land and received no reply.

The Church Position, so far from Headquarters and the first post to its left, I regarded as the most hazardous of any we held. Its isolation was an invitation to the enemy—if he knew of it—to try to capture the men stationed there. A spy among our droshky drivers—a real possibility—or an alert patrol might locate the post.

Morning found us undisturbed by the Bolos and still on guard or huddled around the fire. I had had no sleep. Late in the forenoon, while I was alone, a large yellow-and-white dog appeared. Not having seen one in our lines, I suspected it came from the Bolo side of the river. Believing the dog might reveal my position behind a young, thin pine tree, I tried to frighten it away. Suddenly I was startled when a sharp report broke the stillness. "A rifle shot from across the river," I told myself, though I heard no bullet's whistle.

I hurried behind another tree a few feet back. The dog followed at my heels. I hit it lightly across the rump, but it was not to be easily chased away. Scarcely was I squatted behind the tree when a second shot was fired. Believing I had been seen, I ran back farther to the sheltering bole of a large pine. The third shot was followed by the sound of a bursting shell on our left wing.

Realizing the three reports were enemy artillery fire, I became calm. The dog lay flat in the trail with its tail to the enemy, trembling. I laughed. "You damn fool! You're as badly scared as I was."

The corporal appeared but could not convince me the fire came from the Canadian artillery. The first two shells were duds. The acoustics of the river and forest made the reports sound like a nearby rifle. The Canadians soon commenced rapid fire; and how the woods did ring.

The corporal returned with my relief and I departed for Headquarters. Too late for dinner, I had to be content, as did others, with a tin of bully.

A long log shack was built by our men for quarters while in reserve. Ottney and I bunked here for the night.

I arose about 0800 and was getting warm by the sheet-iron heater when all hell broke loose at the first outpost south of the Artillery Position. The enemy had located the post and opened fire. With rifles, machine guns, and artillery firing, pandemonium reigned for a few moments. Our men, among them DePue and Clyde Miller #1, had not been under fire before, but like veterans they unflinchingly fought with rifles and Lewis guns.

One shell felled a large pine near their position. No one was injured, but fingers were frosted as men operated their rifles in the morning cold. The Canadian artillery went into action and the fighting ceased.

Though this skirmish was a mile from Headquarters—due to the river's winding—no orders were issued to get the reserve force ready to aid the outpost or defend the camp. On my way to breakfast I heard the high-pitched zing of a stray bullet passing overhead. Fortunately, the Bolos were shooting high.

Instead of making our quarters in the barn when we returned to Mejovskayia before noon, Ottney and I occupied a small, overcrowded room in one of the houses. The afternoon was cold and stormy and our quarters agreeable, though we had to make our bunks under a bed. After dinner I enjoyed reading letters from Muriel and Albert, Mother, and friends. This was my first mail while at the front and it was especially welcome. Mother's letter of 22 September had been over nine weeks in reaching me; Muriel's, a week longer.

While reading two *Charlotte Tribunes* of 21 and 28 August, I was saddened to learn my Olivet College classmate Lt. Harold "Christie"

Pagette was killed in France on 11 July. There was also a campaign advertisement of Uncle John Nichols, candidate for the state legislature, with a quotation from one of my letters. All this news plus Clyde Miller's exciting tale of the Bolos' attack made it a memorable day.

My fifth trip to the front was with Corporal Metcalf. The outpost was under a large tree a few yards from the river. Tangled growth made it scarcely discernible. In a slight depression behind, we had a good fire, where we spent our time when not on post. The Bolos ineffectively shelled our left flank during the day. At dusk Maj. "Mike" Donoghue, commander of the Seletskoe Sector, visited the front; an unusual occurrence. Apparently, not having found sufficient excitement from the bottle, he attempted to find it by firing on the enemy with a machine gun and throwing a couple hand grenades into the river. Receiving no return fire, he ventured onto the bridge.

This was not the first of Donoghue's drunken deeds. The preceding Monday evening he'd entertained Captain Heil by throwing grenades down the road in front of officers' quarters. I'd heard their muffled explosions. His conduct did not elicit respect or confidence. He was far from the gentleman that Maj. J. Brooks Nichols was.

I was fortunate in having Corporal Hahn for a companion on post. Corporals were not required to stand post, but for some slight negligence of duty at Bakaritza, Hahn incurred the displeasure of Lieutenant Baker, who ordered him temporarily assigned a private's duties. This was one of the darkest nights I experienced in Russia. We slipped on the inclines and stumbled over roots and sticks as we felt our way to and from the post. I fell more than twenty-five times on that rough and slippery trail.

At daylight I enjoyed a breakfast of stew made by cooking a half tin of bully with two hardtack and a little water. Until becoming supersaturated with it, I had liked cold corned beef. Freezing weather now necessitated thawing it. Some warmed their beef in the tin, but I found a stew more palatable. Soon my mess kit was black with the smoke of many campfires. Since I could not make three satisfying meals of our scant frontline rations, I usually divided mine into two: one early in the evening and the other the following morning.

Upon being relieved we returned to Headquarters and were treated to a Thanksgiving dinner of bread, butter, tea, and beans—so scorched it was almost impossible to eat them. A thankless meal and men justifiably cursed.

From the President's Thanksgiving message—read to the troops before our return from the front—I gathered we were in Russia for a definite, though unexplained, purpose and that we would remain until the administration saw fit to withdraw us. The message also brought the first positive information of the Allied triumph on the Western Front.

We were depressed. The effect of such a dinner and message couldn't be otherwise. Even the cloudy weather was in harmony with our gloom. A punk supper differing from dinner only in the substitution of M&V—usually called slum—for the scorched beans, added nothing to our pleasure. M&V—meat and vegetables—contained beef and many vegetables; sixteen, I was told.

Metcalf, Hahn, and I occupied a small pine bough shack close to the road. Metcalf and I were especially dispirited, but Hahn's jokes and good nature were contagious and somewhat relieved our depression.

Upon arriving in Mejovskayia, Ottney took me to an excellent upstairs room in the first house we came to. Here, for nearly a month, we made our quarters when not in reserve or at the front. It was comfortable, fairly free of cockroaches, well-lit by windows on the south and east sides, and accommodated fifteen to twenty men, many of them corporals. The adjoining room was occupied by sergeants. A stove built into the partition at a corner heated the two rooms.

After shaving I leisurely enjoyed the afternoon. Intermingled with my reading were the voices of sergeants Reynolds and Bygden and corporals Mylon and McIntyre singing popular songs. I laid aside the paper and listened while the Arctic twilight gradually encompassed us. It was a cheerful and pleasing moment.

Dusk came early—as early as 1530—and dawn did not break before 0745. The days were short and usually gloomy, as the sun seldom shone. The nights were long, especially on duty at the front, but rarely real dark. The snow seemed to emit light. With nothing to read, I usually retired about six or seven at Mejovskayia and arose about the same hours in the morning, but at Headquarters, often got up as late as 0800.

In case of attack it was the policy to tenaciously hold the line. A wedge driven between the Seletskoe-Kodish Sector would endanger the Railroad and Dvina River sectors. During our first days at the front our posts were poorly screened from view and we were told not to provoke the Bolos. Life was dear and this was agreeable, so no initial shot was fired by E Company, if the drunken spree of Major Donoghue be excepted.

This morning we were instructed to snipe at the foe, if seen; a change of policy that was temporary.

I was stationed near the bullet-riddled post. During the day I kept well under cover by lying prone in a small hollow at the foot of a tree a few yards from the river. At night I stood along the river bank. In the afternoon Sergeant Rogers lay beside me for some time vainly watching, hoping to pick off a Bolo. This did not please me. His shot could reveal my post, and though he could leave, I had to stay. Other noncoms also made themselves obnoxious by selecting some private's post from which to snipe instead of choosing an unoccupied point. Except for a few rifle shots, probably ineffectually fired, our front was quiet.

I was well supplied with food when I left Mejovskayia this morning. Besides a tin of M&V, hardtack, tea, sugar, and butter, I had my ration of bacon that I ate for dinner, as I was too ill to eat it for breakfast. After dark I cooked a satisfying supper over a fire. The tin of M&V contained a generous piece of beef. It was a good change, but for a steady diet became unpalatable sooner than bully beef. The butter was really margarine, packed in cylindrical tins. In civilian life I'd used it sparingly, if at all. Here I ate it clear to satisfy my craving for fats.

I arose at 0600 and, being assigned no front line duty, leisurely spent the day resting and rereading most of my latest mail, then writing Muriel. Just after I pocketed my pen a sergeant entered and detailed a group of us to get mud and moss to chink a small log building for the officers' quarters. Private Frank Mueller was excused because he was writing a letter. It may have been his last letter home, for he was the first man killed in the battle of Kodish.

Somewhere in northern Russia, 3 December 1918

Dear Muriel,

I've been to the front six times and under artillery fire four times. Those old shrapnel shells certainly can whistle. It doesn't amuse a guy very much to hear them, but I never imagined I'd go to the front with so little nervousness as I did the first time. However, I've had a couple good scares. The fighting is intermittent and at times there is absolutely nothing doing. So far I have not seen a Bolsheviki except as a prisoner, and I've not fired a shot since at Stoney Castle, England. I hope this affair ends quickly and that I needn't raise my rifle toward anyone.

Congress met yesterday and I understand Wilson is planning to come to Europe soon. I suppose peace will be concluded before 17 December, when the armistice ends. I hope it brings an end to this Bolsheviki fracas. Did Congress go Republican or Democratic?

I wish all of you a Merry Christmas and a Happy New Year. Don't let my absence hinder your usual celebration.

With much love, Donald

(Muriel received this letter in February.)

Our room was too hot for comfortable sleeping, so I was not rested when I arose. As we approached Headquarters on our way to the front I saw, in the early morning twilight, the red lightninglike muzzle flashes of the Canadian artillery.

I was given a post under a large pine tree. The river was gradually freezing. The noise of grinding, breaking, bumping ice carried on the swift-flowing river impaired my listening, in case the Bolos tried to duplicate Washington's crossing of the Delaware.

Before midnight and amid the uproar of the river I plainly heard the footsteps of someone stealthily walking at my left in no-man's-land. Occasionally a twig snapped. With my rifle ready, and determined to kill the first man who appeared, I kept in the dark shadows close to the bole of the pine, also watching my flanks and rear. The open area was light enough to see anyone, so if I was knifed it would be only my fault. Realizing that an animal might be prowling about did not lessen my alertness.

Nothing came into view. Knowing my imagination had not tricked me, I was not satisfied until I learned that two members of the guard at my left had become lost and wandered into my vicinity. It was fortunate that I did not see them.

Upon returning to Mejovskayia I cleaned up and rested. The day was cold and stormy. To avoid going to a boat with a detail after supper, Hahn and I took our chow to Shaw and Muetze's camp, where we spent the early part of the evening. They had an excellent camp in the forest, protected from the cold by a cozy fire, and with pine boughs for their bunks. They led a healthy life sleeping in the open with no restless nights due to hot, stuffy rooms. It was especially attractive to Shaw, the Chippewa Indian.

We were routed out at 0400 and left for the front, being told that a Red attack was expected, and that intelligence was brought by a Russian spy. We doubled the force at the front and were exceptionally alert. Upon reaching my post I fired my first shot in Russia—accidently—sending a bullet over the trees into Bolo-land. Corporal Damagalski rushed up: "Great God, you'll kill somebody!"

"Why in hell do you suppose I've got the muzzle in the air?" I savagely replied.

Two of us stood beside an old dead tree a few yards from the river, and in the dark could only listen for the approach of our foe. We distinctly heard him moving about in the bush on the opposite side, heard his relief arrive and clear his throat occasionally. The Bolo made little noise compared to my companion, who had a severe cold and coughed loudly and incessantly.

Our force was not relieved before noon, as was customary, but remained on guard until dusk. This necessitated bringing up additional supplies for dinner. Captain Heil and Lieutenant Baker were on the line or sat around one of the campfires. The front was quiet, though we heard artillery fire from the sector to our left.

The sun broke through in the afternoon, so low that its rays struck only the treetops. Finally we returned to Headquarters. I slept in a pine shack with DePue and Conwell. A cold night.

At 0500 we crawled out of our blankets. At the front I was assigned a forward position near the bridge. I sneaked to that dangerous post in the brushy lowland, covered by machine-gun nests on the rise to the rear. Charred pilings of the old bridge and a portion of the new one were visible to my left.

At 1030 we were relieved and returned to Headquarters. After dinner, and thoroughly tired, I spread my blankets under a bunk and slept, but was disturbed by our Canadian artillery firing over fifty rounds. Every round shook the ground. The Bolos did not reply.

Though I'd never been instructed in operating a Lewis gun, I was assigned to Corporal Krooyer's crew. Arriving at the Church Position we sat on four logs arranged around a fire in front of a large, half-completed brush shack. Our Lewis gun crew did not perform guard duty; that was done by privates who had regular shifts. We made ourselves comfortable, got firewood, and when disposed patrolled upstream through the forest.

Soon after our arrival two jovial Canadian artillery observers stopped by to talk with us after checking the effect of their bombardment of the church. They appeared to care little when the war ended.

Before dark Krooyer made a long patrol upstream and reported that all was quiet. After midnight I patrolled the moonlit forest alone. Except for the soughing of the trees, all was quiet. Appreciating how easily a small patrol could cut me off, I walked cautiously, halting often to look and listen.

Upon returning to camp I curled up on a log and slept. I soon awoke, desperately sick, vomiting all of my greasy concoction of bully, butter, pea soup mix, and hardtack that I'd eaten just before midnight. Such a mixture was enough to make any man's stomach revolt. The corporal covered me with his overcoat when I lay down beside the fire to sleep.

Though still sick and weak I walked into Headquarters when we were relieved. Thanks to Krooyer, I was sent to Mejovskayia on a droshky. I went on sick report and was given some pills—more #9s, such as I'd received for the flu.

I remained in Mejovskayia for two days, though after a night's sleep I felt much better. With only two other men in the room, after the detail left for the front, it was strangely quiet and peaceful. I reread Mother's letter received yesterday and read the *Vermontville*

Echo of 11 September containing the obituary of Uncle John Cary. I slept, shaved, and washed, feeling more respectable, though a good bath was much needed.

Another rumor that we were to be relieved about 22 December was floating around, boosting our morale, then leaving us more disgusted than ever.

A real treat on that stormy Sunday was the advent of *The American Sentinel,* a weekly printed in Archangel for our troops. The 10 December issue was, I believe, the first published. Designed for men isolated from the world's fast-moving events, it had a vast assortment of newsy items. It verified that the war in Western Europe had ceased; American troops entered Germany on 1 December, and President Wilson sailed for Europe on 4 or 5 December. Germany was in a state of revolution, and the Kaiser and Crown Prince were interned in Holland. The President's message to Congress was discussed and in the midterm elections a Republican Congress was elected. Michigan and Oklahoma adopted women's suffrage. There are now twenty-eight dry states. With great pleasure I learned of these events and read the paper—already five days old—as though it were the latest.

The room was too hot to sleep, so I spent a restless night until about 0130, when Ottney entered, grinning broadly and waving a short-handled ax he'd stolen from a droshky. We joked about this valuable acquisition, and he gave me his small ax that I'd often borrowed. An ax was virtually a necessity for our life in the woods and by no more honest means could one be obtained.

At 0600 I arose and left for the front. This time I went to the Church Position with a group under Corporal Murphy of Chicago. Posts here were frequently changed and I never saw the same one twice. After cutting fuel and sitting by the campfire I was posted at 1400 under an exceptionally large pine within two yards of the river. The church was about five hundred yards away. The day was not cold, although it snowed. The quiet fall of fine snow never melted, but gradually accumulated all winter until it was of considerable depth.

The river was frozen and the ice covered with snow. For an hour each in the afternoon and evening I stood between the tree and the ice, protected from view by thick, low-hanging branches. When the deep, swift-flowing river separated our lines I felt comparatively safe. With the river converted into an excellent roadway, the situation was different.

At midnight I was at my post again. Just before being relieved our Canadian artillery opened fire. For the first time in about two weeks the Bolos responded. Had their guns been withdrawn to another sector, or had it been indifference?

Relieved after twenty-four hours of duty, we quickly hiked to Headquarters—beneath the artillery fire of friend and foe. As the Bolo fire increased I donned my helmet. Just after stepping out of the woods and into the road a sharp, ear-splitting crash like that of a bursting shell sounded directly overhead. My fright was momentary, for I realized it was the report of our guns. I was squarely in front of them, and the sound was enhanced by the tree-lined roadway.

After a late dinner, a group of us, including DePue, Shaw, Muetze, and myself, secured a sufficient supply of wood to keep a bright, cozy fire in front of our brush shack all night. We sat around cracking jokes until bedtime. Though it snowed and was cold, we were comfortable and as usual slept well in our thoroughly ventilated shack.

Tuesday, 17 December 1918. This was my twenty-sixth birthday. And spent in a manner I do not wish to repeat.

> *Somewhere in northern Russia, 18 December 1918*
> *Dear Folks at home,*
> *I stepped across my twenty-sixth year yesterday. I was at the front and came back to Headquarters about noon, where I remained in reserve till this morning. Just before leaving my post our artillery opened up and then the Bolos let loose. They did no particular damage, but those old three-inch shells can whistle as they pass overhead. It was the fifth time I've been under fire and about the twelfth time at the front. We are usually there for twenty-four hours at a time.*
> *The ground is covered with four to six inches of snow. It is cold occasionally. I'm surprised it isn't colder. One gets cold standing an hour on post, but a few minutes around a good pine fire soon fixes him up. I'm well dressed, and here we sleep in Russian houses.*

I go to the front again in the morning. Don't worry about me. I can't figure out this Russian puzzle. May peace come soon—for us as well as those in France. I wish you all a Merry Christmas and a Happy New Year.
With love to all, Donald

Our extreme left flank rested on the Artillery Position, which was inaptly named, for there is no artillery there—none nearer than the two guns behind Headquarters. Though having approached that position on patrol, I never saw it until sent there with a Lewis gun crew under Cpl. George Benson. Originally from St. Louis, Missouri, Benson was employed at a milk condensery at Eaton Rapids, Michigan, when drafted, so he arrived at Camp Custer with us. He is a tall, raw-boned fellow gifted with a vast fund of dry humor and is often the occasion for much hilarity.

The Artillery Position, in contrast with other posts along the Emtsa, was situated on a high bluff some fifty feet above the river. Divided by an island, the gurgling waters flowed so swiftly that it had not yet frozen. Of the twenty-four hours of duty, I was on post only two, these during the beautiful moonlit night. There was no sign of the enemy. I doubt if their outposts extended this far downstream. The other hours I spent about the fire, sleeping, cutting wood, and cooking my bread, bully, and canned beans.

No war would quite conform to the conventional if there were no fraternization. During the evening Lieutenant Baker spent some time on the bridge south of Headquarters talking with a Bolo officer—a brigadier general, I believe. They shook hands and the Bolo apologized for the untidiness of his uniform. Then they discussed—through interpreters—an exchange of prisoners. None of our company had been captured, but one man from I Company was taken 3 November, and three from C Company on 29 November. That courageous act of our dashing lieutenant afforded us something to speculate about.

We had a substantial breakfast before returning to Mejovskayia. Trivial as this may appear, good food was greatly appreciated. At the village I arranged my bunk beside Ottney's. Threatened with a recurrence of congestion of the lungs, he had not been to the front for a few days, but did kitchen guard. Though it was cold and the shortest day of the year, I saw the sun peeping through a rift in the clouds as it hung low in the southwestern horizon.

I had a haircut, slept some, and after chow finished a letter to Max, telling him that "hell itself couldn't heat and light Russia."

I went to the left flank with Benson's Lewis gun crew, where our post was south of the Artillery Position and a few yards from the river. The day was cold and stormy. I was short of food and hungry. It was impossible to get a seat around our campfire when patrols from other posts crowded in.

When would this devilish war end? I wanted to go back to a real country and do something besides tramp down all the snow in hell's half-acre.

Corporal Leo Baker and some of his men returned after six weeks on detached service guarding boats taking supplies up the Dvina, or one of its tributaries, for our troops or allies. That took them farther into the interior of Archangel than we went.

Despite their many handicaps our cooks undertook to give us something better than ordinary for Christmas Eve dinner. All of us, tired of bully and M&V, were in a mood for a change. We lined up around the kitchen and each was given a cup of tea, along with bread, beans, and bully beef mixed into an unpalatable stew. And wonder of wonders, a piece of excellent peach pie.

I retired early but had not slept when I heard someone in the sergeants' room report the arrival of mail from the States. Many of us received Christmas boxes. Mine, from home, though torn and battered, was received most joyfully. It contained candy, gum, broken maple sugar cakes, towels, handkerchiefs, toothbrush and paste, shaving soap, and a box of Pacal Balm for colds, plus a few other items. Temporarily my intense craving for sweets could be satiated. I treated some of the fellows and saved some for Ottney and DePue.

It was ridiculous how wild we went for joy. We talked and acted like a gang of wild kids. It was the better because I had no intimation that such a box would be sent or that the government would permit shipment of such nonnecessities. No youngster ever appreciated a Christmas gift more than I did in that giftless land of Christmas trees. Only an honorable discharge would have been more appreciated.

Letters were distributed. I received eight; four from Mother, the latest dated 1 November. They related how the terrible epidemic of flu was sweeping through the country. (The worldwide epidemic of Spanish influenza in 1918–19 took more lives than did combat during the years of World War I.) It was 0025 before I put away my letters and retired.

Just as I spent Thanksgiving and my birthday at the front, so I spent Christmas Day, a unique manner to celebrate any or all of those occasions. Contrary to persistent rumors that we would be home for Christmas, we were still marooned in snowbound Russia and at war with the Bolsheviks. Dreaming or wishing could not alter this.

I arose at 0600 and went to the Artillery Position, this time under Cpl. Anthony Naugzemis, a Chicagoan of Polish ancestry. Since my first day there, a comfortable log shack with a sheet-iron stove had been erected by the 310th Engineers; shelter from the winter, and defense against attack. This was the beginning of a policy of constructing blockhouses along our line—a policy later abandoned, only to be renewed still later with redoubled effort and haste.

I was immediately put on guard behind an enormous pine near the water's edge. I stood nibbling a bar of sweet chocolate, viewing the picturesque area and listening to the frigid water rushing over the rocks around wooded islands farther downstream. For northern Russia, it was a beautiful scene.

I had been on watch forty minutes when the corporal appeared, looked over the situation, and took me off guard. No one did guard duty until the following morning. Had we been enveloped in a flanking movement, such as we later inflicted upon the enemy, we would have had no opportunity to escape. Men occasionally went outside and looked around. Though realizing the possibility of a surprise, we had no fear of it.

In the shack I warmed my bacon and fried some bread; an appetizing dinner. At night I enjoyed bully stew and hardtack. I slept fairly well though I heard men talking throughout the night. It was a great Christmas, probably more pleasantly spent by our guard force than any other along the River Front. During the night a gentle fall of snow obliterated our tracks, revealing that no one had stood guard. Not to be caught by the forenoon patrol or the possible inspecting officer, Conwell supplied the necessary tracks by pacing between the shack and tree.

Upon being relieved we returned to Headquarters, where a group of us, including Conwell and Corporal Baker, made our quarters in a large brush shack. More wood than usual was obtained and we were a hilarious gang that roughly joked, told crude yarns, and ate our none-too-satisfying supper around a cheerful fire.

Anyone seeing this group of bread and bean engines might have thought us a hard-boiled and carefree lot without a thought of war. However, the reminder of our deadly duty was the always loaded rifle either leaning against the shack or standing butt in the air with the bayonet thrust into the frozen earth.

Two long, low log shacks were erected near the artillery by the engineers who had recently arrived to construct shelters and defenses along the front. One of their earliest structures was a first aid station, a small log shack close to Headquarters and operated by two English medical men.

I arose three times during the night to build up our dying fire before getting up at 0600. While in reserve we were supposed to sleep in full dress, prepared for any emergency, but the order was indifferently observed and never enforced. I usually removed my shoes and blouse, using the latter and my fur cap for a pillow. Dressing beside the fire was especially comfortable.

Somewhere in northern Russia, 27 December 1918
Dear Folks at home,
I had hoped to write you on Christmas Day, but just as I spent Thanksgiving and my birthday at the front, so I spent Christmas there. So you can see that I didn't eat a turkey dinner, but I did have chocolate and maple sugar.
The most unexpected thing happened Christmas Eve. I received your box and eight letters. They came at just the proper time, and the best part was that I never expected the box. Believe me, I appreciated everything you sent and all of it comes in handy. Many thanks.

Others also got boxes and we all acted like kids. That maple sugar couldn't have been better. I crave sweets more than anything else in the category of eatables. Altogether I thought it a pretty good Christmas—considering the circumstances.

I have five months' pay coming. I have nearly as much cash as when I left Camp Custer. There is little need of it here, so don't worry about my finances.

No, I haven't any cooties. I took off my shirt a few days ago to make a louse investigation, but found none of the creatures. However, many have or had them. I am pretty dirty.

At Headquarters we can sleep in log shacks, but I usually sleep in huts built of branches and have a fire in front. It is healthier in the open, at least at present. Here I sleep in a Russian house which has a regular Russian stove.

I'm sure I'll never be able to express my gratitude for those presents. If I ever appreciated a Christmas gift, I did this one.

With love to all, Donald

Not being ordered to the front, I returned to my bunk after a good breakfast and spent the forenoon eating the last of my sugar cakes, writing a long letter to Max, and sleeping.

That was my last day in the warm, comfortable room. In the afternoon we were ordered to vacate it for two platoons of K Company. It was the most pleasant room I found in Russia and I regretted being deprived of its comforts. Ottney and I, as did others, took our equipment to an old barn across the street, made our bunks on some straw, and managed to keep warm.

Thus for six weeks—it seemed like as many months—we guarded the Emtsa River Front, hiking back and forth between Mejovskayia and Headquarters and camping in the depths of the pine forest. It was not a disagreeable life. It was healthful, and despite short rations we looked well and were in good spirits. As far as the customs of military life, there were no restrictions so characteristic of life in the cantonments. We were not required to salute, and on our hikes we straggled along carrying our rifles promiscuously on either shoulder or unslung. I would have been satisfied to continue in this unmilitary manner so long as we remained in north Russia.

Chapter 12
The Battle of Kodish
29 December 1918 to 15 January 1919

For days I'd heard rumors that a drive would soon be made. The arrival of K Company men at Mejovskayia during the afternoon of 28 December confirmed this. At the new first aid station men were instructed in the use of stretchers.

We were to participate in a concerted attack on Plesetskaya, a strategic town sixty versts southwest of the bridge we were defending, and on the Archangel-Vologda Railroad, about thirty-four versts south of Emtsa; a town behind the enemy battle line of the Railroad Front. Our force and that of the Railroad Sector would converge on the objective. Our route along the Archangel-Plesetskaya-Petrograd highway was fairly straight and passed through Kodish, Avda, and Kochmas. The latter, about twenty miles from our front, was our first day's objective.

To accomplish this, Major Donoghue was given an inadequate force of 450 men, composed of E Company under Captain Heil, two platoons of K Company, one platoon of Machine Gun Company, a trench mortar section, a detachment of 310th Engineers, the two guns of Canadian Artillery, and a small group of medical men. To relieve our men of frontline duty while making preparations, part of L Company was brought up a day before the attack.

Most of the cold and stormy day was devoted to preparing. Part of E Company was at Headquarters, where they waited to assault the bridge. Those of us at Mejovskayia were given definite assignments. I was placed in Cpl. Roch LaPres's Lewis gun squad and spent the afternoon in a cold room listening to instructions on how to operate this deadly weapon, though I could not get close enough to get a comprehensive explanation. Eighteen poorly trained White Guards arrived.

Just before dusk the rat-tat-tat of two Lewis guns made sufficient noise, I thought, to arouse the Bolo's suspicions. Then we lined up at the kitchen and received two days' rations of hardtack and bully beef. As we passed a case of canned milk, Conwell helped himself to a can and handed one to me.

Suspecting we would need all the sleep we could obtain, Ottney and I retired early, but we were awakened at 2230 to make up our blanket rolls and fall into line. Our officers must have been quite confident, for in the road were Russian drivers with loaded droshkies ready to convey all of our equipment to Avda and Kochmas.

While we waited, a driver was roundly bawled out for permitting his horse to run amok among the droshkies and overturn the load. We were given a few instructions and informed the enemy was "a bunch of damned cowards" that would run at the first shot. I did not believe this, but hoped the officer was right.

With First Lieutenant Baker in command of that part of E Company not in reserve at Headquarters and two platoons of K Company, we set out from Mejovskayia about midnight. After following the road for some distance we left the droshky train—which continued southward along the road—and turned left into a narrow forest trail leading to the river. This trail was used by our patrols while reconnoitering the enemy's right flank and in making at least one reconnaissance under Lieutenant Baker to view Kodish. Apparently the Bolos patrolled to our left. During their conversation on the bridge, the Bolo general told Lieutenant Baker that his patrols had quietly watched the E Company patrol pass by on the way to Mejovskayia.

Being a member of LaPres's Lewis gun crew entailed hard labor for Horton, Ficht, and myself, who took turns carrying a bandoleer of loaded machine-gun pans. This khaki-colored canvas device was designed to be worn over the shoulder and contained ten pans, each loaded with forty-seven cartridges. Added to one's clothing, Shackleton boots, leather jacket, small pack containing iron rations, canteen of water, and loaded cartridge belt, it made traveling through snow—nearly knee deep—exceedingly difficult. The rifle of the person carrying the bandoleer was carried by one of the other two men.

While carrying two rifles I lost my bayonet. It had never fit my rifle properly and undoubtedly caught on a bush. I hated to go into battle without my bayonet.

Our long, irregular column passed down a steep declivity onto the snow-covered river ice and to the enemy side of the Emtsa. Walking was much easier. The ice cracked ominously and the order to spread out was unhesitatingly obeyed. Shielded by trees lining the bank, we moved upstream toward the Bolo right flank—somewhere between our Artillery Position and the bridge. Opposite the Artillery Position we halted for nearly an hour, awaiting time to attack. Groups of dark figures whispered or talked in low tones as they stood in the deep gloom.

Finally, we proceeded along the ice for a short way before entering the dense woods on the Bolo side of the Emtsa River. In single file we continued along the low bank.

About 0600, Monday, 30 December, we came upon a survey line— one of those long, straight, narrow lanes cut through the forest— and were ordered to form abreast on it and "Give the enemy a couple clips." The formation was executed amid confusion and under the light of a Very flare that for seconds illuminated the blended green and white of the snow-covered pines with a color both weird and beautiful.

Flames leaped from the muzzles as our uneven volleys broke the early morning stillness. I never understood the reason for this firing unless it was expected to scare the Bolos into retreating. They did not reply.

Immediately after firing, we advanced in line as nearly perpendicular to the river as possible, hoping to strike the right wing of the Bolo's picket line. Fallen trees and uneven ground made it impossible to maintain alignment. Commands were loudly given. Comments and curses ensued. Sergeants endeavored to keep the line straight as we hurried and stumbled along. From time to time we were ordered to form up under the light of a Very flare.

Often it was necessary to half-circle a large pine whose snow-loaded branches hung to the ground. Blows, followed by snow dashed in the face or down the neck, were delivered by branches indistinctly seen. More than once I was catapulted headlong into the snow when I struck a fallen branch or other covered obstacle.

"Fire another clip!"

As I hurried to get in line I saw two stragglers endangering the lives of their comrades by firing from behind. I was pleased to hear them rebuked by an officer. I feared their lack of judgment more than Bolo bullets.

When we first opened fire I succeeded in firing eight shots before being ordered to cease fire. Now, after a couple shots my rifle was empty. Hurrying to reload, I jammed the cartridges. When I attempted to close the bolt I could scarcely move it. Intending to remove the cartridges from below, I opened the floor plate. It and the magazine spring flew into the loose snow. Frantically I searched, while muttering, "This wouldn't have happened with a U.S. rifle." Failing to find the pieces, I hurried to catch up with the rapidly advancing line.

Loss of my bayonet was serious, but losing my rifle's floor plate and spring was more so. Though I could reload after each shot, I did not. Thus after firing ten shots into the air I ceased to be a useful participant. Carrying the heavy bandoleer, I followed just behind the line.

Suddenly, as we passed about an acre of scattered pines and underbrush, we struck the Bolo picket line. The sharp crackling of rifle and machine-gun fire was accompanied by the whine and zing of bullets. That first burst instantly killed Pvt. Frank Mueller of Marshfield, Wisconsin. Clyde Miller #2 was at his side and later told me that Mueller fell with such force, he was nearly knocked down.

Our line was ordered to get down. Men dropped into the snow. Being behind, I hastened to get beside my squad and was among the last to obey. Near a cluster of underbrush we prepared to give the enemy a pan of Lewis gun fire. But the gun, and the pans I was carrying, were so clogged with snow that it was useless.

The noise of battle greatly increased as our line got into action. Bullets whizzed and sang. I thought little of danger, but became indignant at August Rumptz, who was firing his rifle with the muzzle dangerously close to my head.

The platoons of K Company took no part in this skirmish lasting fifteen or twenty minutes. When asked if he had anything to report, I heard Lieutenant Baker's laconic reply: "All Okay, and K Company lost." I suspect K Company's absence was intentional. After their au- tumn' experience here they had little enthusiasm for our drive. Routing the enemy without them redounded to the greater credit of E Company.

Cooperating with our flanking movement was the direct assault by a platoon of E Company under 2d Lt. Carl Berger. These men pre- maturely crossed the bridge to attack, but soon returned to their side of the river. Later, they again crossed the bridge in the face of ma- chine-gun fire and joined our force in driving the Bolos toward Kodish. This daring feat was executed without casualties. One of the first to cross was Pvt. Howard DePue of Charlotte, Michigan, gunner of a Lewis gun crew who displayed considerable courage.

Also, early in the morning, our company attacked a third point when Sergeant Masterson of Detroit, with fifteen men, crossed the river's ice at our extreme right and drove a much larger force of Reds from the Church Position.

By then it was quite light. As we hurried along we caught glimpses of the enemy's defenses. They were better than anything we had. Somewhat back from the river a structure of neatly hewn pine logs was under construction, with a deep cellar as large as its floor area. The pounding and chopping we had heard nightly while on guard was explained—Old John Bolo was endeavoring to make his posi- tion impregnable.

At other points they had erected pine-bough shelters for the guards and protected machine-gun nests with a thick breastworks of ice. In some of these, dead and wounded were found. A few prison- ers were taken.

During the pursuit our formation was parallel with and on each side of the road. Walking the road was generally avoided as an un- necessary exposure to danger, though Lieutenant Baker followed it for some distance. I was on the east side of the road. Most of my squad was on the west. With my burdensome load I struggled along.

I attempted to shift my load to Ficht, but he had reopened an appendicitis incision made just before coming to Camp Custer. Horton relieved me. At least twice as I staggered along Lieutenant Jeffers patted me on the back and encouraged me. Finally, after having again carried the bandoleer for a seemingly interminable time, I was afforded respite by George Wedtke, to whom I was most grateful.

Between the river and Kodish the Bolos made at least two efforts to check our progress. The last of these stands was along a slight rise about a verst from town. In each of these skirmishes our line dropped and fighting immediately resumed. Though the ground was uneven, there was no place so outstanding as to afford military advantage. The most striking irregularity was a long, deep oval depression undoubtedly made by glacial action.

Exhausted and sweating profusely, I was relieved to drop flat and plunge my burning face into the snow. However, I quickly became chilled and the aching muscles of my legs so painfully cramped that it was difficult to rise and walk. I saw Conwell, indifferent to danger, standing erect as he rapidly fired his rifle.

When the bullets ceased to zip and whine, I distinctly heard—from a considerable distance—Lieutenant Baker's "Ready, Jeff? Ready, Mac? All right. Forward!" The first syllable of the last word being long drawn out and delivered with a rising inflection. His loud, high-pitched voice at all times carried above the confusion and din of battle as he kept the two platoons in a straight line by calling out, "Steady on the right," or addressing his subordinates, lieutenants Jeffers and McClung, before ordering the troops to advance.

Lieutenant Baker was a splendid officer in battle: daring—almost reckless—heedless of danger, and visiting all parts of the line. I saw him under fire as he returned from inspecting our extreme left, just after our line formed the position to dislodge the enemy from Kodish. As he hurried along—head high as on parade—he inquired why I was not on the line.

"My rifle's out of order, sir." I had just traded bolts with Corporal McIntyre, who could not reassemble his in the cold.

There was no hint of the lieutenant's wasting time behind trees dodging Bolo bullets, as was rumored of our captain. Just as at Camp Custer during maneuvers, the captain permitted Lieutenant Baker to command in this attack. Of our other officers, I saw only Lieutenant Jeffers. He was at all times alert, cautious, self-possessed, and got down when the firing was severe. Sometime before the town was captured, Lieutenant O'Brien was severely wounded—a bullet shattering the bone just above the knee.

Our force, including the two platoons of K Company that joined us somewhere between the river and the town, reached Kodish at noon. While under fire, a curving line of battle was formed on the edge of the forest that skirted the north and east sides of the village. There, the men in various positions—prone or kneeling behind trees or rail fences—poured deadly fire into the village, using rifles, machine guns, trench mortars, and the Canadians' eighteen-pounders at Headquarters.

The enemy, reported to have 2,700 men in Kodish, were supported by four pieces of artillery and a reserve force of 500. From every door and window they fired rifles or machine guns. Most bullets passed overhead.

Bullets whizzed, whined, and sang in varying intonations; some resembling the long, drawn-out, high-pitched twang of a tightly drawn wire. Dumdums—jacketed bullets with soft tips satanically devised to flatten upon striking and make large, jagged wounds, like hunting bullets—cracked with the explosive report of a small-caliber rifle.

Though the Bolos usually fired high, I saw two men wounded. Neither was from E Company. The first quickly gripped his upper arm and cried: "I got it! I got it!" To my inquiry, "Where, in the arm or shoulder?" he replied, "Yes," and started for the rear. The other I first mistook for Ottney as he rubbed his left leg just above the knee and limped rearward.

I was east of town and near the left of the line. When the fire was especially severe I lay in the snow, but it was too cold to remain inactive and I frequently changed position. Once as I lay flat a twig cut off by a bullet fell on my leg. Later, while erect, I distinctly heard above the din the steady fire of a machine gun as it combed the woods from left to right. Its dumdums snapped with great regularity. As it approached I dropped flat until it passed over. It was all exciting and thrilling. Strange as it seemed, there was an element of fascination about this.

After an hour of severe fighting the Bolos left—not all at once, but in groups. Part of our force on the right attempted to occupy the place, but withdrew until the Canadians were ordered to cease their bombardment; this was done by telephone, for we were in communication with Headquarters at all times during our advance. Our entire force quickly occupied the village at 1300.

Kodish is a typical north Russian village, situated on a small rise and near the northeast corner of a large clearing surrounded by forest. Nearby, frozen Lake Kodi appeared as a level portion of the snow plain. Weather-beaten, unpainted log structures serving the dual purpose of house and barn were situated on both sides of the road. A few small shacks stood at the clearing's edge. A dirty place with odorous and vile drinking water. Unfortified, it was militarily unimportant except that it barred our progress to Avda and Kochmas.

Without chow for twenty-four hours, most men took advantage of this delay to eat. With others I entered a partly enclosed barn and, amid filth and dead horses, ate some hardtack. As I stepped outside, I saw my platoon leaving in company formation. Hastily preparing to join, I encountered LaPres, who said: "The lieutenant ordered our squad to stay and put the Lewis gun in working order."

My chief concern was to secure a serviceable rifle. I selected one from a large number left leaning against the house by the Bolos. Upon inspecting it the next morning I found its bore so rusty that firing it would have been dangerous.

When I requested permission to exchange it, Lieutenant Baker remarked as he consented: "You have a hell of a time with your rifle."

Within the house a dead Bolo lay at the foot of the stairs. His upturned pale, yellowish face was gruesome. Later, in the dark, I stumbled over his stiff feet. Another dead Bolo lay in the snow outside.

Pushing my way through a group of E Company men crowded about a cheerless fire in the first room off the hall where the Bolo lay, I entered a smaller but better-lit room. Though unheated, it afforded protection from the cold, penetrating breeze. On a wide bunk in the corner and on benches around the sides sat a number of men, including Corporal Geyman.

The steady fire of rifles and machine guns in the forest southwest of town was heard as I stood eating my bully beef and hardtack. The platoon of E Company, those of K Company, and the Machine Gun detachment had again struck the Red line. As the sounds of battle developed I realized that a general engagement was in progress.

Corporal Geyman was wounded when a bullet entered the window, was deflected by a helmet, and struck his hand. In another room, Seidenstricker, the bugler, was wounded under similar circumstances. The rooms were vacated.

Not content with merely resisting our forces, the enemy subjected the town to a severe, though harmless, bombardment of three-inch shrapnel. Their first shells exploded at the wood's edge, where our line had been during the attack. The forest's gloom made the flames of bursting shells plainly visible. Some struck within the clearing, shaking the ground and throwing dirt and snow high and in all directions. Occasionally two or three rounds would burst within as many seconds. Leaning against the side of the house, I was, with others, an interested spectator.

Fascinated, we listened to their shrill screech and watched the explosions creep closer and closer. At what moment would one drop in our midst? Yet none sought shelter. Perhaps all felt as I, that it was as safe to remain in one place as in another. As dusk gradually set in, the bursting shells were more distinctly seen. Far to the northeast the long, dull red flashes of our Canadian artillery streaked skyward above the forest as they played upon the Bolo line.

The shelling ceased at dusk. It was twilight when the wounded began to arrive. I was still standing beside the house when the first appeared. It was "Banker" Burnham, with a bullet in his arm. He had scarcely left in a droshky for Mejovskayia, as Geyman and Seidenstricker had earlier, when Aaron Shaw and Everett Roe—who was badly wounded in the arm and shoulder—walked in from the firing line. These men were taken to the rear in droshkies, ultimately arriving in one of the hospitals in Archangel, where they recovered. Lieutenant Baker supervised their departure. He swore vehemently moments later when two more men, including Joe Ross, his dog-robber (an officer's servant), arrived.

The attack on Kodish was exhausting. Nevertheless, I was fascinated. To flirt with death was novel; to be under fire in battle was exhilarating. To have possessed a serviceable rifle and been able to fire at human targets would have made it even more so. In my dreams of being in battle I had always been so terror-stricken that now I was surprised to find myself scarcely frightened and saw no evidence that others were. Arrival of the wounded produced a different effect. It was unnerving. I had concluded from the noise that the battle was severe. Now I was certain that it was a veritable hell. My dread of the line because of exposure to the cold was now augmented by an aversion for other obvious reasons.

Compared to the battles along the Western Front, that of Kodish pales to insignificance. Nevertheless, for those involved, Death stalked here. It proved the Bolos were not entirely deficient in military strategy. They regarded Kodish as untenable. However, they appreciated the strategic value of the road to Plesetskaya, and at Verst 12—where they had fought K Company in the fall—were well prepared in numbers and defenses to check our drive.

Our forces were stopped. Establishing a line, we settled down to fight.

Soon after the wounded arrived I was drafted with about fourteen others by Sergeant Untener to carry ammunition to the line. The order for more ammunition was brought by a Machine Gun or K Company NCO, who was to act as our guide. He soon disappeared. We halted in the protection of a house and one of the men went back for our guide. He failed to return. Others did likewise until our group dwindled to not more than four. Regarding it imperative that the fighting force should have ammunition, I reported the situation to the sergeant, who quickly secured seven or eight more men, among whom were corporals Munkwitz and McIntyre.

With only the sound of firing to guide us, we left in single file and crossed the clearing. I was so weak and exhausted that it was impossible to keep up. The rifle ammunition, in a double tin box enclosed by one of wood with a rope handle on two sides, was heavy and more awkward to handle than the Lewis gun bandoleer. In an effort to bear it with some degree of ease, I carried it in every conceivable manner: by the handles; on my shoulder; slung on my rifle over my back. I even dragged it. Bullets whistled past and above us. I paid little heed. My chief concern was to keep up. When others dropped to rest or avoid the fire I caught up. At times I had a moment or so to rest and cool my hot face in the snow before they resumed their way. About two-thirds of the distance across the opening we found, in a sheltered vale, the first sergeant with a reserve force of thirty or forty men. Opposite them, under a bare tree, were two telephone operators. My companions disappeared into the underbrush. Following their trail was impossible, for the snow was tracked in every direction. Plunging into the thicket, I found Sergeant Reynolds just back of the line. He was half reclining with his head resting on his right hand. "What I should I do with the ammunition?"

"Open it," he ordered. After doing so with his hatchet, I asked whether I should stay to fight or return.

"What are your orders, Carey?"

"Take ammunition to the front."

He ordered me to aid some of the wounded.

Responding to the repeated call: *"Medical man! Medical man!"* I came upon a Lewis gun crew, including corporals Baker and Benson, and Pvt. Walter Franklin, on the edge of a wooded crest. Franklin, terribly wounded in the small of the back by a number of machine gun bullets, lay groaning in a slight hollow. He had been hit while loading pans. Though firing in short bursts, the spurts of flame from the muzzle revealed their position and the Bolos subjected them to severe fire.

I concluded Franklin's wounds were mortal and had no heart to talk to him. He told the corporals that he was in too much pain to be carried except on a litter. In my condition I could not have carried him anyway. Sad that this fine Tennessee lad should meet such a fate so far from wife and home, I returned to the sergeant, who ordered me to have First Sergeant Comstock send a number of men and litters for the wounded. Franklin died the next day after being removed to the rear.

Corporal Baker narrowly escaped death when a bullet punched four holes through the Red Cross muffler wrapped around his neck.

On my return through the underbrush I came upon Corporal Kooyers and other E Company men. Four of them were squatting in an open space around 2d Lt. Carl Berger of Mayville, Wisconsin, who lay on his back with his head downhill. He had been hit in the

mouth by a bullet—almost immediately after lighting a cigarette—
and died the next day.

The men asked me to help carry him to the rear. Regretfully, I refused, telling them I had all I could do to get myself back to the village. While I stooped and talked with them, a dumdum struck a
branch a couple feet to my left, knocking bark into my face and exploding so close and with such a report that my head rang for some
time. Getting down still lower I finished my conversation and departed.

Just after leaving the forest I tripped on some hard object and
went down just as a bullet whistled over me. The oath I was about to
utter underwent a remarkable metamorphosis, emerging as a calm
appreciative remark that it was all right; for it sounded as if the bullet passed exactly where my head had been. Regardless of flying bullets and of being so physically weary that death would have been a
delightful end, I stumbled on, often falling, until finally reaching the
village and reporting to Sergeant Comstock.

Entering the room opposite the dead Bolo, I found enough floor
space to lie down. I was awakened by a voice saying, "For God's sake,
men, help those poor wounded fellows. They're freezing to death!"
I was ordered to get up and did so, but recognizing Ottney's cough,
instead of going outside, I entered the smaller room, where I lay under the bunk beside him. With the sound of rifle and machine-gun
shots still ringing in my ears, I fell asleep.

Thus closed the longest day of my life. It was a severe strain. I felt
ten years older. It was not until nearly a year later that I felt like my
former self.

For many the day had not closed. For some it had closed forever.
After 2300 the firing lulled and gave to all a much-needed respite.
Bitter cold—many degrees below zero—greatly added to the suffering on that tenaciously held line. The hands and feet of some were
frostbitten.

In the first day, K Company lost sergeants Crowe and Kenny and
Private Fuller. E Company lost privates Austin, Mueller, and Wagner.
Mortally wounded and dying the next day were Second Lieutenant
Berger, Corporal Mylon, and Private Franklin. There were also a
number of wounded.

Wagner, a graduate of Albion College, had stripped a pair of soft leather boots from a dead Bolo and died with them strapped on his back. Austin, according to DePue—who lay with one man between them, after being hit in the head—lay unconscious in the snow for an hour before he died. Ironically, I had often envied Austin and Mueller for their great size and strength.

Firing was vigorously resumed before daylight on Tuesday, the thirty-first. For a long time before I completely awoke I heard it distinctly. It seemed the fiendish noise had been ringing in my ears all night. We were to push on toward Avda. Those of us in E Company not on the line were drawn up in company formation behind the town and held in readiness for over an hour, standing under a fall of fine snow. I did not anticipate our southward march. At my right was Ottney, suffering from the cold, but he would not exercise as I urged him to do. While we were in line, our commander received orders not to advance, but to hold Kodish; though Colonel Lucas, a French officer of the Allied command, had pronounced it strategically untenable.

Of the forces involved in the drive for Plesetskaya, only ours had accomplished anything.

At last we were dismissed. I entered the barn to rest. Soon Van Randwyk and I were told by a sergeant to find an English medical officer to treat those whose feet were frostbitten. "He might be in Kodish or on the line." We found him in the village.

During our search we found Sergeant Bygden, Corporal Bosma, and privates Kemperman, Sullivan, and Leventhal occupying a large room comfortably heated by a big stove. It was not crowded, so we returned to it. I brought Ottney along. Seated on a bench in front of the fire, we dried our wet socks and boots and cooked our bully beef. Ottney's frostbitten feet pained him greatly and his usual joviality gave way to abject despair. He cried.

On a small table were some uncleaned fish resembling large smoked herring—Red Army food. We remained there all day, undisturbed, though I expected to be called out at any moment. I slept on a small scaffold near the top of the stove.

Throughout the day both sides showered each other with rifle and machine-gun bullets. In the afternoon the village was severely bombarded, the fire more accurate than yesterday. With every explosion the house shook and the windows rattled. One shell struck the north wing—the barn portion—bursting with a terrific crash. Removing cardboard that replaced a broken pane, I looked out just in time to see another projectile burst only a few rods away, throwing snow and earth in all directions. As darkness settled, the din of battle ceased.

New Year's Day, 1919, found us still in our hazardous position. Under cover of the dense forest surrounding Kodish, a Bolo movement on our flanks or rear, executed with determination, could turn our partial success into a complete disaster. The enemy, greatly outnumbering us, could drive our front line into town and subject us to a far more withering fire than had compelled them to retreat. Guards were stationed to alert us in case the Bolos attempted to drive a wedge between the town and river, cutting off our best line of retreat. The trail north to the church—where some of the men remained—was frequently patrolled.

The men appreciated the gravity of the situation and some planned to evacuate the village. Two days of fighting under adverse conditions for an unexplained cause was sufficient to stir their grumbling into action.

We were aroused about 1000 on 1 January. Indistinctly seen in the twilight was a large group of men prepared to desert Kodish. Sergeant Rogers reported to Captain Heil. The captain, in the absence of Lieutenant Baker—who had severely injured his spine in a fall downstairs and was in the hospital—appeared and explained that a retreat would endanger men on the line. Of course, it was intended that they should follow. Lacking a leader, the men returned to their quarters and the contemplated retreat ended.

DePue, Ottney, and I returned to our quarters, but the comfortable bunk by the stove was occupied, so we slept on the floor. Firing woke us. DePue left for the front with his Lewis gun crew.

Our kitchen crew was established between two buildings, and James McGehee and his dirty assistants gave us a much-needed warm breakfast. It was good regardless that I picked a nasty cigarette butt out of my oatmeal. While waiting for chow I said to Corporal Osborne, who had served in the Philippines with the regular army, "Do you suppose we'll live to see another New Year's?" His doubtful reply was so serious that it was amusing.

During the third day of battle an effort was made to systematize affairs so that all men should serve equally at the front.

In the afternoon, mail from the States was distributed. I received five letters. Dusk was fast gathering as I stood by a window reading my last letter when the Bolos commenced their severest bombardment. Windows rattled and buildings shook as screaming three-inch shells dropped into the village. To my knowledge no one was injured. Windows were covered with blankets, candles lit, and the artillery fire ignored.

This bombardment was the enemy's farewell. As it ceased and the rifle fire died, darkness and quiet settled upon the three-day battle of Kodish. Neither combatant succeeded in driving back the other and both rested on their arms. The advantage lay with the Bolos, who had checked our advance and brought about the failure of our drive.

E Company sustained a loss of six killed: one lieutenant, one corporal, and four privates; plus eighteen wounded: one lieutenant, four corporals, one bugler, and twelve privates. K Company had three killed, and I do not know how many were wounded.

A piece of shrapnel hit the edge of Corporal LaPres's helmet and a narrow chunk curled, broke off, then struck his left eye, cutting out the ball. Private Carlo Arini, who had served in the army of Italy, lost a leg. Conwell was shell-shocked and saw no more active service, but returned home with E Company.

During a lull in the firing, Clyde Miller #2 raised up on his knees to light a cigarette and discovered seven Bolos approaching. Excitedly reporting it to a nearby lieutenant, he and others opened fire, but the Bolos escaped by dropping and rolling down the slope. It was probably a patrol, but the men, fearing they were armed with grenades, gave them no opportunity to come nearer. Later, a Bolo deserter came running and yelling toward our front line; fearing treachery, Joseph Wisz shot him. Mortally wounded, he came on and talked to our men until he died.

While on patrol, Edwin Waterstreet met an enemy patrol. Becoming separated from his comrades, he was pursued through the forest's deep snow for a considerable distance while he headed toward our former position along the river. Bent on his capture, the Bolos did not fire until it was evident he could not be caught. However, the nervous strain was such that he was unfit for duty for a short time.

Considering the excitement of the previous three days, the second day of 1919 was quiet and dull. Both battle-weary forces apparently regarded further struggle futile and were reluctant to open fire.

Having voluntarily slept with the front line relief, I left with them at 1100. Quietly and cautiously we picked our way through the thicket and took positions at the front. The line was irregular, but considered in its entirety, was somewhat curved. At points narrow trenches had been, or were being, dug. At other places trees served as defenses.

I lay behind a stump. In front was no-man's-land. Aptly named, for only bushes, scattered trees, and snow were there, sloping down toward our unseen foe. As all was quiet my chief concern was to keep warm, so I kicked the ground until we were ordered to "dig in." That afforded exercise and warmth. With pick and shovel from my light pack I excavated a hole in the frozen earth sufficiently large to kneel in. Below the frost line work progressed rapidly and by the time we were relieved at 1730 I had an adequate breastwork of yellow gravel.

Detroit Free Press 2 January 1919

BOLSHEVISTS IN NORTH RUSSIA ARE DEFEATED BY YANKS AND ALLIES

Enemy Pushed Back 14 Miles

Americans End Campaign Fought Without Shelter or Fires, in Extreme Weather; Objectives Are Won

Archangel, Dec. 30—The recapture of Kadish (sic) gives American troops a good winter position in the blockhouses they have built.

Since the retirement from the town early in November the troops in this section had had virtually no shelter. The front line being unable to build fires for fear of the artillery or snipers on the opposite bank of the narrow Emtsa river.

Preparations for yesterday's attack on Kadish (sic) carried out under conditions met with nowhere except in a semi-Arctic wilderness. A battery of naval howitzers had to be brought on sleighs 80 miles on a rough trail through wilderness in a few hours of daylight. . . .

I arose at 0845, had breakfast, and helped clean our quarters. Afterward, twelve of us under Sergeant Reynolds patrolled around the right wing of our front toward the enemy position. The cold, stormy weather added no pleasure to this. Ever on the alert for the enemy, we advanced cautiously, halting frequently to survey the thick pine forest. We saw nothing unusual except a belt of machine-gun ammunition near a dead Bolo gunner—a victim of the first day's fight. Halting the patrol, the sergeant and a corporal proceeded farther, saying upon their return that they had seen a Bolo outpost.

It was exceedingly cold between 0430 and 0630 on the fourth, when I guarded the supply train. I rifled a droshky for a pair of mittens to replace those lost earlier in the first day's battle.

Early in the morning E Company was withdrawn from Kodish and quietly returned with all of its equipment to Headquarters. More than one old soldier mentioned how easily we could be ambushed as we marched four abreast along the narrow, thicket-fringed road.

K Company remained in possession of Kodish while our company and a detachment of engineers erected blockhouses on the north side of the river and cleared the timber for some distance on each side of the road along the enemy side of the river. We worked all afternoon—without dinner—cutting, piling, and burning brush and trees. Working near the road, I saw the enemy defenses.

Dead Bolos were rifled for rubles; Private Zukas being especially proficient in appropriating his erstwhile countrymen's possessions. They were also buried. Sam Gordon, from Coney Island, created some hilarity as he shouldered the frozen fallen and carried them to the grave to the tune and words of "The Battle Hymn of the Republic."

As we worked, Radus Kemperman cut a dumdum bullet from a tree. The Bolos had cut off the jacketed tip to make a wicked wound.

A group of men were inspecting their clothing beside a burning brush pile. Opening my undershirt at the neck, I found it well occupied by a colony of small cooties. Some men had acquired them a month before, but I failed to find any while at Mejovskayia. Since entering Kodish my body had itched incessantly. I doubt if any man who slept in that foul, dirty, lice-ridden village escaped this physical torture.

"Reading shirts" became a popular pastime, and the nonsense written about cootie "squads left" and "squads right" or platoons of cooties marching and countermarching could be applied to me. I entertained my quota of vermin. The mental and physical discomfort was terrible. They used the belt-line and seams of clothing as runways. When cold they were not so active, but when warmed became extremely annoying. They were typical gray backs—body lice. Some men mailed specimens home.

I was returning from the hole in the river ice, where I'd obtained drinking water, when First Sergeant Comstock passed by in a droshky bearing Mueller's body, one leg projecting upward. For five days his body lay in the snow where he fell. I believe that Mueller and all others killed at Kodish were buried in the cemetery at Seletskoe.

We returned to work along the Emtsa on Sunday, the fifth. The day was cold and it was good to see the sun shine even for a short time. The work was not disagreeable and the policy of feeding us twice a day—before and after work—necessitated a fairly short working day.

Just before 2100 we were told that Kodish was burning. Stepping outside our large log shack, I saw the bright red glow reflected on the sky. How little when reading in 1914–15 of the burning of French and Belgian villages did I dream that I should ever be in the midst of such horrors of war.

On that evening a lieutenant with a single platoon of K Company held Kodish. Evidently fearing an enveloping movement, they fired and evacuated the village without authority. No doubt K Company was susceptible to such fears; their experiences there in the fall were enough to unnerve veterans. The Bolos shelled the burning village. K Company retreated to the north side of the river. E Company was ordered to fall out, then finally dismissed with orders to be prepared to move at a moment's notice. I spent an uncomfortable night sleeping in my overcoat and cartridge belt with my rifle by my side.

Related to the burning of Kodish was the refusal of E Company corporals Baker and Naugzemis to accompany Major Donoghue back to the village. The major, under the influence of liquor, had been left alone in a shack on the outskirts of Kodish, but finally had the presence of mind to return to Headquarters, where he ordered the corporals to cross the river with him. Appreciating his condition, they refused to do so. Had not Lieutenant Jeffers falsely informed the major that he had not even talked to E Company men, the corporals would have been court-martialed. The lieutenant told Baker and Naugzemis to obey a superior's orders in the future. Later, an attempt was made to court-martial the major.

Detroit Free Press 5 January 1919
ENGAGEMENT LARGELY ONE OF ENDURING IN COLD

Archangel, Jan. 4—Fighting about the village of Kadish (sic), which was recaptured by American forces December 30, is continuing.

The American artillery has moved up slightly and is almost continually shelling the enemy. There have been numerous outpost encounters in the thick woods bordering on the Petrograd road.

The Bolsheviki force outnumbers the Americans nearly three to one, and is seeking to outflank them, but the American soldiers, though tired after five days and nights of fighting activity in the extreme cold, are bearing up splendidly. The battle is largely a question of endurance in the Arctic winter.

Now and then in the course of the fighting the Americans encounter hidden machine gun positions in the woods or along the road. One of these held out five hours until the Americans, advancing step by step or crawling in the snow, succeeded in flanking it.

There is some respite with darkness, which descends at 3 o'clock in the afternoon, but the shelling at night is making perilous the matter of the transport of munitions and provisions along the highroad in sleighs or on men's backs through the forest.

The Russian peasant drivers of these sleighs, stricken with fear, in some instances turned and bolted, only to be forced to proceed by American soldiers.

At 0430 we were called out, and without breakfast a force of forty E Company men followed doughty old Major Donoghue back to Kodish. With loaded rifles and Lewis guns we silently and sullenly marched in the dark along the familiar road. One survey of the village—embers glowing and smoking—revealed the effectiveness of K Company's work; only a few dilapidated shacks on the outskirts remained. Kodish had been unoccupied all night. On the edge of the village we were halted and addressed by the major. He said he did not know what "Old John Bolo" thought about burning the town, but we would hold it until otherwise ordered. His speech depressed me, as I concluded we were sacrifice troops sent to hold the place at all hazards. I believe all expected an attack at daybreak.

We were stationed at various points throughout town. With ten men I was sent to a forward position at the left of the road where, in a partly open barn, we kept a keen lookout. With daylight and still no attack our spirits lifted. Iron rations—hardtack and bully beef or M&V—were finally brought and we risked a small fire to thaw our frozen fare. On the edge of the forest, a half mile distant, we watched a Red guard walking his post. We did nothing to disturb him.

After 1830, having spent more than fourteen hours on duty, we were relieved and returned to Headquarters, thoroughly tired.

Detroit Free Press 6 January 1919

FIERCE FIGHTING WON IN SNOW 4 FEET DEEP

Few Americans Slain in Battle.

With the Allied Army of the Dvina, Jan. 5—American troops, composed largely of Detroiters in the 339th infantry, fighting desperately near Kadish (sic), have driven back bolshevist troops which made an advance thrust.

Bolsheviki also launched attacks on the Onega sector and bombarded the Allied front. Americans came into battle along the Petrograd road and in the frozen swamps that border it. The battle was fought in snow from two to four feet in depth.

American forces captured Kadish (sic) Monday after a display of gallantry that evoked admiration of the Allied commanders. . . . There were some casualties Monday, but they were small in comparison to those inflicted upon the enemy.

• • •

The severe, bitter cold during the period of our attack abated somewhat. We spent the day cutting, piling, and burning brush on the south side of the river. I distinctly heard machine-gun and rifle fire at Kodish.

Soon after I began work near the bridge First Sergeant Comstock detailed me to guard the right wing of our working party. We were recalled at noon, and at 1630 our guard detail was sent to Kodish. As a member of Private First Class Ogea's Lewis gun crew I did not stand post but spent the night sleeping in a dirty shack where the trail to the church entered the forest.

Detroit Free Press 8 January 1919

U.S. FORCES LIST 132 DEATHS FOR RUSSIAN FRONT

LaFollette Criticism of Anti-Soviet War Is Delivered to Senate.

Bolsheviki Not Pro-German, Is Assertion of Senator, Who Wants to Know Why Wisconsin Fighters Are in Campaign.

Washington, Jan. 7—Total deaths among American expeditionary forces in northern Russia to January 4 were given as six officers and 126 men in a cablegram received at the war department today from Colonel James A. Ruggles, American military attaché with Ambassador Francis at Archangel.

Casualties were given as follows: Killed in action and died of wounds, 3 officers and 57 men; died of disease, 2 officers and 63 men; accidently killed, 4 enlisted men; drowned, 1 officer and 2 men; missing in action, 16 enlisted men; wounded in action, 159; accidently wounded, 15.

Colonel Ruggles said equipment of the troops was complete, health excellent and morale very good. Food conditions were described as very good, the greatest defect being lack of fresh vegetables.

On Friday, 10 January, I piled brush and carried logs along the river until recalled at 1400. The remainder of the day Hahn, Baker, Ottney, and I spent constructing a comfortable pine-bough shack; our quarters until we were withdrawn from the Emtsa River Front.

It was intentionally located some distance south of the camp to escape the sergeants' annoying details. We kept a cheerful fire in front and made ourselves quite comfortable.

After working along the river until 1400 Saturday, I was sent with the guard detail of fifteen men on my only visit to the church. The hike on the ice of the broad, winding river was tiresome. The small church was crowded when the patrol from Kodish joined us. Though a dangerous position familiar to the foe and far from any support, it did have telephone communications with Kodish and Headquarters. An operator was always on duty, and about every fifteen minutes informed Headquarters that the place had not been attacked or the line cut. His "Church OK" soon became a familiar report.

Being a member of Ogea's Lewis gun crew did not excuse me from standing guard one out of every three hours of darkness. Watching the river from beside a pile of lumber was agreeable enough, but patrolling a short, winding forest trail in the rear was nervous work. The most undesirable assignment was standing alone in the forest some distance from the church, and I did not envy young Philip Burlak as he left with fixed bayonet.

This was an exceptionally cold night, so quiet and cold that the pines cracked and snapped like pistol shots. Those across the river were especially loud, and once I was startled by a sudden snap of the lumber pile.

Sunday was especially cold when I was on duty between 0300 and 0400 and the snapping of the trees was more pronounced than last night. After breakfast, Ogea sent Muetze, Horton, and me across the river to investigate the possibility of the enemy having been there during the night. Weary almost to the limit, we were in no mood to enthusiastically perform what we considered a fool's errand, so we leisurely strolled about criticizing Ogea for not accompanying us.

While not on duty I spent the long hours sleeping, attending the telephone, or cooking rolled oats. Without seasoning it was unappetizing and scarcely better than the monotonous M&V or corned willie.

After dark we were relieved. Hahn, DePue, and Ottney were at our quarters. Seated around a bright fire, we joked, told stories, and recounted incidents of the day. We were about to turn in as soon as I finished an Indian story, when the stillness was suddenly broken. "That's rifle fire!" I declared.

The others claimed it was cartridges exploding under the kitchen fire, as others had done, when the cooks were preparing supper over a fire built in a place heretofore unused. It was logical; cartridges were often lost or thrown away. Shots followed from other locations, then the shrill blast of the first sergeant's whistle.

Believing a Bolo had prematurely fired a shot as they approached to flank or attack our rear, I hurriedly laced my Shackleton boots. Grasping my loaded rifle I hastened to the center of camp. Ottney, ignoring our demands that he take a rifle, sauntered leisurely after us without one.

All was confusion. The sergeants were hastily attempting to form a skirmish line in the woods across from officers' quarters. Some in that ragged line faced one way and others the opposite. A shot fired near the artillery convinced me the enemy was at our rear. I shivered with cold and trembled with fear. A guard detail, including DePue, rushed to the bridge, probably the last place the Bolos would have considered crossing the frozen river. Guards were stationed about the camp. The first sergeant assigned me a post near the kitchen. Hahn was posted near our shack. Ottney alone escaped a detail and claimed that had we also left our rifles behind we would have been equally fortunate. Undoubtedly the first reports were cartridges exploding in the cooks' fire. The engineers or Canadians fired the others.

My contempt for danger of attack on this front had vanished with our drive, and I feared a counterattack. I keenly anticipated our withdrawal. Heretofore I would have gladly stayed on this front so long as we remained in Russia. I considered our officers negligent in not assigning guards other than the one walking in front of their quarters. Our camps in friendly America and England were guarded. In the presence of our enemy, this essential security measure was disregarded. The excitement abated and I crawled into my sleeping bag and slept well.

I spent the next day, a clear, cold Monday, on our side of the river helping carry heavy logs for a blockhouse the engineers were erecting. Late in the afternoon about fifty engineers left Headquarters for Archangel. Hahn, Ottney, Baker, DePue, and I slept in our comfortable quarters and had the usual hilarious time around our fire.

The morning of the fourteenth was bitter cold. The moisture of our breaths froze on our whiskers, fur caps, and collars—noticeably more than usual. My steel mirror revealed a most unkempt face bristling with stiff, red, frost-covered whiskers over a quarter-inch long. Having no opportunity to shave, everyone presented a similar appearance and many a joke was cracked at the expense of someone's looks.

Hahn, DePue, and I did not respond when the fatigue detail was called out, and escaping detection in our secluded place, lazily spent the day around the campfire. It was seldom we took such a vacation.

We were not so fortunate the next morning, for the first sergeant, quite amused, called at our shack to get us out for fatigue duty along the river. Baker had a sore foot, and I faked illness, so we went to the Red Cross (first aid) station for treatment—mine being "number nines." To avoid the fatigue detail we returned to our shack by a circuitous route through deep snow. Late in the afternoon as we sat around our fire awaiting the order to fall out preparatory to our withdrawal, the Bolos began a severe bombardment of Kodish. Perhaps the Bolos could not resist firing a departing salute in our honor.

After dusk on 15 January we left Headquarters—never to return—and hiked to Mejovskayia, where I slept in a cold room.

Editor's Note:
In 1920 First Sergeant George E. Comstock was awarded the United States *Distinguished Service Cross* for three times going forward of U.S. lines and returning with blinded or wounded men on 30–31 December 1918 during the Battle of Kodish.

Major Michael J. Donoghue, awarded the *British Distinguished Service Order* as commanding officer of American and Allied troops, for the Kodish offensive in fall and winter defensive campaigns of the Seletskoe Detachment of Vologda Force.

Major Michael J. Donoghue, awarded the *French croix de guerre*.

First Lieutenant John J. Baker, awarded the *French croix de guerre*.

Chapter 13
"Rest" at Smolny
16 January to 19 March 1919

On 16 January 1919 we left Mejovskayia shortly after noon and hiked nineteen versts to Seletskoe, on our way to Archangel, where—rumor again—all U.S. troops were to assemble for departure to the United States. It was cold, but we were not chilled. This was a hot, tiresome march, for we traveled ridiculously fast over a rough and frozen road. I felt like a man of sixty years, but stood up better than some, who panted along bent under the weight of rifle and light pack.

We reached Seletskoe before dusk and were billeted with civilians. I was assigned to a house with Ottney and four others. Our small, dingy, unventilated room was overrun with cockroaches and harbored a stench. Its double windows were so covered with frost that we could not see out. To reach our room we passed through the living room, where the family spent the winter. A few benches, a cradle hung from the ceiling, a large stove for heating and cooking, and an unmade bunk bed without springs and covered with faded quilts constituted the furnishings.

Hung in one corner and facing the door was the inevitable icon: a framed painting of Christ, the Madonna, or some saint. Besides the cooties and cockroaches, the occupants were a cobbler, his wife, and a boy of about two years. I never saw the boy clothed in more than a short shirt; all he needed for comfort as the room was always hot.

We visited the YMCA to purchase anything eatable besides hardtack, M&V, and bully beef. I bought a can of honey.

I wanted a good night's rest. Instead I accompanied a large group with the first sergeant to the Red Cross hospital to convince the English medical officer that our outfit was physically unfit to hike to Obozerskaya, and that droshkies should be provided for us. Some men were examined, but most of us failed to get within the building.

We left Seletskoe at 1000, men and equipment riding on droshkies. It was well that we did, for nine weeks at the front had depleted our strength and endurance. Instead of being delayed by wheeled droshkies jolting through mud and water, as on our way to the front, we now had excellent sleighing and made fast time with these curious, homemade sleds without steel runners, frail in appearance but capable of carrying heavy loads. The driver wore a parka—a greatcoat of reindeer fur with an attached head covering. Being without a front opening, it was slipped over the head. Walking or running in this was difficult and undoubtedly accounted for the driver's seldom leaving his seat on the sled. Removing the coat was exceedingly awkward and required assistance, or motions that might be mistaken for a native polka or Russian calisthenics.

Nature, too, had greatly changed since November. The deep green of the gloomy pine forest assumed a lighter tinge—with white predominating. Every branch hung low with its heavy burden. Survey lanes were long white avenues. The verst poles stood as tall, silent sentinels decorated with a fluffy white crown a foot high. We were in the midst of an Arctic winter.

Exercise was imperative. We usually walked up the hills, leaping aboard our sleds at the crest. Then the galloping horses were pushed downhill by speeding droshkies skidding wildly from side to side. Bumping into a tree or nearly upsetting as a runner bounced over the end of a log added to the excitement. Our route was greatly shortened by leaving the road and following a narrow trail to one of the Emtsa's icebound tributaries. How those small, wiry ponies scurried for miles along this level, winding ice-paved highway!

At 1600 we reached Volshenitsa, about twenty-six versts southeast of Obozerskaya. This is the junction of the Seletskoe-Obozerskaya trail with that from verst 444—leading south to Emtsa, where the Reds were holding up progress along the Railroad Front. To prevent the enemy from sending a force from Emtsa to cut the trail, it was alternately guarded by British and Russian troops from Seletskoe, and Americans from Obozerskaya.

For troops passing to and from the Emtsa River Front, quarters had been built since we camped there in November. The crowded barracks were uncomfortably hot and reeked of tobacco smoke. My cootie colony became so active that I spent a restless night on the floor under a bunk, where it was cooler.

We left Volshenitsa about 0900 and continued toward Obozer-skaya. It was colder than yesterday (about 50 below zero). To keep warm we walked more and at a faster pace. A monotonous stretch of forest heavily bedecked with snow was all I saw. The glint of bril-liant moonlight on the smooth tracks; the deep shadows under the pines; the creak of sled runners; the still cold: these beautiful scenes just before the end of our day's journey made a lasting impression.

Leaving our droshkies at Obozerskaya, we entrained in boxcars. Though cold, they were fitted with comfortable bunks. After visiting the YMCA, we slept as the train lay on the tracks.

Sunday was clear and cold. After many of us revisited the YMCA to buy candy or food, our boxcar/passenger train pulled out of Obozerskaya at 1015 and slowly traveled northward, reaching Bakar-itza about 1700. Then on to a station across the broad Dvina River from Smolny. Upon detraining, we hiked across the ice, frozen to a depth of twelve to eighteen feet. Rails were laid on ties across the ice and cars rolled down the incline to the west side and hauled back by cable. The heavy locomotives were not run over this temporary track.

At Smolny we were quartered in comfortable, warm, electric-lit barracks. The mud we waded through in the fall was now frozen, and the filthy area about the buildings was covered with clean snow. Near the officers' quarters was a YMCA, where we obtained luxuries: gum, hot coffee or cocoa, and tasteless crackerlike biscuits. Movies rallied our low morale. Mess halls were nearly ready to use. New latrines—heated by sheet-iron stoves—were built. These comforts relieved the hardships of winter camp life and were greatly appreciated.

Ottney paternally provided for my physical welfare by swiping five blankets to replace mine, which disappeared in a similar manner.

I was happy to be relieved of front line duty and return to Smolny so I could clean up. For months we had been without a bath or change of clothing. For weeks we had not shaved or washed. Our bodies were overrun with vermin, and in some cases covered with a rash.

I had shaved and cleaned up in Mejovskayia on 27 December, but for twenty-four days had not so much as washed my face and hands. A bath was impossible. Had I desired to feign insanity, taking one in the shade of a snow-laden pine with a mess kit for my bathtub would have procured a recommendation for the nuthouse. Even my mess kit was neglected, for it was only occasionally rinsed by melting snow in it.

"If Ma could only see me now," was never more appropriate. Had she been present, more than one filial hero would have been passed unrecognized. Or unclaimed. Long, sandy-red whiskers intensified the grimy appearance of my dirty face. Long hair added to my un- kempt aspect.

My clothes, especially the underwear, were extremely filthy. Soon after arrival at the front I had added a second pair of heavy under- wear, and later "changed" by putting the outside pair next to my body. My breeches were comparatively clean, for on 11 January I had received a new pair to replace those worn since August.

I was literally crawling with body lice, and a fine red rash covered my skin. The filth and cooties produced such irritation that at times it seemed I would become insane.

I was not aware of the rash until this morning when I removed my shirt at Smolny Convalescent Hospital, where we were examined and given a powder that fattened instead of killed the lice. The medical officer explained the rash was due to too much bully beef and cor- rectly stated it would disappear with our change of diet. After a shave and an attempt to remove the smoke and grime of many a campfire, I felt something like my former self, though a bath and clean clothes were needed for comfort.

A recent copy of *The American Sentinel* told of the death on 6 Jan- uary of ex-President Roosevelt. Though he lost a son in service, he had lived to see our country emerge victorious in the world's great- est war.

After dinner E Company was assembled in the barracks and re-organized. With Lynch, Moore, DePue, Leemaster, Clyde Miller #2, and McCarthy, I was assigned to Cpl. Anthony Naugzemis's squad; the first of the first platoon. We remained with this agreeable squad leader until discharged.

The YMCA was the best feature of camp and relieved the monotony of army life. There I whiled away many hours reading magazines and books. In the reading room were tables with ink and paper bearing the YMCA circle stamped over the "Service in Russia" triangle, for our use. Finding *The Review of Reviews, The Outlook, The Literary Digest,* and other magazines was like meeting old friends. Accounts of President Wilson's Independence Day address and the American fight at St.-Mihiel only whetted my desire to get into civilian life, that I might follow current affairs with continuity.

In the evening I attended a movie presented for the special entertainment of our company, heard some music, and bought candy, biscuits, and hot cocoa. These features were of considerable benefit to us, but there was much criticism of the YMCA, chiefly because the Y men seldom came to the front, and we were obligated to pay for cigarettes and eatables. That these had been paid for by drives in the States and should be distributed free was the popular conception.

Tuesday forenoon I accompanied a group across the river to the railroad station, where we got our barracks bags and carried them to camp. In no hurry to return to where some disagreeable task might await us, we took time to investigate the trestle work of the temporary railroad and to examine the deep cracks in the river's ice. It was cold, noticeably colder than in our forest camps along the Emtsa. Smolny is about 110 miles farther north and exposed to winds sweeping down from the Arctic Ocean and White Sea.

Dinner of beef, gravy, mashed potatoes, bread, and tea contrasted with our scant rations of tin willie and hardtack.

Twenty of us were taken to a large Russian bathhouse on the outskirts of Archangel. After a long wait—the place was crowded with soldiers and civilians of both sexes—I took my second bath since arriving in Russia four and a half months earlier. I felt much better in clean clothes, but failed to rid myself of cooties until after leaving the country.

"Rest" at Smolny

My first letter of 1919 was written at the Y and sent to my parents. Chancing censorship, I described our drive to Kodish. I could have written much more: a scathing indictment of our officers; how we supplied ourselves at Bakaritza; and criticism of the march, but deemed it better to give an account of the battle than possibly lose all by relating carping details. The letter passed. Soon, due to newspaper clippings and letters from the States criticizing the expedition and our Allies based on accounts sent home by other soldiers, censorship was made doubly strict.

After getting my hair cut, Ottney and I applied for a pass to Archangel. The cold had somewhat abated and snow fell quietly. At the YMCA—a massive, cheerless, and nearly deserted building in the heart of the city—Ottney beat me at a game of checkers.

We then went to the hospital to visit E Company wounded. Resting in individual cots, all appeared to be doing well. After talking for some time with Cpl. Frank Goodson, who had been severely wounded, we returned to the Y for something to eat before going to the Red Cross, where we sent cablegrams home. My message, with the address, consisted of eleven words: "Well. Don't worry. Love to all. Donald." It cost twenty rubles and was received on 29 January. I hoped it might relieve the tension at home, for I was sure newspapers would contain accounts of our struggle with the Bolos at Kodish.

A team of three reindeer was across the street. The driver, a Laplander, was short, Mongolian in appearance, shabbily dressed, and as I told Ottney was , "a dirty-looking cuss." I petted one of the surprisingly small deer. Two ropes around its neck were all that attached it to the merest skeleton of a sled.

Apparently a bath, after surviving three months without one, was a greater shock than my system could endure, for I returned to the barracks with a severe cold in my throat and lungs.

My cold being no better on Friday, I "went on sick report" as accompanying "the sick, lame, and lazy" to the dispensary was called; not that I expected medical aid, but that I might be excused from duty.

In the evening I attended an illustrated lecture on this godforsaken country in which we were marooned.

I went to the dispensary today and was marked "duty," so stood an outdoor inspection of heavy packs with the company. For supper we had Australian rabbit, a tasty new item on our menu.

Our "rest" was short. We were being prepared for future campaigning. This included learning to use the French Chauchat automatic rifle, lighter and less effective than the Lewis gun, and firing twenty rounds. (Col. Frederic M. Wise, USMC, in his book *A Marine Tells It To You,* says: "Those damnable French Chauchat automatic rifles . . . they were heavy, clumsy, and inaccurate.")

Training at the Archangel school—more intensive than that at Smolny—was designed for instructors, and to it were ordered a number of E Company men, including myself. Suspecting the school was conducted by the English and recalling how one of our men complained about poor food while being trained by them at Stoney Castle, I determined to exploit my cold to avoid being separated from my comrades and deprived of good food, comfortable quarters, and the YMCA. Upon accosting the first sergeant I was referred to Lieutenant McClung, whom I found in the midst of a number of officers in their quarters. He inquired if I was listed for duty.

"Yes, sir," I said. "I'm sure those at the medical department don't appreciate just how I feel."

He half smothered an oath, then with others laughed as he told me the medical officer was in the room. The latter made some inquiries and finally the lieutenant said he was not particular if I didn't feel well, just so some intelligent man went. The next day I attended the first session of the Chauchat gun school held in our barracks at Smolny.

The weather continued cloudy and milder. I was still ill, but instead of reporting to the dispensary cared for myself. At 1600 our company was placed under arrest because someone stole a razor from the company barber.

On Tuesday forenoon we drilled for a few minutes for the first time since at Seletskoe in November. In the afternoon we marched through a snow-bound cemetery to the rifle range and fired the Chauchats.

At the barracks I learned that part of the company was to leave the following morning for the Railroad Front. Knowing how orders are often changed, I felt there was a possibility I might be included, though was informed I was not.

In the forenoon two platoons of E Company departed for the Railroad Front, where they remained with other American units under the command of Major Nichols until early March. Though subjected to intermittent artillery fire, they spent a comparatively quiet month, sustaining no loss except Walter Ciesielski, of Detroit, who died of pneumonia on 27 February.

As our bunkmates Baker and Ottney went to the front, Hahn and I moved into an upper tier; warmer and also less likely to be noticed and drafted for some detail.

Archangel, Russia, 30 January 1919

Dear Folks,

I came off guard duty this afternoon and for the most part have been enjoying the YMCA. It is a real pleasure to have a place to write, read, and buy a few cups of cocoa or coffee. You'd be surprised to know how much of it I can get away with in an evening.

I'm going on my ninth month in the army, and more than six of those have been spent overseas. You can never realize the vast difference between our country and that of other nations. Our advantages, conveniences, and customs are far superior to those of the two great nations I've seen. The soldiers who came across will appreciate the U.S. if anyone does.

There'll be no more school teaching for me; that old farm will have to put up with me when I get a good rest after my return.

Tomorrow I'm booked for a little kitchen work—fine training for a bachelor whose prospects are as good as mine.

By the way, Father, get your stand-up collar, for you and I, and Mother if she can, are due to make an auto trip to Washington, DC, about October 1920 if all goes well. It's at my expense. I've not signed the payroll since August, so have a neat little wad coming when I hit American soil. It would be a shame to save it!

With much love to all, Donald

KP duty was a snap. All I did was help clean the dining room tables after two meals. At 1400 I chased three prisoners with my loaded and bayoneted rifle. These were recalcitrant or venereal Americans, who in the latter case, having been treated at the hospital, were obliged by regulations to serve a turn in the stockade without pay. More than one NCO's rank was sacrificed on the seductive altar of immorality. Commissioned officers, too, were not guiltless.

Much could be written about this phase of army life, which is hushed in official circles and polite society. The smutty yarns; the foul, suggestive expressions; inexcusable, insulting comments at the sight of a woman; and the shameful attitude that it is an evil necessarily characteristic of the service. The fact that prophylactic stations are provided is a confession of such an attitude, and a veritable encouragement to many who otherwise would have hesitated because of possible disease.

Being required to wash my mess kit in the same water with such companions did not add to my love for army life. I feared infection from this source or from latrines. There were seats marked For Venereal Only. It was a standing joke that those were the least dangerous. Little wonder I feared that upon our return home the world would turn its face and blush for shame. Great was my surprise that we should be aided to employment for having been in service. There were those who followed the straight and narrow path, but they were a minority.

I detested guarding prisoners, who were assigned tasks ranging from cleaning the latrines to bringing in the camp's wood supply. At this time of year there was no harder work than providing an adequate supply of fuel. In a region abounding in vast forests this would appear a simple task, but it was not. With the river frozen solid, the Archangel-Economia Railroad was put in operation and carloads of scantlings were shipped in from the great sawmills at Solombala, Economia, and perhaps elsewhere. I chased prisoners who unloaded these cars near camp, then hauled the scantlings on commandeered droshkies to the barracks, where daily a large group cut and carried them into the buildings. With someone to stoke our two huge stoves day and night, we kept our barracks well heated.

A Laplander and his team of four reindeer passed while a railroad car was being unloaded. Though the team was panting and running with tongues hanging out, the driver urged them on with a weird moaning cry and a long, slender pole used to guide them.

A ten-day Lewis machine-gun school began on 5 February for all E Company men in Smolny. Morning and afternoon we gathered in the theater, where groups of eight or ten assembled around the tables for instruction by men with previous training or experience with these efficient, death-dealing weapons of modern warfare.

The head instructor was an English lieutenant who had served in a machine-gun unit on the Western Front. His assistants were two English sergeants whose patronizing airs, peculiar inflection of voice, and habit of pacing the room together during the frequent cigarette breaks were sources of amusement and ridicule.

Our gun crew instructor was Cpl. F. W. Wilkie, a modest and unassuming young man of K Company. In the autumn campaign near Kodish he wrought such havoc with his Lewis gun among a battalion of Trotsky's troops fresh from southern Russia that he was awarded the British Military Medal. In our crew, besides our squad, was George Washington Miller, the youngest man in E Company, a seventeen-year-old Mississippi lad.

Practical application of our training was offered at the rifle range, where each man fired short bursts of machine-gun bullets across the desolate wastes. I fired about thirty-six rounds, then spent the rest of the cold, stormy morning tramping snow in an effort to keep warm. The afternoon was devoted to cleaning the guns.

In the evening while reading at the Y, I was told that mail had been called. I received eleven letters. Three from Mother; the latest dated 18 December. Returning to the Y's comparative quiet, I spent an enjoyable evening reading my mail.

The Lewis gun school was dismissed at noon, so I went to the bathhouse in the afternoon. After a tedious wait I obtained a room where I could bathe privately. Apparently Saturday afternoon bathing is a Russian custom, for the hot, poorly ventilated waiting room was crowded with civilians and a few American soldiers. Two tall, handsome girls about twenty years of age laughed and mimicked my poor Russian when, upon paying my fee, I inquired "*Skulks uhr?*"—"At what time?" I, too, laughed, but left it to other soldiers to entertain them.

In the evening I attended a movie and drank hot cocoa and coffee. Occasionally I drank so much that I retired in distress, if not sick.

A report arrived that Clifford B. Ballard of Cambridge, Massachusetts, a second lieutenant of Machine Gun Company was killed in severe fighting near Kodish. I felt a personal loss, for he had spent a night about our campfire while we were guarding the Emtsa River in the fall.

On Sunday afternoon, while reading at the Y, I was happily surprised when Vern Slout, a schoolmate from Vermontville, entered to see me. A corporal in the 310th Engineers, he served as a clerk in the great sawmill at Solombala. I had not known he was in Russia. Vern wrote and directed a play given in Archangel, and after the war toured the United States on the Chautauqua circuit.

In the evening I attended a YMCA service, where Mr. Watts gave us a scathing lecture and severely criticized our morals. "Had I a daughter," he said, "I would do all in my power to prevent her marrying a soldier!"

Our Lewis gun school was dismissed early so we could hear Major Young, who undertook to stem the rising discontent among the troops in Smolny. With the war on the Western Front ended, we were anxious to return home. Rumors that we were soon to leave always failed to materialize. Every evidence indicated further campaigning. His attempt to explain our presence in Russia and why we should remain only made matters worse. It was a poor effort to camouflage the situation.

We were tested on the operation and care of the Lewis gun. Gunners were assigned on this ability. I am not a gunner.

Rumor again had us going home. We liked to believe these recurring reports, which in our hearts we knew to be false. They buoyed the spirits, giving us new hope and courage, only, in due time, to leave us more dejected than ever.

Archangel, Russia, 14 February 1919

Dear Folks,

I'm writing this at the Y. Here I find my greatest pleasure. Last Sunday evening I attended services and believe me it was good to sing a few hymns and hear a minister talk. Before this I had attended a Bible class or so, mostly accidental. I happened to get caught where they were held.

The Y and Red Cross certainly help out. January 24th we received our Red Cross socks containing dates, candy, raisins, nuts,

and a sock to match the filled one. Coffee, cocoa, crackers, gum, and
tobacco may be had. There is a fairly decent map of England here
and I saw that my two trips across the island took in a great part of
the country.

I'm dressed in my reddish-brown sheepskin overcoat, a black fur
cap, heavy socks that nearly reach my knee, and Shackleton boots of
canvas. This is my extra apparel for out-of-doors.

On the way back from the front we were billeted in a house occu-
pied by natives, numerous cockroaches and an army of some other
type of bug. Anyone not having cooties before should have them now.
The standards of morality, living, knowledge, wages, and ideals are
considerably lower than in America. It is not uncommon to see people
relieving themselves on the street. The men do less physical labor than
the women. Begging cigarette butts or driving a horse and droshky
are their main occupations.

I used to see icicles or frost on men's beards and thought it a dis-
agreeable feeling I'd never experience. One snappy day at the front I
took out my steel mirror to see if I looked as mean as I felt. The fel-
lows and I had quite a laugh for I had a fine white outfit in place of
my fierce Irish red whiskers.

You may consider this my Valentine. I don't imagine these old
Russkies ever heard of a Valentine card, or I'd try to send one.

With love to all, Donald

I was detailed to bring some Russian troops of the British Slavic
Legion from our camp to the theater where they were to be instructed on the Lewis gun. They were boys, a few in their twenties.
The long overcoat concealed my uniform and they mistook me for
an English soldier. Pointing to myself I said, "Americanski," and
showed them my collar ornament. They then demonstrated their
friendship for Americans by patting me on the back and gleefully
talking to me.

Our mess kits, blackened by the smoke of numerous campfires,
were inspected by Captain Heil. We were ordered to clean them.
With Cosmoline and brick dust I readily shined my kit and passed
inspection. One man appeared with an unfastened button. Another
dropped his knife. Both were awarded extra duty.

In the afternoon the corporals and sergeants were given the warrants of their noncommissioned rank, dated 17 August 1918.

Sunday at 1400 I mounted guard at the post regarded as least desirable—near Headquarters. The guard continually presented arms as officers came and went. Upon appearance of the camp commander the guard called, "Post number one! Turn out the guard!" If the officer saluted, he then said, "Never mind the guard." Otherwise those lounging about the guardhouse hurried outside, assumed a military formation, and performed the formalities.

To obtain our meals we presented a small cardboard ticket at the kitchen window—a recent innovation. I ate no dinner, but presented my ticket and mess kit for a second helping at supper. As tea, mashed potatoes, gravy, roast beef, bread and butter, and date pudding constituted the meal, I fared sumptuously. It was well worth going without dinner, as noon meals were exceedingly poor in quality and quantity.

DePue and I had scarcely stepped into the crowded Y when First Sergeant Comstock told me to report to Captain Oldfield's quarters. The captain was an American in the British service, temporarily stationed in our camp with a few Tommies. One of them, during my shift after dark—when I was required to halt and advance everyone who approached—failed to halt even after I ordered him to do so for the fourth time. How the captain learned of the private's refusal I do not know.

After affirming in the presence of both that the Tommy had not halted, the captain said to him: "Now what do you have to say for yourself?" adding that I had a perfect right to kill him for not stopping. I knew this but had no intention of murdering a harmless Britisher whom I could plainly see in the light of a nearby arc. The captain listed a vast amount of extra duty for the private.

After a good supper, and its duplicate obtained as last night, I went with two E Company platoons to the theater, where a lunch and smoker were held. There were pillow fights, boxing bouts with Hahn and Baker participating, musical numbers, a pie-eating contest, and similar stunts. Afterward we were treated to a feed and I obtained two pieces of pie, cake, cocoa, coffee, and gum. I was indifferent to the entertainment, but wide awake to my responsibilities concerning the eats. I could have been a winner in the pie-eating contest.

Though there was no parade ground in camp, our two platoons were often drilled during the inaptly named "rest period" of sixty days in Smolny. During severe weather we practiced—in the barracks—the manual of arms or use of the bayonet. Normally we lined up between the barracks for drill. Sometimes we hiked south, beyond Smolny's limits. Drill in extended order was impossible. During the manual of arms Captain Heil bawled me out for not giving my rifle the precise twist as I brought it from order arms to port arms.

Again I went without dinner and at 1400 mounted guard, this time going as acting corporal to a comfortable dwelling. After a good supper of tea, bread, jam, and rabbit stew, we returned to our guardhouse. While Corporal Metcalf slept the first half of the night, I settled down to spend the long winter evening posting the guards, stoking the huge stove with pine scantlings, and writing. This was a fortunate assignment, for the night was bitter cold. The coldest I experienced. The mercury must have dropped out of sight. The guards—strong, tough men—could stand post only a half hour at a time. The wind howled and blew. It caught one's breath; chilling through in almost no time, shooting its intense cold to the very marrow.

Though it snowed little, it swirled the snow high, drifting it in deep, fantastic formations almost hard enough to support one's weight, and making walking difficult. This was the Terror of the North. (Other accounts of the winter of 1918–19 in Archangel and at the front record temperatures of 40 to 50 degrees below zero—not calculating the wind chill factor.)

Living in rooms adjoining our guardhouse was a tall, elderly, wrinkle-faced Russian civilian who occasionally called on us though he could speak little English. To him—in the dead of night—I sold six packages of cigarettes. The transaction was conducted by my asking: *"Skulka rubles?"* as I held up my wares, and he replying in Russian and showing me paper money. Shaking my head and saying, *"Nyet, nyet,"* I succeeded in getting him to raise the amount. Another time I could not do business with him because my British Scissors cigarettes were not as desirable as American brands.

After waking Metcalf, I retired at 0215. With my overcoat for a bed as well as a covering I lay on the floor. How I appreciated the comfortable guardhouse on this terrible night. With daybreak the fury of the storm was more plainly seen. Great drifts of snow blocked our paths. Men, even while exercising, had frosted cheeks and noses. The terror of the storm did not deter me from walking to camp for a double breakfast of rice. Though the storm raged all day, camp activities were conducted as usual.

While we were guarding the warehouses and wharf area and fortifying ourselves against the increasing cold, other men were at the camp YMCA enjoying a movie. At its end, a photograph of President Wilson and one of the American flag were thrown on the screen. The audience was American troops with a scattering of English. The two views were hissed at. A few English soldiers applauded that which should have brought a patriotic response from every American.

It was a shameful act and when DePue told me of it I felt the men were much in the wrong. At no time, however discouraging the situation, could I have participated in such an act. Though a Republican, I admired the president and never felt he had sent us into north Russia without good reason. As for the flag, my respect for it could not be diminished by a dozen north Russian campaigns.

Sergeant Marten, who misappropriated some of our money in England, was reduced to buck private.

After supper I attended a Russian concert at the Y. Among the musicians presenting a varied program of vocal, cello, piano, and violin numbers was a girl graduate of the Moscow Conservatory, a dissipated violinist, and a fine tenor from the Russian Grand Opera. All were accompanied by an elderly lady pianist. I most enjoyed the tenor, who sang in Russian, which of course was "all Greek to me."

Among the guardhouse prisoners was a tall, young American from another unit in solitary confinement. While at the front during the winter he suddenly became violently insane, shooting and killing a British officer. Pitiful as the case was, his ravings were amusing—so fanciful that we wondered if he were not feigning insanity. He required much attention. Once he donned hat and overcoat and insisted on being taken for a bath. It took all of my tact—of which I have little—to get him to give up the idea.

One afternoon, while I was acting corporal, he set fire to the dry moss chinking between the logs of the guardhouse. The guard was called out. With axes and water they went to work while I, contrary to regulations of which I was quite ignorant, ran to Headquarters for a chemical fire extinguisher.

In the meantime the prisoner called an American officer every kind of a Jew and concluded his profane tirade by hurling his tin cuspidor at the officer, hitting his target.

I was dejected. How I wished I was out of Russia so I could see my people, read, study, learn, and amount to something. I'm tired of rotten food, irregular life, vile companions and conditions, and of hearing Wilson and England damned.

In the evening we were again subjected to one of Major Young's harangues; this time at the theater and on the subject of venereal disease, apparently of much concern to the officers.

Communiqués posted daily at the Y were of interest to all. These, with *The American Sentinel,* were our only means of getting up-to-date news, for magazines and papers were invariably weeks, if not months, old.

In the afternoon of 28 February our two platoons of E Company moved into a newly remodeled barracks, where Hahn and I obtained an upper bunk at one side of the room. Our move was made to accommodate part of L Company, which arrived the next day.

The two E Company platoons at the Railroad Front were about to return, and this move made it possible to quarter the company in one barracks. The one we vacated was shared with a detachment of Machine Gun Company.

On 3 March I was ordered to report to Major Young, the camp commander, and to testify regarding the reputed drunkenness of Major Donoghue on the morning of 6 January when we reentered Kodish after K Company burned it. No doubt the major was drunk when he accosted corporals Baker and Naugzemis—who testified to that effect. When I saw him in the morning he was sufficiently sober that I could not swear that he was or had been intoxicated. I angered Major Young by telling him I did not know if Major Donoghue was drunk. "My ignorance is due," I added, "to not having associated in civilian life with people addicted to such habits." He curtly dismissed me.

The two platoons of E Company from the Railroad Front returned, having spent over a month in practical training and front line duty. They blustered in an attempt to impress the camp that they were seasoned, hard-boiled troops.

While looking out the window overlooking the nearly snow-covered, icebound Dvina River, I saw three reindeer teams hurrying toward Archangel. A weak sun peeped on this frozen part of the globe. As I watched the raw, penetrating wind swirl the fine snow, I thought that riding the Laplander's crude, open sled was not an enviable task. I am grateful to be an American.

The forenoon was taken in outdoor drill under our new replacement officer, 2d Lt. Edwin Broer, of Toledo, Ohio; soon known among the troops as "Dizzy." He did not appear in the afternoon and Corporal Bygden—later promoted to sergeant—conducted the drill.

On 7 March the sun rode in a clear sky and was much higher than two months earlier. Places sheltered from the chilling breeze thawed slightly. This was not the advent of spring, for bleak, stormy days immediately followed to remind us the long, cold winter was not over.

Though it was long past the hour for lights out, the noisy barracks was well lit by numerous candles. For weeks our outfit had been keeping late hours, gambling, smoking, and swapping yarns. Nearly everyone sucked a cigarette. The dense, foul-smelling atmosphere of the poorly ventilated barracks was blue with smoke. It was almost unbearable and nearly everyone had a cigarette cough. Often above the din of blended voices and shuffling feet one could hear the foulest remarks shouted in jest.

That evening was no exception until the arrival of our little captain, who should have been asleep and not paternally worrying about our affairs. Noticing his entrance, I immediately snuffed my candle and feigned sleep, but could not escape the bawling out administered to all of us.

All members of E Company were given a service stripe while on the way to supper. I sewed this unnecessary reminder that we had served overseas six months on my blouse. It was a beautiful golden *V* and worn seven inches above the cuff of the left sleeve. Though proud to have the privilege of wearing it, I wrote my parents: "I'll be perfectly satisfied with one—another will represent too long a period of service abroad."

At the Y, I concluded a letter to my parents with: "It was eight months yesterday when I last saw you. Do you suppose I'll get back before next July 7th? I'm inclined to believe I will."

My parents were no fans of the Wilson administration. In case of my death in Russia, I believed they would feel quite bitter toward the president for sanctioning this expedition, so I wrote: "President Wilson has less than two years to serve. I read that two attempts to assassinate him have occurred. He is a great statesman, and I'd hate to see him leave his work unfinished. No matter what happens to me, by all means give him the credit due his greatness. I'm sure he'll go down in history beside our first and sixteenth presidents."

After turning in our blankets at the Smolny Annex of the Convalescent Hospital to be deloused, we spent the mild day drilling. In the evening the Y presented a thrilling holdup movie set in California. The educational program featured beautiful Washington, DC, and photographs of Admiral Sims in action with torpedoes and smokescreen; so interesting that DePue and I stayed for the second showing.

The twelfth of March was stormy. In the morning before beginning our routine drill I was sent across the river for a new gas mask. From a train—run down from Bakaritza, where Supply Company was stationed—we were issued new masks to replace those lost or converted into haversacks while holding the Emtsa River Front.

The day's most important event was the return of 1st Lt. J. J. Baker, confined to the hospital since the last day of 1918, when he injured his spine at Kodish. He scrutinized us with his customary eagle eye, and I felt our days of lax discipline and comparative ease were past.

Not infrequently on Russian festival days—of which there are too many for the welfare of the people—we were held in our quarters as an emergency guard in case of riot. I do not know that such ever occurred. Because of this, I was not permitted to leave the barracks on this cold Sabbath until 2000, when I visited the Y. I spent the afternoon reading *The Review of Reviews*. Father had ordered it sent to me for four months. Some unscrupulous party appropriated the other three copies.

Instead of taking the usual route to the rifle range on this St. Patrick's Day, Lieutenant Baker—unacquainted with the trail—led us along a path that ended at the church door. Rather than retrace his steps, he confidently struck out in a direct line toward the range. He soon found wading the waist-deep snow—to the amusement of his troops—so slow and laborious that he took the regular trail.

I frosted two fingers as I operated my rifle. It became useless after the sixth shot. More serious, nearly half of the company's rifles became useless this afternoon. Such damnably unserviceable rifles were a sad example of equipping American soldiers with anything except U.S. army rifles. This failure—under favorable conditions, compared with battle—was demoralizing.

For some time it had been rumored that we were to move. I was in a state of nervous expectancy. There was so much speculation that I finally ceased to believe any of it. This ended the following morning, when we were ordered to pack our barracks bags. I carried mine to a boxcar a short distance north of camp, a convenience made possible by a railroad spur laid over the frozen river. Rumor also said that the enemy had captured our mail, fortunately false. It was a cold day and, not feeling well, I rested much, except for a visit to the Y, where I obtained some pie, a real luxury in cursed Russia.

Chapter 14
Defending the Line of Communications
20 March to 19 May 1919

On the morning of 20 March we left Smolny Barracks and began our second trip into the interior of the state of Archangel. We marched across the icebound Dvina River and boarded a freight train going south to Bakaritza, now so wrapped in snow that it appeared inactive. Then a comfortable ride through Isaka Gora to Obozerskaya. On 16–17 March the Reds had surprised a small force of French and White Russians at Bolshie Ozerki, forty miles west of Obozerskaya, and by occupying the town cut our vital Archangel-Obozerskaya route to Kola, the all-year open port of north Russia. Mail, supplies, and reinforcements passed over this vital route through Bolshie Ozerki, Chekuevo, Onega, and Kem.

This drive, launched by the Reds from a base sixty versts distant, drove a wedge between our force on the Railroad Front and that along the Onega River, threatening Obozerskaya on the line of communications between Archangel and the Railroad Front. If successful, this might fulfill the Bolo's boast to drive us into the White Sea by spring. This was the critical situation when we reached Obozerskaya just before a glorious sunset. Expecting an attack on the poorly defended town, soldiers patrolled the woods during the night.

We did not stay to defend the place. Though it was dusk our equipment was loaded on droshkies. Marching westward, we soon arrived at Maliozorki, a small lakeside village.

After delay and confusion we were billeted in private dwellings. Two squads of us were assigned a large room in a house in a remote part of town near the forest. The evening was spent loading pans (circular magazines) and cleaning the Lewis gun. It was late when we wrapped up in our blankets to sleep on the floor, only to spend a restless night in the hot, smoky, unventilated room overrun with cockroaches. One woke me by crawling over my face. Men bayoneted them as they appeared from between moss-chinked logs.

The Russians were plagued with body and head lice. I saw a boy of ten or eleven eating lice combed from his hair.

Swarthy, unkempt Russian men frequently entered our room to beg cigarettes or stare at us. From my bunk on the floor I saw them seated around a crude table eating their noon meal—a frugal affair. They dipped large wooden spoons into a wooden bowl containing thin, milky soup. It did nothing to whet my appetite. The women wore soiled, varicolored cloths tied about their heads while they ate.

Late in the afternoon I procured a sleeping bag and new Shackleton boots to replace the pair I'd charred while seated by campfires on the Emtsa River Front.

The most important incident was the corporals' meeting, held after supper. Every corporal attended. It bordered on mutiny. The men—privates and corporals—were satiated with fighting at Kodish and did not relish a similar experience. The feasibility of refusing to leave for the front was thoroughly discussed. Most, if not all but one, favored refusing to fight. Corporal Earl Metcalf, whom I esteemed for his courage and good judgment, opposed their action. As no one would accept responsibility for leading the mutiny, it came to naught.

Asked what I would do if the men refused to obey orders, I said, "I have no intention of going to the front line alone. Neither do I intend to lead the revolt."

I preferred to take my chances in battle with poor Bolo marksmen than at sunrise with an American firing squad.

The day was somewhat warmer and we spent it resting for the anticipated move and battle. About 1800 orders to fall in were received; all obeyed, though not without considerable grumbling and cussing. With depressed spirits and morale exceedingly low, we set out across the north end of the lake.

In advance was a well-guarded train of droshkies carrying our supplies and equipment. Almost immediately one man slipped through a hole in the ice and into the water. He was relieved of making the tiresome hike. Probably many felt as I and wished he might have enjoyed the consequences of that cold plunge.

Our hike of twenty-one versts along a winding road thickly lined with snow-clad pines and across rolling land was tedious. We crossed a bridge carelessly guarded by a Russian of the British Slavic Legion. It was never dark enough to hamper our marching. I could plainly see—against the white background—the dark forms of the convoy and soldiers. Our flat-soled, slippery Shackletons made walking difficult and precarious. I welcomed the few halts we made.

At 0100 we reached the Eighteenth Verst Pole. This was a poorly fortified position on the road twelve miles west of Obozerskaya, and four miles east of Bolshie Ozerki, where the enemy was concentrated. In a low area across this road—so essential to the enemy for transporting the artillery he'd require to take Obozerskaya—was a hurriedly improvised front. It faced west and consisted of a few pieces of artillery and an inadequate force of Americans, eighty Royal Yorks, and Russians of the British Slavic Legion. If outposts were established, they were not held by Americans.

This was the front—ominously silent. Men conversed in low tones as they huddled around cheerless, low-burning fires beside the road, well screened by the dense coniferous forest. The hilarious campfire jokes so characteristic of our Emtsa River duty were conspicuously absent.

After spending two joyless hours mingling with this group and jostling for places by the fires, we were ordered to fall into company formation on the road. During this tedious wait we were given a cup of hot cocoa and an English biscuit—comparable in size and appearance to our soda cracker. Cold, shivering, and unable to get near the fires that produced more smoke than heat, I marked time in an effort to keep from freezing.

While we stood on the road a large force of the British Slavic Legion passed in front of us, headed toward Bolshie Ozerki. They were preceded by a squad or so from another unit detailed to patrol the forest in no-man's-land. Camouflaged in white sheetlike hood and cape—the first I saw—they reminded me of descriptions of the Ku Klux Klan.

The Bolos, to warn of approaching patrols, tied dogs in the forest. We have no such canine allies.

About 0400—a propitious moment for zero hour, as our spirits and temperatures were equally low—we were ordered to "Push off," as Lieutenant Baker casually phrased it. With two of our lieutenants stupefied with liquor, we started toward the Bolo stronghold. Almost immediately we passed four French 75s, two on each side of the road, manned by stolid Russian gunners, and protected on the flanks and front by a strong barricade.

Shortly after passing the guns we were halted and Lieutenant Broer, reeling and swearing, aligned us in an attacking formation. To lead this column he selected Pfc. Lynch Noone, an irrepressible Chicago Irishman, whose keen sense of humor immediately departed when he was ordered along the right track, with me following a couple rods behind on the left track. Alternating right and left at regular intervals followed the rest of E Company.

Though it may have been the most feasible plan of attack, to those of us at the head of the column slowly—almost pussyfooting—marching down the narrow, snow- and forest-flanked road winding over uneven country, it was preposterous. An alert Bolo force, screened by the dense snow-laden branches, would have us at its mercy, for escape through the waist-deep snow was virtually impossible. At their leisure they could end our promising careers.

Despite an indescribable physical weariness, I was mentally alert. The conglomerate panorama of ideas crowding through my mind has always interested me psychologically. Thoughts of home and those close to my heart were uppermost. Would they ever realize how I sympathized with them for their anxiety concerning my welfare, and if death befell me, would that anxiety be increased by their inability to obtain a satisfactory account of the circumstances?

Though the odds were apparently against us—especially those at the head of the line—I could not convince myself that death awaited me in this war. At least not today. However, did not every man feel the same, and were not some usually killed in battle? It was like reasoning in a circle, or with a false premise. Capture or being wounded might be my fate, but not death. Someday, only a matter of time, tedious as that might be, I would return to my people and relate my military experiences and all that I had seen. How utterly futile our efforts. Why should we waste our lives in this godforsaken hellhole?

As we eased down a gentle grade, I saw—near the road and some distance ahead—a faint glow. Could it be a cigarette? For a second it seemed inexplicable—a thing of fascination. Then I dimly perceived the dark forms of men squatting in the snow. Were these Bolos? Just as I emitted a low whistle to Noone, he halted and looked back, only to be ordered forward by a second lieutenant who said, "Those are troops of the British Slavic Legion." These Russians, sent in advance, were to attack the enemy position.

We proceeded a few yards farther before the Russians hurriedly shifted their position. For a second or so it resembled a flight. Immediately there was a sharp volley of rifle fire. The Bolos had discovered them. Poorly aimed shots cut the air above us. We were ordered back a few rods before dropping in the road. So far it was turning out better than my gloomy foreboding warranted. The battle had begun before we were entrapped.

I was told this slight withdrawal was because the plan precluded our making the attack. We were to give moral support to the Russians. Expecting we would soon be recalled from Russia, precautions were taken to prevent needless loss of American lives. Corporals Anthony Naugzemis and Ora Wagner got off a six- or eight-shot burst from our Lewis gun before it jammed; the only shots fired by E Company men.

We were exposed to flying bullets. My position on the crest of a gently sloping knoll afforded no protection.

As we lay in the road enveloped by Arctic twilight, there suddenly appeared ahead, just below the treetops, a burst of red flame, followed immediately by a loud report. Artillery fire. Startled, I ducked my steel-helmeted head at the proper angle to ward off shrapnel. None hit in my vicinity. With their first shot the Bolo gunners had nearly located our range. I believe it burst over our Slavic allies, who had checked a slight retreat and were returning the fire of their countrymen. Other shells burst without injury to our company. Our Russian gunners soon had the French 75s behind us in action.

While hugging the snow I noticed that none kept closer to it than our captain who was now just ahead of me. His "bravery" at Kodish had been held up to ridicule at one of the company smokers.

Our force, exposed to this fire, was withdrawn and sent northward into the forest to attack the enemy's left flank. As we left the road and plunged single file into the forest, what had been the rear became the head of the column. Breaking trail through that waist-deep snow was exhausting. Our formation was not an exact reverse, for now twelve or fifteen men were behind me.

As we entered the woods the din of rifle- and machine-gun fire and exploding shells became terrific. Our line of march gradually swerved northwest. Moving through the snow was difficult. None hastened to reach our destination. Rests were frequent and our progress slow. A repetition of the Kodish fiasco and hours of fighting in the snow and cold appealed to no one.

Finally, after what seemed hours of struggling through deep snow, we received—over a line the telephone gang strung as we proceeded—the order to retreat. Drooping spirits immediately revived. Every man turned in his tracks and that slow, reluctantly moving line executed our retrograde movement with vigor.

As we neared the road, shattered treetops, scattered snow, and shell-blown earth testified to the severity of the Bolo artillery fire. The south end of our trail was so shelled that, had we been there, our force would have suffered many casualties. Our withdrawal could not have been timed with greater precision. As we entered the road, the repulsed British Slavic Legion slowly approached and their van fell in directly behind our rear. Their unsuccessful attack was responsible for our recall.

Our Russians suffered at least three killed and a number of wounded. Some were bandaged; others, supported by their uninjured comrades. The dead, partly covered with a carpet-like material, lay beside the road in the rear of the artillery. One, a gunner, carelessly stepped in front of a French 75 just in time to have part of his head blown off.

Our nearest approach to a casualty was Charles Givens of Bellaire, Ohio. As he entered the woods a piece of shrapnel pierced his leather jacket and the tin case of his snow goggles, leaving without breaking the skin. He had a black-and-blue spot on his left leg above the knee. So anxious were our officers to make the best possible showing that he was awarded a wound stripe for this mark, which ordinarily would not have been reported. Givens, a quiet, modest fellow, shared this joke with mingled amusement and disgust.

We reached the artillery about noon. Though weak from hunger and exhaustion, I was detailed with ten men to guard the guns. Our position in front and to the right of the 75s was behind a log barricade camouflaged with snow and pine boughs.

For three hours we awaited our reliefs. Coffee and oatmeal for supper. Tired unto death as I had never been in civilian life, I found DePue and made arrangements to bunk though it was early in the evening.

In a partially cleared area of the forest just off the road and behind the artillery were fifteen or twenty inconspicuous white canvas tents; as cold and cheerless as they looked, they at least afforded protection from the wind. With no fire in front to radiate warmth inside, and with not all of the snow removed from the ground, they were less comfortable than our open brush shacks along the Emtsa. This was the poorest excuse for a camp I experienced.

DePue and I hurriedly made up our bed of ten blankets. It was a great relief to turn in after nearly twenty-four hours of strenuous duty. Soon after the first shivers gave way to some degree of warmth we were sleeping soundly. The dangers of the night attack were the least of our worries compared to the corporal's statement that he would call us during the night to relieve the guard. Neither occurred, though we were awakened by noncoms endeavoring to wake other tired men.

About 0600, before daybreak on Monday, 24 March, Sergeant Rogers routed us for "stand to." This was new. I was sure it was nothing pleasing.

With my ever-ready loaded and bayoneted rifle I stepped out into the cold morning dusk to ascertain just what in hell was in store for us. The good-natured sergeant, somewhat amused, grinned and told me it was the "stand to arms" to repel a possible attack on the guardhouse. Of course. It was quite military, but why had we not been introduced to it along the Emtsa? We had been too negligent there.

Our stand to was without incident. Finally, without breakfast, I was posted with six others in the forest a few rods outside of camp. We had no fire, so exercised to keep warm. With no particular degree of suspicion we eyed the dense forest and noisily conversed. How beautiful when twilight gave place to daylight and objects could be clearly seen, and yet how cold and uninviting. Branches, weighed with the heavy accumulation of weeks of snow, hung low and often rested on the ground.

Walking was difficult and the patrol did not comply with the order to reach a trail some distance south of our road. Ottney blusteringly told how they deemed it unnecessary to wallow so far and returned when it suited their mood. And this was a dangerous position.

The 18th Verst Pole Position was the first obstacle the enemy must overcome in his plan to cut the Allies' lines of communication. In view of M Company's later fight for life, I now fully appreciate the peril of our situation. Our officers must have realized this—or been quite incompetent.

When we came off post after midafternoon, the Bolo artillery was firing at our Allied bombing plane. I watched it circle over Bolshie Ozerki. Daily, and many times oftener, this lone scout left his aerodrome northwest of Obozerskaya to make observations for the artillery and to drop bombs on the enemy stronghold.

Our artillery went into action. From the road a few yards in the rear, I observed this triune battle. The sharp Russian commands; the rapid loading of the four 75s; the almost simultaneous fire and recoil; the loud reports, followed by ones less distinct and more distant. My attention was on the aeroplane. Bursting one-pound shells were a pretty spectacle. Like small patches of suddenly appearing cumulus clouds the smoke of exploding shells appeared, then drifted away.

Breakfast was long over when we returned to camp. Nothing was saved, so we were obliged to cook our own rolled oats. While here we were usually fed only twice a day and the food was fairly good. Occasionally a YMCA man furnished us with gum, chocolate, and peppermints—a real treat—plus cigarettes. The Red Cross had a couple ambulances mounted on runners, each drawn by a horse.

Conditions were not ideal for campaigning. There was no water, so we melted snow in our mess kits and cooled it in our canteens. Worse, there was no warm place to spend our time off duty. The campfires—always crowded with huddling men—were nearly devoid of heat. The tents were too cold unless one covered up with a blanket, so we found it necessary to exercise regardless of our need to rest.

During the afternoon I was again posted in front of the artillery. According to rumor, the Bolos had cut the line between Obozerskaya and Seletskoe at the point where our squad expected to be stationed. If this was true, communications were soon to be reestablished.

"What would Mother and Father think if they could see me now?" I thought. "Would to God that we could get out of here soon."

Many a time while on guard at Bakaritza or on the long march to Seletskoe or in camp along the Emtsa, I fervently wished my people could see me amid my surroundings. But here, at the 18th Verst Pole, I was thankful they could not see the circumstances under which we existed.

Two pieces of artillery were brought up and placed one on each side of the road in the rear of our camp. Had the enemy not delayed to amass more troops, but taken advantage of their success on the twenty-third and attacked our small force, we would have been compelled to retreat, or if surrounded—as M Company was later—possibly forced to surrender, for our supply of food and ammunition was negligible. During the days we were here, supplies were brought by droshky from Obozerskaya, and by the time we left, the necessities to withstand a serious attack were available.

Though we were shifted from post to post, our hours of guard duty were regular: two hours on and four off. Men could not endure this indefinitely. We were still suffering from the strain of Sunday's drive. It was usual for us to eat, then turn in upon returning from duty.

Our bed of two groundsheets next to the earth, two shelter halves, and ten heavy woolen blankets equally divided beneath and over us, plus our heavy sheepskin or goatskin overcoats on top was inadequate to keep us warm. After a couple hours the cold penetrated from beneath, chilling us to the marrow, driving us out to the fire or to exercise long before the end of our four hours off duty.

This was particularly the case when one slept alone, as I usually did during the day. Two could, by sleeping close together, withstand the cold much longer. My hip and shoulder protested with an occasional twinge of rheumatism. Short as this campaign was, it was too long.

About noon, the approach of our aeroplane—mistaken for the enemy—created a flurry of excitement. Lewis guns were hurriedly placed to repel an attack. Some men sought cover in the woods. As the plane sped westward sanity reappeared.

Creating almost as much excitement was the news that our force would take over the extreme forward position held by the White Russians. This met with much protest. Campfire conversations were outspoken and sullen. Corporal Jim Sanders informed the officers of this attitude. At 0800 when his guard detail was called out, he refused to go unless accompanied by a commissioned officer. A heated argument ensued with Second Lieutenant Broer before he agreed to accompany the corporal. They spent two hours at the front, having relieved the White Russians.

Leaving camp long after dark we cautiously followed a path just within the forest's edge. At 2000 I was posted behind a large, dead pine, as desolate and lonely a post as any I ever stood. The foreboding silence was not broken. In front was no-man's-land. With eye and ear I was keenly alert. My relief, due at 2200, did not appear until 2300.

During the next twenty-four hours I made four more trips to the front. I felt more secure during the day when a group of 310th Engineers commenced erecting log barricades and defenses just to my rear. These were of inestimable importance after we were withdrawn. Except for the sound of our plane and the French 75s, it was an uneventful day.

My last shift on this lonely post occurred between 0200 and 0400, the eerie hours before daybreak when man's resistance is at its lowest. At that hour—four days later—the Reds burst upon camp. Had the attack occurred this morning, would I have seen the advancing troops or been enveloped by them before I could reach my comrades? It was a dangerous place, and I was happy to be assigned a position within the new barricade guarding our two pieces of artillery. This change and the bright day brought up my spirits, and I felt better than at any time since leaving Smolny.

I interested myself less in watching the forest than in getting some French rifle bullets for souvenirs and inspecting the artillery; the barrels were being heated preparatory to action. The barricade was breast high, constructed of three or four tiers of logs, and protected the front and flanks of the 75s. Mills and French hand grenades lay on the barricade. More were handy in boxes on the ground.

From 2000 to 2200 I was with ten men at a new post in the forest northwest of camp. As we picked our way in single file over the rough trail, our artillery went into action. The bright, lightning-like flashes vividly illuminated the forest. I caught glimpses of the trees' huge boles, their low-hanging, snow-laden branches creating dark shadows. Our day and night bombardment of the Bolos was intended to demoralize them.

This post was a partially completed blockhouse: The roof and one side were yet to be constructed. Three guards were posted in front. The rest of us idly waited our shift. Behind was a fire where we kept warm and roasted slices of bacon on the ends of branches. Seldom did I eat with keener relish. What a scene for a camera as we squatted about that comforting fire enjoying our late noonday meal.

Our afternoon shift was shortened an hour by the arrival at 1500 of M Company, who relieved us at Verst 18. We hastened to camp to find our outfit already some distance along the road. Half running, we hurried to catch the long, irregular column of men and droshkies. We arrived at Maliozorki just after sunset. With part of the company I was quartered in a schoolhouse.

We spent two days and three nights at Maliozorki resting from the arduous duties of the past six days. During this stay no work was required of most of us. With fifty of my comrades I was quartered in a large, warm, well-lit schoolroom. It was a model of neatness. For arithmetical calculations there was a large, vertically supported abacus. Large maps of Russia and the continents hung on the walls. I attempted to trace the routes of our campaigns, but found the Cyrillic alphabet undecipherable.

Spreading my blankets on the floor, I slept soundly. After 0900 we got up. A good breakfast awaited us. It snowed during the morning. I spent most of the day reading the *Saturday Evening Post* of 28 December 1918.

After six days at the 18th Verst we got away just in time to miss one of the most stubbornly fought defensive actions of the north Russian campaign when, three days later, M Company began a three-day struggle for its life. During the short interval before this attack, while the Bolos were finishing preparations for their seven thousand troops to open the road to Obozerskaya, M Company worked on the barricades and blockhouses. Though not completed, they were adequate to withstand a serious attack.

The attack came early Wednesday morning, 31 March. A surprise attack in the rear severed all communications. The Canadian artillery officer quickly reversed his two guns and fired shrapnel set for muzzle burst into the Bolos, averting the loss of these weapons. A direct assault was made on the forward defenses, but they were resolutely held by M Company, supported on the flanks by raw White Russian troops. Darkness found the Allies still in position. During the night everything possible was done to make their defenses impregnable.

During the second day's fight—lasting from daybreak till dark—large numbers of Bolos were repulsed at every point. The commander of the 96th Saratov, one of three regiments employed, was killed as he rode forward on his white horse during a lull in the fighting at noon.

Severe artillery fire preceded the infantry attack on the third day. That attack failed before noon. The battle ended. Allied losses of three killed, one wounded, three missing, and three shell-shocked were insignificant compared to the loss of over two thousand Reds. On 4 April, M Company was relieved, and on 19 April the enemy withdrew to Shelaxa.

Sunday, 30 March, was a beautiful day, but the Arctic cold was still with us. It was gratifying to see the sun get higher day by day. I spent much of the day on my bunk reading a late copy of *The American Sentinel* and sleeping.

Military operations were in progress along the Railroad Front, for the continuous roar of guns was plainly audible when outside the school. Two Allied planes flew over. Our supper of bread, coffee, salmon, and applesauce was good.

We were awakened about 0630. Rolling our blankets, we prepared to leave our comfortable quarters and move to the Railroad Front. We left Maliozorki and marched to Obozerskaya. After a short time in the large YMCA near the tracks, we boarded a freight train and rode southward eight versts to Verst 466. Horse manure was frozen to the floor of my unheated car.

The train stopped long enough for our squad and three other squads to get off at the north edge of a large clearing embracing each side of the tracks. Carrying our rolls and equipment, we crossed the deep snow to an isolated log house, where I was immediately placed on guard at 1100. For two hours I stood behind a barricade, looking for Bolos that might appear in the thin forest a few rods to the west.

Verst 466 was twenty-two versts behind the front line of the Railroad Sector. For nine days E Company was in reserve, guarding the line of communication. The rest of E Company were quartered in buildings clustered near the tracks at the south of the clearing.

Our riflemen and Lewis gun crew occupied a one-room house at the north end of the clearing and a considerable distance from other buildings. We were the rear outpost. The building was heated by a stove and furnished with comfortable bunks—probably constructed by Americans. The only door was at the north end. There were no windows on the south and west sides. A breast-high barricade of three or four tiers of logs described an irregular triangle about the building.

We were well equipped with a Lewis gun, grenades, and ammunition and could have repelled a force much larger than our own. In the afternoon Lieutenant Baker inspected our defenses and set a stake to limit the leftward arc of our Lewis gun's fire, so we should not rake the main defense in case of attack.

Duty at Verst 466, compared with that at the 18th Verst, was a sinecure. Besides standing guard, little was required of me. Frequently I prayed that we might soon be withdrawn from old, war-cursed Europe and returned home.

By this time of year the sun was rising about 0530 and getting high in the heavens. On clear days its bright light flooded the clearing and penetrated the dense forest. Its light, dazzlingly reflected from the snow, was almost blinding. Furrows between the eyes appeared or deepened as men, not wearing their snow goggles, scowled or squinted.

It was the first of April and the men, having little else to do, made the most of it. Everyone—even the cadaverous, long-faced Paulo

Giorno—appeared good-natured. April Fools' Day jokes were rife, especially as we followed the narrow trail through deep snow on the way to dinner. I was finally tricked.

While on duty during our first nights at Verst 466 I saw the dull red flash of artillery fire in the direction of Bolshie Ozerki. It lit the sky like spiteful discharges of heat lightning playing among the distant clouds on hot summer evenings. It was fascinating, yet produced a sensation of horror, just as it had at Kodish. Occasionally a flash was followed by a report so barely audible that it was nearer a suggestion than a sound.

While on post in the early morning, DePue and I distinctly heard the boom of artillery. Little did we realize that we were listening to the last phase of the three-day struggle by M Company to hold the 18th Verst Position. Ignorant of what was occurring, we thought it was merely the day-and-night shelling of the enemy town. The sound of artillery on another front while ours was quiet was not new. We regarded it casually. I will always wonder why M Company was left to its own resources and no force sent to its relief during those three days.

I received four letters from Mother written between 28 January and 31 January, and a report that my cablegram sent from Archangel on 23 January had been forwarded from Washington, DC, and received on 29 January. Seven years later Mother told me how Father received the message over the telephone. It had been a particularly blue evening and the cablegram was reassuring—so elating that she cried. Looking up when Father asked her why she was crying, she saw tears streaming down his cheeks. They had been closely following the press accounts of the Kodish battle. Mother inquired if I had participated in the reoccupation of Kodish after it was burned.

In the afternoon, Lieutenant Baker, on a tour of inspection, entered our shack and told how the work detail taken to Verst 444—the front line of the Railroad Sector—had been attacked the night before. No one was injured. This was my first hint that troops in reserve were obliged to repair and strengthen the forward fortifications. The lieutenant appeared pleased that he had been there.

In the afternoon I went to the canteen car—brought down the railroad tracks—and purchased gum, cocoa, cake, syrup, peppermints, sardines, and Christmas pudding. An extravagant outlay for one of Uncle Sam's soldiers supposedly getting three squares a day. I needed this to satisfy my craving for sweets and to furnish variety to our monotonous rations. The Christmas pudding proved to be a mass of soggy, dark dough mixed with some fruit, perhaps raisins.

While on post between 2300 and 0100, it rained and snowed— the first rain of the year, another harbinger of spring.

Except for distant artillery fire in the direction of Bolshie Ozerki, all appeared quiet and peaceful. It scarcely seemed possible that death could break in anytime. Now it seems like a strange dream. Yet there I stood within a log barricade with loaded rifle and fixed bayonet carefully scanning the forest's shadows for the approach of an enemy.

While on post in the morning, DePue pointed out an ermine. It was like a weasel, and except for a black tail, all white. Its color and the glare of the snow made it difficult to distinguish as it ran through the snow at the edge of the forest.

When I went to the train for dinner—where the kitchen force issues our rations—Lieutenant Baker was sitting just inside the door to see that every E Company man took a cup of lime juice. The art of making coffee had so deteriorated in our company that I had ceased to drink the black, bitter concoction that some sincerely said was made by boiling fine-cut tobacco. Noticing I had no cup, the lieutenant said: "Carey, where's your cup?"

"I've not been drinking coffee," I replied, "so I left it at our quarters."

"Every man is obliged to drink a cup of lime juice."

"All right, I'll attend to that, sir." It was a considerable distance from the car to our shack, but I returned, not so much to obey the order, but to benefit from the drink.

In the afternoon I had my first bath since 26 February. A few heated cars provided with hot water and tubs—some of wood—were sidetracked opposite our quarters. I was glad to get rid of the grime and put on clean underwear.

North of our triangular defense and near the edge of the forest was a large pile of dry pine logs used for firewood. In the afternoon while helping get a supply of fuel for the stove, I entertained the squad by attempting to teach Paulo Giorno how to use a crosscut saw. His inclination to ride the saw afforded me an opportunity to keep up a running fire of ridicule and sarcasm until he disgustedly surrendered it to one who had a speaking acquaintance with the tool.

My guard duty at Verst 466 ended at 0300. It was a bright day, warmer than any so far that spring. Making up our blanket rolls, we impatiently awaited the arrival of M Company, who apparently followed us from place to place as we moved to the front. They arrived about 1500. Boarding a train, we were taken to Verst 455 where we remained for two or three hours.

Verst 455 was the field headquarters of Major Nichols, commander of the Railroad Sector. It was an unimposing cluster of log houses beside the track in a large clearing. High on one of the buildings was a watchtower. Barbed-wire entanglements were an important part of its defense. Numerous shell holes were scattered about the area.

Long lines of boxcars, some equipped with stoves and used for quartering the men, stood on the two sidetracks. Mounted on a steel flatcar in front of a locomotive was a long naval gun capable of firing twenty versts. I was told that after it effectively dropped numerous shells into Emtsa—a large town on the enemy side of the line— the Reds sent a warning to our Railroad Force that a repetition would result in their blowing our forces to pieces. Such bravado implied that they were not conducting their part of the war to the limit.

While standing in the doorway of the car I saw a group of five French and American officers, including Major Nichols and Col. George E. Stewart, commander of the 339th Infantry, passing alongside. At once I recognized the major, but so seldom did I see the colonel that, had I not seen the silver eagle on each shoulder, I would not have known him.

We left Verst 455 about 1900 and rode seven versts nearer the front to Verst 448, where most of E Company detrained. The train pulled out at 2030 with Sanders's and Naugzemis's squads, who were ordered off at Verst 447.

After the train passed on its way to the front, Lynch Noone picked up the muster roll and began calling off the names. Coming to his own he called, "Noone. *Noone!* several times, increasing the severity with each failure to obtain a response. At last, looking half apologetically at his amused comrades, he slipped the roll under his arm and said, "Well, damn it, they've got to be called off, haven't they?"

Leaving the forest-lined track, we followed a rough trail to a small, circular clearing. In the middle was a new log blockhouse. Inside we found Corporal Haynes and his squad. Though crowded with one squad, both squads spent the night in this warm structure. I found a place on the floor and regardless of possible attack was soon asleep.

My rest was broken at 0250 to spend thirty minutes on guard behind the blockhouse. As I quickly made my preparations by the light of a flickering candle, I noted the weary men breathing heavily as they lay in various positions on the floor. Outside, the scene was dismal and unfamiliar. The ragged edge of treetops against the skyline was plainly distinguished, but in the deep shadows utter darkness reigned.

Our clearing, seen after daybreak, bore the air of disorder due to work hastily accomplished and left unfinished. The rough ground, gently sloping away from the blockhouse toward the forest, was dotted with stumps and strewn with small branches. There were a few logs. The trampled snow revealed an occasional shell hole.

The blockhouse was practically completed. The sides and roof, substantially built of at least three tiers of pine logs and camouflaged with branches and a few small trees, provided fair protection against bullets and shrapnel. The only door faced the track. Within was a sheet-iron stove. We made our beds on the floor. About shoulder high were two long, narrow portholes situated so rifles and Lewis guns could command the open forest into which—now that the branches were not weighted with snow—we could see for considerable distance. These narrow ports could be closed by a drop door. With a reasonable degree of alertness on our part, an approaching enemy could not, during the day, reach the clearing unseen.

A few rods away, nearly screened from view by trees and bushes, was the railroad. Occasionally we saw the armored train pass to and from the front. This consisted of a flatcar with riflemen and machine gunners protected by sandbags, then a steel coal car mounting a naval gun buttressed with sandbags, pushed by a funnel-topped locomotive pulling two or three boxcars. It was a moving fortress, formidable in either offensive or defensive warfare.

On the other side of the tracks and somewhat farther in the rear than our blockhouse was a battery of one heavy gun—perhaps a six-inch—and six French 75s. These, with the mounted naval gun, constituted the supporting artillery of the front line force at Verst 444, the extreme forward position of the Railroad Sector. This was the strongest battery I saw; possibly our strongest in north Russia. Screened from aeroplane view, it was located in a cluster of pines near the edge of the clearing at Verst 448.

Some of the guns were sheltered in partly enclosed structures and all were protected by strong log barricades. They were manned by White Russian gunners and guarded by men of E Company.

Another blockhouse, occupied by Cpl. Jim Sanders's squad on the left and somewhat in front of the battery, provided, with our position, additional protection for these guns. To make our defenses still more impregnable, lanes of fire—long, narrow avenues cut in the forest much like the Russian government's survey lines—were established so the machine-gun fire of the two blockhouses would intersect, raking the lanes and cutting to pieces an advancing foe.

Early in the morning, without awaiting breakfast, Corporal Haynes took his men to Verst 448, where most of the company were in reserve. Our situation was not secure. No barricade had been constructed, and barbed wire for entanglements had not arrived. Of greater concern was our lack of munitions.

Considerable work was necessary to put our position into a fair state of readiness. At first little time was wasted. We cut trees and erected a strong barricade near the door. Another Lewis gun and a good supply of grenades and ammunition were brought from Verst 448. When not on guard during the day, we labored. More or less. Usually less.

One guard at the end of the blockhouse, where every dangerous point could be seen, was sufficient during daylight. After the first two days one of the privates, or even our obliging corporal, kept watch from within, peering through the porthole. After dark two men were posted outside.

To keep our fighting force at full strength, a man from Verst 448—where company cooks prepared our food—brought our chow and told us of affairs there. One meal today included bully, toast, syrup, and coffee. Our meals were not served in courses, nor did we sit around a table graced with a white cloth and order from menu cards; we sat on blanket rolls and bolted our food like hungry animals.

I helped cut trees for the barricade and was under artillery fire while on guard from 1600 to 1700. Putting the place in a better defensive status slowly continued. During the day a telephone was installed connecting us with those in the rear and with 448. We no longer felt completely isolated. Construction of entanglements began after rolls of barbed wire were dropped beside the track when the work train made one of its frequent trips to the front. A zigzagging fence was built by stretching wires from tree to tree along the forest's edge.

For some reason I was sent to Verst 448. With my rifle as my companion, I made a leisurely trip along the railroad and greatly enjoyed the lovely warm day. Along the tracks were numerous large holes, perhaps twenty feet below the elevation of the railroad. Like small craters, they exposed the rich black earth, revealing the nearly accurate fire of the Bolos' attempt to destroy the track carrying our troops and supplies to the front.

In the evening we were surprised to learn that Captain Heil had been relieved by First Lieutenant Baker. Though I never learned the official reason for the captain's replacement, it might be explained by incompetency. Captain Heil was assigned to Machine Gun Company, and I did not see him again until we were about to leave Russia. At Camp Custer I had heard him described as a "snappy soldier," but never detected that characteristic. In dress and appearance, not to mention ability, he was surpassed by the lieutenant.

Lieutenant Baker had so completely commanded the company during maneuvers that though I heartily hated him, I desired that he command us if we ever went into battle—and he did that at Kodish. Due to restrictions by the War Department, since fighting on the Western Front had ceased, Lieutenant Baker was not promoted to captain when he assumed command of E Company. This assignment was one of merit; a fitting recognition of Lieutenant Baker's courage, ability, and service. Our struggle was still raging in Russia, but petty regulations prevented a deserving lieutenant from being rewarded with a captaincy.

Along with news of the change of command came the rumor that mail from home awaited us, and that our new commander said we would leave Russia between the fifteenth and twentieth of May.

After spending an hour on guard behind the barricade I retired on the floor shortly after 0100 on Sunday, 13 April, and at 0255 was suddenly awakened by the corporal kicking the soles of my feet. Startled, my first impression was of confusion and fear. Everyone was excited. The men moved about, speaking in whispers. Except for our confusion, everything in the vicinity was quiet, but distinctly heard was the unmistakable uproar of an attack on the front. Rifle and machine-gun fire predominated. Not since the battle of Kodish had I heard such firing. We stood ready to repel an attack. The firing ceased before daybreak. We concluded it was a sporadic effort of the Bolos to surprise those at the front, and not a general assault. The entertainment was sufficiently close and never failed to give me a thrill.

Having lost sleep eavesdropping on a dispute not involving us, and trusting the Bolos to wait till our blockhouse was fully prepared, we deemed it more necessary to rest than strengthen our position. We slept till noon. It is scarcely creditable that a group of intelligent men fully aware of their danger could so neglect their duty for the comforts of bunk fatigue.

In the afternoon I made another trip to Verst 448 for staples, then helped string our barbed-wire entanglements. Later, DePue and I cut shrapnel from the pines for souvenirs. In the woods we saw a large gray owl that soon took flight. While our artillery dropped shells on the Bolo line, I sat on the barricade rereading Mother's letters and writing in my diary. The moon shone brightly while I was on duty from 2100 to 2200.

A volume might be written on "British–American Discord in North Russia." The "limeys," as they were contemptuously called— when not designated by some foul names—were anathema to most of our troops. The snobbish self-assurance and patronizing air of English soldiers, even in colonial times, never met favorably with Americans. I know some were overbearing, but what American soldier cannot cite similar examples in his own army? One E Company corporal told me he said to an English officer, "We licked you twice and can do it again."

There was a general attitude that the British command "was putting something over on us." I had no sympathy for this idea. There was the feeling that the British were leaving an undue proportion of the fighting to the Americans, and were not adequately supplying us with food—food we knew to be stored in abundance in Bakaritza and Archangel.

It was frequently said that this was a British war to secure the region's timber and mineral wealth. It was also said that we never renovated a barracks or completed the defenses, but that we received orders to vacate and the Tommies occupied the place. It became a mental attitude.

Regardless of the order that we were not to write home criticizing our allies, Cpl. John Czerwinski of E Company stated in a letter to his fiancée: "Never in my life was I ashamed of being an American till now, and I have to be, because I know the British are putting something over on us." Passed through censorship, his letter was published in the *Detroit Free Press* of 24 or 25 February and, boomeranglike, returned to Russia in printed form. I saw a copy on 13 April. It created much discussion and met with almost unanimous approval.

One fortunate aspect was that it stimulated Detroit's efforts to get the 339th—"Detroit's Own"—out of Russia.

Mail arrived from the States and as I was about to go on guard at midnight I was given five letters. Those from Mother were especially welcome. Upon being relieved at 0100 I read them. Her statement that five large roosters awaited my return created amusement when I told the squad in the morning. One man remarked, "They'll be pretty tough by the time we get out of Russia."

About a half hour after I was relieved at 0400, the Bolos cut loose with rifles and machine guns, as they did yesterday morning. We stood to. The attack was not as severe nor as long. After breakfast I helped stretch barbed wire. At noon a rare delicacy, apple pie, reached our camp.

Around 1300 our artillery opened fire and started a real battle involving rifles and machine guns at the front. There was good reason for shelling the enemy lines. Yesterday an enemy patrol or small combat force was reported by one of our outposts near the 26th Verst on the Obozerskaya-Seletskoe road, which we had taken in November on our way to the Emtsa River Front. A strong combat patrol of a platoon of E Company was sent to the vicinity of the 26th Verst to impress on the Bolos that this road was a military necessity to the Americans. The fight lasted most of the afternoon. The enemy left the road in possession of our force, which, with no loss and considerable elation, returned to Verst 448. The Bolos lost at least one man, for Cpl. Fred Johnson of Cadillac, Michigan, by slightly swerving a Lewis gun, nearly cut one of them in two.

The Bolos soon replied, and for the first time since leaving the 18th Verst on the road to Bolshie Ozerki we were under fire. How those shells directed at our artillery or at Verst 448 shrieked and whined! Our position near their target was not reassuring. I never lost my respect for them and evidently there were others who felt the same. It was amusing how like a strong dose of physic it affected some.

Outside of the blockhouse there was no particular place of safety, and as I sat on my bedroll I had ample time to consider how easily one of those screaming demons might pierce the roof and send us all into eternity. Passing over, they exploded in the woods beyond. Falling short, they dropped in front. They fell all around our clearing. In spite of that indescribable apprehension when flirting with death, there was a peculiar and equally indescribable fascination.

The White Russian gunners manning our artillery were magnificent. Occasionally they fired in unison, and frequently fired one after the other in such rapid succession that they sounded like a short burst of magnified machine-gun fire. Plainly our allies were superior to the Bolos in rapidity.

We easily distinguished the deeper tone of the great naval gun. After dropping shells on the Bolo line opposite the Railroad Front, they pivoted the guns and dropped neat barrages on the patrol opposing our platoon at the 26th Verst. We calmly listened to the bursting shells and enjoyed the uproar. For more than an hour and a half this artillery duel continued. Then the small-arms fire that we distinctly heard in front and at the 26th Verst ceased.

Gradually the artillery fire died. Finally it degenerated into a contest of who would fire the last shot. Serious as it was, it was amusing to hear the enemy returning a single shot a few moments after our salvo, then get our reply. Half an hour after the Bolos had seemingly been permitted to have the last word, our gunners fired the closing shot of the day's battle. This desultory firing may have been effective, but if it did no more damage than the Bolos, it was wasted energy.

Though we spent much of the afternoon observing the action and speculating its outcome, we did not confine ourselves to the block-house except at first when the Bolo shelling was most severe. It was a warm day, too lovely to remain indoors. We cut firewood and finished stringing the third strand of wire for our entanglements, now nearing completion.

On Wednesday forenoon we added a section to the barricade beside the blockhouse. After dinner we heard rifle fire at the front, and we were again under Bolo artillery fire. Fortunately, these sporadic outbursts were ineffectual, but did vary the monotony of life at 447.

It was warm and the snow disappeared fast. This early approach of spring scarcely seemed credible, but after the long, cold, dreary winter was doubly welcome. In the afternoon, at a boxcar at Verst 448, we turned in our snow goggles, mittens, mufflers, long heavy socks, Shackleton boots, fur caps, and fur overcoats. In return we received overseas caps and O.D. overcoats, and ordinary army shoes—either American or English. This added to our comfort and mobility.

On one of my visits to 448 I saw an unexploded Bolo three-inch shell embedded in one of the ties between the rails. Its base projected two or three inches above the tie. The workmen gave it a wide berth.

On this beautiful warm day we worked on the barricade, and were better able to see into the forest, cut brush, small trees, and low branches along its edge.

For most of us, army life was irksome and monotonous and had dangers from which even our high $10,000 insurance policies could not guarantee immunity. Yet it is peculiar how indifferent to these dangers we became and how easily we dropped our cares and responsibilities to enjoy ourselves as best we could.

Getting up at any hour of the night to watch for Bolos, who apparently had no desire to see us, sleeping on a hard bed, keeping cooties from becoming too aggressive, melting snow for drinking water, and doing similar disagreeable duties only emphasized the ease and pleasures of civilian life, and awakened a keener appreciation of home.

Probably no Bolo knew of our blockhouse, but we knew the possibility of his running into it if he chose to attack 448, so at night lights were extinguished and we were quiet. During the day we were quite careless. Frequently we indulged in heated arguments concerning Wilson's war policies and our political relations with England, or we joked and swapped yarns. We became uproarious when Clyde Miller #2 told how crudely the elephant performed when he took a young lady to the circus.

Just after our artillery opened fire, Sergeant Rogers came to tell us that we were to be relieved 10 May, and would sail in American vessels direct for the States between 30 May and 31 May. This encouraging information was exactly what we wanted to hear. Most of us regarded it as rumor.

On Friday, 18 April, I hiked to Verst 448 to get our breakfast, which was usually delivered to us.

In the afternoon, while seated beside the blockhouse, I wrote my people. The letter was censored by First Lieutenant Jeffers—"Examined by Base Censor"—and received 12 June. In two places on one page portions relating to our barbed-wire entanglements and our morning stand to arms were cut out with a penknife.

I was awakened after 2300 by the men talking about seeing Very flares and hearing shots, explosions, and Bolo trains at the front. I did not get up to see what was occurring. Rumor had the Bolos withdrawing from Kodish, Shred Mehrenga, Bolshie Ozerki, and the Railroad Front. The enemy was still there when we arrived.

The Bolos evacuated Bolshie Ozerki 18–19 April. Their heavy forces were withdrawn from the various Allied sectors—including the Railroad Front—to stem the advance of the northern wing of the Siberian Anti-Bolshevik Army under (General) Kolchak, and (General) Denikin's unit operating in southeastern Russia. Westward movement of Kolchak's men might unite them with our Dvina River force and cut the Reds off in the northeast. The Bolsheviki reverses on every front were a serious threat to their power and necessitated greater attention to fighting the White Russians rather than our force.

The Reds boasted of driving us into the White Sea in the spring. But the advance of these White Russian forces, together with the Reds' desire not to offend the United States and endanger securing their hoped-for recognition at the European Peace Council, may have been important factors in saving us from destruction or at least more serious fighting. And there was always the possibility of driving out the English after the U.S. withdrawal.

I went on guard at midnight. It was dark—one of the few dark nights I experienced in Russia. The sky was heavily overcast and nearly all of the snow in our clearing had melted. The Arctic twilight with its semidarkness, so much to our advantage, had vanished as if an ominous shroud were drawn over it. As I took my place with loaded and bayoneted rifle behind the barricade, I could see nothing but the deeper darkness of the forest. I thought this was an excellent night to surprise and overpower us before we could do a thing in self-defense. A stiff breeze rustled loose papers in our yard, making it difficult to detect the stealthy approach of an enemy.

Time slowly passed. Abruptly, at 0100, two rifle shots were fired near Sanders's blockhouse. It gave me a thrill that quickly changed to fear when a few bursts of machine-gun fire were followed by two more rifle shots. The rifle fire came from slightly ahead of the Lewis gun. Shivering like a leaf in an autumn breeze, I snapped off my rifle's safety and awaited developments. Had an attacking force come upon a guard, or had a guard prematurely commenced firing?

The firing ceased as suddenly as it began. We stood to, but nothing occurred. The corporal, listening on the telephone, learned that Ogea, a guard, had seen a light, probably phosphorescence, and fired at it. The Lewis gunners, supposing Ogea had seen something and opened fire. A good example of nerves. It did not relieve our tensions keyed to detect the approach of a Bolo force.

Recuperation after a period of tense guard duty was necessary and I slept—except for breakfast—from 0300 till noon. In my most recent letter home I complained of my inability to get sufficient sleep. These accounts of so much rest would not appear to corroborate that. Nevertheless, our sleep being broken by guard duty and the stand to arms early in the morning made us as tired as though we had been born that way.

After dinner Leemaster and I cut up a large dead pine for firewood, an enjoyable task. Then we joined the rest of the squad idly talking in the bunkhouse. We had more to discuss when Lieutenant Jeffers paid his respects and administered a mild but effective rebuke. The place was not in a good state of defense. We had little to show for our ten days here. Naugzemis's apologetic explanation failed to impress the lieutenant.

Corporal Naugzemis could criticize no one but himself. We were not unwilling; but not being ordered to work, we did what all good soldiers do. Once or twice Naugzemis called us from our labors, saying we had done enough for that day. He liked his squad and it was not in his nature to drive us.

I slept from midnight till 0530 and during the day, in spite of Lieutenant Jeffers's rebuke. It was Easter Sunday, but as I said in a letter to my people: "Our old hens failed to turn out any byproducts, so we didn't have eggs for breakfast." Some of the men sent farther into the interior had meals that included eggs and milk, but I had seen none since leaving the States.

After supper we rolled our blankets and prepared to leave our quiet clearing for the front. It became colder and the fast-falling, sticky snow changed everything to a beautiful white. About 2030 our relief from M Company arrived. We boarded a freight train that slowly and quietly took E Company near the north edge of the Railroad Front. It was well that our movement was made quietly, for recently a relief had to take over its position under severe enemy fire.

Our squad was divided. DePue, Noone, Wagner, and Miller #2 left us. Following the tracks for a few yards, we turned right and took over barricade #1. I was immediately detailed for guard and stood behind a tree carefully watching the thin forest just north of my post. It was colder and the snowflakes were fine. In spite of the storm I could see distinctly for some distance.

My view of the Railroad Front revealed a circular clearing of 300 to 360 acres. Through its center ran the railroad to Emtsa and the Bolo front lines. Numerous large piles of wood, cut by German prisoners of war when Russia was doing her duty with the Allies, constituted part of our defenses.

This important area, the southernmost point attained by our

forces on the railroad, was captured on 17 October 1918. Though frequently attacked by the Reds, it was resolutely held throughout the long winter.

Our barricade was along the north edge of the clearing and just west of the tracks. Amid piles of wood and in a shack built into the side of a large unpiled mass we made our quarters for the next four days. With four men from a machine-gun detachment it was crowded, and frequently I was obliged to sit up when I needed sleep. A stove grudgingly furnished sufficient heat to take off the chill. On the west side, protecting this poor excuse of a dwelling, was a breast-high double tier of wood that intersected with barricade #1. In the forest were lanes of fire and a blockhouse so concealed that I did not learn of it till one night when I saw sparks from its chimney.

If the report was true that an eight-day truce had been arranged so the Bolos might celebrate their Easter festivities, we were fortunate to reach the front at this time, for there was practically no action till 26 April.

During the day a more efficient stove was installed. In the afternoon I received letters from Father, Mother, Max, and Mrs. Haughey, at whose home I roomed and boarded during my last year of teaching in Camden, informing me that Mr. Haughey died of heart failure in November. Max's witty letter had two snapshots of his daughter Caryl. Father said the letter describing my experiences at Kodish had been received.

Late in the afternoon we were called to attention in front of our shack to hear a brief address by Brig. Gen. Wilds P. Richardson, recently ordered from France to assume command of all American forces in north Russia, who was making an inspection of the various fronts. Just as we were about to be withdrawn, we got an officer with a rank higher than colonel. Coming in on a powerful icebreaker that cut its way through the frozen White Sea and lower Dvina, he arrived at Archangel on 17 April.

General Richardson was thickset, inclined to obesity, and of medium height. His long, pointed nose; red, flushed face; mustache, and brutal mouth were outstanding. He was neatly dressed and as he faced us I saw a silver star on each shoulder. I saw him only one other time.

His address, full of praise for our record, was an effort to strengthen our morale and better our attitude toward being marooned in this godforsaken region after the war ended. His statement that he would see that our British allies put nothing further over on us, I regarded as uncalled-for and highly impolite. Some men said we could expect a change for the better. I said he might be sincere, but I'd wager we wouldn't detect any changes. And so it was.

I had a good rest before going on guard with Leemaster at midnight. Our three-hour shift was quiet until about 0245, when the roof of our shack caught fire. A blaze about the size of a half-bushel was making rapid headway in the slabs of dry wood when we routed out our corporal, who climbed onto the roof and tried to blow it out. With every puff the flames burned more fiercely. Convinced that Naugzemis had never been chief of the Chicago fire department, I left my post and climbed to his assistance. By throwing off the burning slabs we soon extinguished the fire and the corporal returned to his rest. Leemaster and I had a good chuckle when he said: "I had to laugh to see Naugzemis trying to put out a fire by blowing on it."

While I was on duty between 0800 and 0900, a blindfolded Bolo was escorted through our lines to the rear. I was told he was an officer who deserted and surrendered to our men at the forward positions. It is also possible that he came concerning an exchange of prisoners.

It was a warm, cloudy day. I shaved and cleaned up as well as our frontline facilities permitted. Lead shrapnel balls lay on the ground in great numbers. I picked up a dozen for souvenirs. About 1530 we were given a cholera shot in the left arm.

Before midnight we were relieved by a small force of Russians of the British Slavic Legion. We then went to a large dugout where we were quartered for our remaining four days at this front. It was a hot, stuffy place and I did not sleep well. The rest of our squad—DePue, Noone, Wagner, and Miller—joined us after midnight.

Daylight afforded a better view of this strongly constructed dugout. Located a few yards east of the railroad, it served as quarters for troops in reserve, on guard, doing fatigue duty, and as a refuge during severe shelling. Built of logs, it was fully a hundred feet in length and faced the north. Partly underground, it was entered by descending one of three short stairs. Inconspicuous, it was made nearly shell-proof by a roof of three or four layers of logs deeply covered with earth. Our quarters were furnished with a double tier of bunks. Overly heated and poorly ventilated, it was uncomfortable—especially when I was obliged to entertain a platoon or so of cooties and had no appetite for cigarette smoke. The kitchen and officers' quarters were in the opposite end.

East of the dugout was a triple tier of wood extending along the side of the clearing and serving as a line of defense against a flanking movement. Beyond was the forest, its outer edge thin and ragged. To the south was a barricade occupied by machine gunners and part of Corporal Hahn's squad. Irregular piles of uncut logs littered the muddy yard. To the west of the track was a vast amount of wood; part was piled. At various points barricades were carefully guarded and ready for action. The most critical position was by the railroad near the clearing's south edge. In front were two dangerous listening posts on the side of no-man's-land.

After dinner I was detailed to a patrol with Sergeant Masterson reconnoitering beyond our left flank. Such patrols went out daily to locate enemy outposts and detect any flanking movement or effort to drive a wedge between our unconnected sectors. Besides the sergeant, our patrol consisted of corporals Naugzemis and Bell, and privates Leemaster, McCarthy, and myself.

Equipped with loaded rifles and ammunition and wearing rubber hip boots, we entered the forest. Screened from view, we turned toward the Bolo right flank. We ran across a survey line near their front where an outpost was believed to be. One of our group, some distance in advance, led the patrol. The rest followed well apart in single file, making a line fully a quarter-mile long. I covered the rear.

As we got farther from our clearing and approached the dense forest there was little undergrowth, and we could see for some distance. We proceeded slowly and alertly. No one talked. Except for the snap of a twig, the splash of a boot, or the monotonous *swash, swash, swash* of our feet in the soft, needle-strewn mud, no sound broke the deathlike quietude of the forest.

Artillery fire began.

We saw no sign of life as we advanced along a narrow, poorly marked path winding among the pines. Occasionally the other men were obscured from view as the trail twisted or turned. Our greatest danger was the possibility of encountering a patrol that might give us a fight or cut off our retreat. As the "get-away-man," supposed to escape and secure reinforcements, my task was perhaps least hazardous. Nevertheless, I kept a keen lookout to my rear and both flanks.

Walking was difficult due to the soft muddy ground, surface water to wade, and an occasional swollen rivulet to cross. Less cautious, we made better time on our return. The beautiful blue sky mottled with lazily drifting cumulus clouds reminded me of warm April days at home. After three and a quarter hours we returned, hot and weary, to a scant supper.

After supper I slept some, but our squad, with the exception of McCarthy, who was exhausted by the patrol, was routed out at 2100 to pile wood until 2330. This fatigue duty—endearing us to this no-man's army—was meted out as a punishment for our lazy life at Verst 447. After some profanity, we good-naturedly set about building a barricade.

Rifle fire and the staccato bursts of machine guns awakened me. It mingled with my last sleeping moments. I arose instantly. It soon ceased, but it stirred my sense of insecurity lest we be required to repel a serious effort by the Bolos to oust us from this stubbornly held position.

Often I speculated on the ease with which a few thousand Bolos could hurl us out of the clearing, or compel us to surrender, or how a real army, determined and willing to make the necessary sacrifices, could make good their boast to drive us into the White Sea. Such contemplation led to the conclusion that the Reds little cared to fight us, or feared an aroused America.

There were no latrines on the Railroad Front during the winter, and conditions in our clearing were foul. With the melting of the snow, human dung—commonly called "snow snakes"—was everywhere. Such a vile condition was inexcusable. The approaching warm weather promised a terrible stench, if not disease.

As a partial remedial measure a small detail—I was included—was given shovels and went about covering this refuse, as I said: "For all the damned American and French companies that have been here!" Our resentment was expressed in emphatic and profane language. Not that we were too good for the work, but it was unjust that we clean up for those who should have built latrines. A detail of the dirty Russian civilians idling about Archangel and possessed with no incentive to fight for their damnable country should have been compelled to contribute to their cause by cleaning up for those who did fight.

My indignation was further incensed by "a hell of a supper"—fried bully, lime juice, and one hardtack. Bully beef was fairly good any way except fried. Lime juice might be a coffee substitute for an Englishman, but not for an American. And an army won't creep very far on its belly with one hardtack per meal. Breakfast had also been unpalatable. One poor meal a day might be excusable. Two were intolerable.

After supper I was sent with four others to the extreme forward position to get Lewis gun ammunition. It was still daylight. We followed a beaten path along the clearing's east barricade, passing a number of posts and machine-gun defenses. Stooping to keep from the enemy's view, we soon came upon some thirty men clustered under the railroad bridge—an excavation through the embankment with the overhead rails supported by piles. This unimposing place was the southernmost point attained by our forces along the railroad running from Archangel to Vologda.

In advance, and screened by undergrowth and scattered pines, were listening posts, one on each side of the embankment. Beyond was no-man's-land. Somewhere farther were the enemy's outposts. The forest was their front, protecting Emtsa from our force. We could drop shells into this important city but could not enter without infantry. As the struggle was about to end we made no effort to force our entrance. The men were quiet, talked in low tones, and kept their rifles handy. Ottney, whom I had not seen for a few days, kidded me about coming so near the enemy. After talking for some time, we got our ammunition and returned to the dugout, where we rested before piling wood from 2100 to 2215.

Sunday afternoon was warm and beautiful while I covered more snow snakes. As I told Leemaster: "This is one damned hell of a job for men of the U.S. Army!"

Before noon three blindfolded Bolos, one an officer, were escorted under a white flag through our lines to the rear. We curiously watched them walk along the track and noted they were not as well dressed as our men. They came to arrange an exchange of prisoners. As we were about to be withdrawn from Russia, special efforts were made to assure the return of the few Americans who had been captured.

About 1800 most of our forces, screened by a detachment of the British Slavic Legion, were withdrawn. Our squad was not so fortunate. As I lay on my bunk, the relief force, smoking and talking a lingo that was a cross between a sneeze and a cough, entered and took possession of the east end of the dugout. I was not enthusiastic about living with this outfit, which I suspected of being dirty and lousy like the typical Russian. Then too, I was apprehensive lest the enemy increase his military activities, as they usually did when European forces took over the front.

Monday afternoon I was seated on a log writing when Lieutenant Baker came up from the rear on his way to the officers' quarters in the dugout. Seeing Corporal Murphy about to leave with a large force of Russians to patrol the left flank, he asked, "Have you got a man who can *oblough* Russky?" Receiving an affirmative reply, he added: "All right, educate 'em." Turning to Corporal Naugzemis, he said, "Tomorrow night we get the hell out of here." I pulled out my diary and recorded his remarks, for they revealed the decisive and emphatic manner in which the lieutenant addressed his men.

Except for the few shells the enemy wasted on our plane during the afternoon, the day was quiet until late in the afternoon when our artillery opened up. The enemy returned the fire. Soon an artillery duel almost as severe as that of 14 April was in progress. Situated in front of the guns of both forces, we could plainly distinguish the shells as they passed over. With others not on special duty I went to the dugout and rested while listening to the firing and the musical whine of the shells. The terrific explosion of those landing within the clearing shook our quarters. It was fascinating. And nerve-racking. Near the close of the action one shell struck a large stump at the corner of Corporal Hahn's shack, a few yards from our dugout, and wounded a Machine Gun Company man, whom I saw carried to the rear on a stretcher.

In the evening the Bolos saw Sergeant Rawlings's fatigue party working near the front and opened fire. No one was injured. Everything was quiet when Leemaster and I went on guard at 2300. We stood behind a tier of wood and alertly looked into the clearing to see that none of the stumps or other shadowy objects moved or crept stealthily nearer. It was difficult to distinguish more than the dark outline of anything, and as we strained our eyes those inanimate objects seemed to change position slightly. Nevertheless, we did not foolishly shoot at them.

> *Somewhere in northern Russia, 28 April 1919*
> *Dear Folks, (written on American Red Cross stationery)*
> *What do you think of my new monogram—the above in red? I don't doubt but that at first sight it alarmed you; probably imagined I'm in some hospital after being shot to pieces. Not at all. They issued this paper, so I'm testing its qualities.*
> *As yet I've seen no angry Bolos and if they only remain as quiet for the next four days as they have since a week ago yesterday, all will be well. One of our large birds flew over this afternoon and the enemy wasted a few shells on it.*
> *I held an inspection this forenoon. I investigated my dirty undershirt for creepers and found none. They are an extremely disagreeable phase of army life. If old Kaiser Bill could have had them as I did, he would have thought at least twice before plunging the world into this living hell.*
> *It is rumored that we are to do some parading when we return to good old U.S. soil. If we do so in Detroit, I want all of you to see it. Be sure Max is with you and make all possible use of my camera.*
> *With love to all, Donald*

After dinner, as we were being relieved on this front, I took my blanket roll to Verst 446. Carrying my rifle, I set out with a small group who were in such haste that I was soon alone. I followed a narrow trail scarcely discernable because of mud and water that led through the thin forest and parallel to the railroad. I enjoyed the sight of the sun streaking through the pines and reflecting from the pools.

As I leisurely walked along, always alert for a lurking Bolo or patrol, I was startled to see a fresh grave with a rough wooden cross and the poorly painted inscription: 8 BOLSHEVIKI. A disagreeable reminder of the horror of war. It was more appropriate than to have Americans resting in this ungrateful foreign soil. The crude cross was almost a boast as well as a mockery; our trophy in a war between supposedly Christian nations. There was no indignity heaped upon these vanquished. I was told that some Bolos were buried with their hands or feet—even both—projecting from the earth.

After returning from 446, I saw part of a three-inch shell the Bolos dropped in front of our dugout. I wanted its copper rifling band as a souvenir. The explosion had blown out the tip and its death-dealing shrapnel, and burst the copper rotating band. With a hammer and chisel and the assistance of a knowing comrade who casually informed me that I knew little about handling tools, I removed the band.

We were relieved about dusk by M Company men and gladly turned our backs on our last front. We then hurried through the rain to a string of boxcars waiting to take us on the cold ride to Obozerskaya. There we went to a new barracks near the track. It was warm, comfortable, and furnished with clean bunks. At 0100 I crawled into a cozy sleeping bag on an upper bunk and, thoroughly tired, slept soundly. It was delightful, in spite of the inevitable cigarette smoke, to feel secure and carefree after nearly six weeks of duty on the front line of communications. Though we were seldom in action or under fire, there was always a mental strain that in time became oppressive and made this barracks seem like a palace.

At 0900 on 30 April I got up to enjoy a good breakfast of rolled oats, bacon, coffee, bread, and jam. Quite in contrast to our fare at the front, this was appreciated and keenly relished.

I sold nineteen packages of cigarettes, valued at twenty-eight rubles, for twenty rubles. With part of this I bought three cans of apricots at the YMCA to add variety to our good meals.

We would have gladly remained in this comfortable barracks until withdrawn from Russia. Though we had seen the front for the last time, we were to hold—at Bolshie Ozerki—the important line of communication between Kola and Obozerskaya. Even this could have been transformed into a front line had our enemy attacked us.

In the morning of 1 May, after the usual delay in making up our blanket rolls and eating breakfast, we began the hike to Bolshie Ozerki. Accompanied by Sergeant McCormick, our squad led the advance. A train of droshkies, driven by Russian civilians and carrying our rolls and company baggage, brought up the rear. We marched with rifles and light packs. Nevertheless, this hike of twenty-three versts (fifteen miles) was long and tiresome.

At intervals cold rain added to our discomfort. The snow, except in shaded nooks, had nearly disappeared. The road, muddy and cut up, was not as bad as in November when we had marched to the Seletskoe Sector. A short hike brought us to Maliozorki, where we spent two days in March. Instead of taking the winter trail across the thawing lake west of the village, we followed the circuitous road around the lake's north end.

As we were carelessly hurrying along the west of Maliozorki, a rifle shot was distinctly heard. We halted. Under the overcautious Sergeant McCormick—whose nerves had been affected at Kodish—our squad deployed as skirmishers and advanced. With the men unjustly ridiculing the sergeant, and the rest of the company following us, we alertly proceeded for about a half hour before coming upon four White Russians camped alongside the road and guarding a bridge. While eating, we learned that one of the Russians had been hunting and fired the worrisome shot.

At 1800 we halted at the 18th Verst Pole. Here, in March, we had spent six miserable days, and just after our departure M Company distinguished itself in the most magnificent defensive fighting of the entire north Russian campaign. While coffee was being boiled we rested in the woods where a small group of White Russians were on guard.

At 1915 we resumed the march and passed the scene of our conflict with the Bolos on Sunday morning, 23 March. As we had been unable to proceed farther, we were unfamiliar with the narrow and winding road to Bolshie Ozerki. About a dozen dead horses had been shoved into an excavation beside the road. Ascending a gentle slope, we emerged from the brush-fringed forest and entered Bolshie Ozerki.

It was still light. The scattered and somewhat dilapidated log houses were, except for Archangel, situated in the largest clearing that I saw in Russia. Along the edge of the village was an abrupt slope, terminating in a lowland of wet black soil near the edge of a small lake.

During my first night in Bolshie Ozerki I was quartered with thirteen others of our company in a large house. Our room was spacious, had many windows, and was provided with a number of benches and a large stove, which was thoroughly examined for Bolo explosives before we built a fire. Except for the cooties and cockroaches, our quarters were satisfactory.

The droshky train was so late in arriving that those of us awaiting our blanket rolls were unable to turn in before midnight. Mine did not come with the first group. Later, when I stepped out to see if it had put in an appearance, I met Lieutenant Baker as I crossed the yard and ventured—without saluting—to address that stickler for discipline. He gave me the once-over in a critical manner and without slacking his pace positively assured me that the rest would be brought in during the night.

Due to a breakdown of the droshky carrying the company stove and my roll, it did not arrive until the following day. Finally, with two benches placed side by side for a bed and an overcoat loaned me by a corporal for cover, I retired after midnight. Negotiating a turnover on those narrow benches required skill and patience. To the discomfort of the corporal sleeping on the floor, I fell off twice.

With no duty till noon we lounged about the room and listened to the gossip concerning Bolo occupancy of the village. Most of the buildings bore marks of rifle and machine-gun fire. Many were badly damaged or nearly destroyed by artillery fire and aerial bombs. I wrote home that "our town is pretty well shot up." An Allied plane had made a direct hit with a bomb and killed a dozen or more Reds playing cards.

The enemy was reported to have raped every female above eleven years of age and killed many civilian males. When retreating, they confiscated every horse and droshky available and compelled many of the women to drive them. True or not, these reports circulated among our men and were generally believed.

Before noon, Hittel's and Naugzemis's squads were transferred for guard duty to a dilapidated shack beside the road at the village's east entrance.

My apprehension concerning our quarters for the night was relieved in the afternoon when our squad was ordered to a large house on the west edge of the village, where four of us were quartered for the next eight days. Though unsure if we would be ordered elsewhere before night, we made ourselves comfortable and rolled out our bunks on the floor of a wide hall.

Nearby were many shell holes, their craters fifteen or twenty feet in diameter. Across the road was a large house, one wing so badly damaged by bomb or shell that it had no roof and only portions of its walls were erect. Perhaps this was where the card players died.

At 0200 Noone and I were routed out to stand guard. At 0230 it was so light we plainly saw two large white rabbits feeding in a field of green rye a quarter mile from us. Daylight arrived before 0300 and the sun did not set till after 2000. Though it was close to freezing during the night, the morning was beautifully clear. I was surprised that so far north the days could be so long and warm so rapidly. The region teemed with wildlife. Flocks of waterfowl flew overhead on their migration to the land of the midnight sun.

Later, DePue, Miller, Noone, and Wagner of our squad were detailed with four others to occupy a blockhouse in the forest some three-quarters of a mile west of the village to guard the approach from that direction.

The post near our quarters was abandoned on Monday, 5 May, and our outfit temporarily relieved of guard duty so that we might be rested for fatigue duty the next day. However, a report that two Bolo scouts had been seen west of the village caused us to be called out on a fruitless patrol.

We were detailed to carry long pine logs to a position midway between the road and the north end of the village. Here on a bluff overlooking the lake a large force of E Company men was busy with picks and shovels, making trenches and a large excavation for a "strong point." Extending east and west, it was admirably situated to cover the town. The strong point was largely underground, and the logs we brought were to reinforce the trenches and form the roof and walls built into the excavation.

> *Somewhere in northern Russia, 6 May 1919*
>
> *Dear Muriel,*
>
> *No, I have no need of money here. There is little in this desolate, poverty-stricken country one can buy. Don't believe all the newspaper junk. Much is true, but one will always find some who love to exaggerate or who have a vivid imagination.*
>
> *Game is plentiful here. From all reports disease germs are still more so during the summer. We always boil our water and drink considerable lime juice. At present we are away from the front. The enemy was here in March and the buildings are badly damaged. Shell holes are on all sides, fences are down and every evidence of war is to be seen.*
>
> *The soil is good, fairly well drained, farmed in long, narrow strips, and should raise pretty good crops. I've noticed a few wheat fields, but crops, I suspect, are terribly uncertain.*
>
> *We are living in a Russian house but none of its inhabitants, unless a few cooties, are with us. The house is typical, pine logs chinked with moss, has a large brick stove, and is more comfortable than our old pine bough shacks on the River or Kodish fronts. It's a crime the way these half-baked birds live; poverty, squalor, filth are their cardinal points. You can be mighty glad that your lot is that of an American instead of a Russian woman.*
>
> *With love to both, Donald*

Our squad and a few other soldiers continued to carry logs to the strong point. A warm breeze rapidly dried the roads and thawed ice on the lake.

Late in the afternoon a large French bombing plane, number 5095, identified with red, white, and blue tail markings and flown by two English officers, was so damaged when it landed near the strong point that it could not take off until repaired a day later.

I received my allotment of five packages of English Scissors cigarettes for use as a medium of exchange or gifts to my cronies. With a menu of bread, potatoes, bully, three doughnuts, and coffee, I felt that I fared well for supper.

About an hour before sunset we were called out to participate in another Bolo hunt. A uniformed man carrying a rifle was seen in front of Corporal Baker's guard post. The guard was in pursuit. Forty or fifty of us hurried in an unmilitary manner to the south end of the clearing. Called on to surrender as he fled through the swamp, the Bolo turned and fired twice at his closest pursuers, Cpl. Leo Baker of Charlotte, Michigan, and Pfc. Charles Benjamin of Rockport, Illinois. Uninjured, they returned his fire. Baker told me he did not hit him. Benjamin fired twice, hitting him in the left upper arm and in the chest. In desperation he attempted suicide, but succeeded only in leaving a black-powder mark on his forehead.

I heard the half dozen shots and arrived to see the prisoner being borne on an improvised stretcher. Probably in his early twenties, the Russian was fully six feet tall and heavy. I helped carry him. Before we reached the village, where he was examined by a British doctor, a death pallor was noticeable on his dark-complexioned, bloodstained face. The poor fellow died before morning. He was a member of the British Slavic Legion and, deserting at either the Railroad Front or along the line of communications, had approached our force, unaware that Americans now occupied Bolshie Ozerki.

Our squad was inspected by Lieutenant Sears, who was not satisfied last night with the condition of our rifles. I was the first to be inspected. As I came to port arms my ramrod flew into the air, nearly hitting the lieutenant. Heedless of formality and with assumed irritation, I said: "That darned thing never would stay screwed in."

Picking up the rod and examining it, the lieutenant found I was right. This amused the men. Some attempted to kid me about it. I said, "It's not everyone who, unaddressed, can get by with speaking during inspection."

We were ordered to leave our Russian billet beside the main street and move to a newly constructed blockhouse. In our group were Corporal Naugzemis, privates McCarthy and Leemaster, and at least three others, and myself. We were pleased to exchange our quarters and its monotonous fatigue duty for the undisturbed comforts of our isolated blockhouse and guard duty.

The blockhouse was south of the road and on a small hill just west of the village, and admirably situated for defense, as it commanded the entire clearing. I had an excellent view of the scattered clusters of log houses stretching a half mile along the bluff to the east. Between the bluff and this hill is an area of lowland badly cut up by shell holes, partially filled with water and ice. To the west underbrush fringed the vast pine forest, concealing the other blockhouse where four of our squad were on duty. Only by coming through the woods could the enemy strike us before encountering the other defenses.

This blockhouse surpassed in every respect all others I saw in Russia. It was a combination dugout/blockhouse projecting not more than four feet above ground. With walls constructed of three or four parallel tiers of logs and its top equally well protected, it was practically bullet- and shrapnel-proof. By descending three steps to a door, one entered a spacious room approximately fifteen feet square heated by a sheet-iron stove. Our bunks were on part of the raised floor. Hinged boards near the top of the wall could be dropped, affording openings to fire through.

Besides our rifles we were equipped with Lewis machine guns, hand grenades, ammunition, and emergency rations: a veritable arsenal that could be taken only at great cost to the enemy. The element of surprise—so vital and disastrous in war—was reduced to a minimum by keeping a sharp lookout from within during the day and by posting a guard near the entrance, where he commanded a complete view of the hill and forest fringe, during the night. We regarded an attack unlikely, for had the Bolos desired this place they would not have evacuated it in April.

We remained here until 21 May. Free from exercise, fatigue duty, and the irritating exactions of officers, we made the best of our situation and enjoyed life as much as possible. When not on duty, we slept, swapped yarns, speculated concerning our withdrawal from Russia, and argued—frequently heatedly. Excepting myself, the squad was infected with Anglophobia, and the administration was damned less from conviction that its policies were poor than from resentment that it had sent us to such a godforsaken place as north Russia.

I was impressed by an encounter with my mirror. I was dirty, tanned, and freckled. It was strange that the glare of the Arctic sun should tan and freckle me. And I weighed more than in civilian life. My clothes were dirty, ragged, and torn from continuous day and night service. I was not so tormented with cooties, though the disagreeable itching sensation was ever present. During the two months at the front I found only four of those horrible crawlers on me. A better record than while at the Seletskoe Sector.

"Had a hell of a dinner." My supper of bread, salmon, bully, and coffee wasn't so bad. No doubt the company cooks were frequently puzzled as to what to set before us, but today it was a greater conundrum as to how to get it down with any semblance of relish.

The day was cold, with a strong wind originating at the North Pole or the icebergs of the White Sea.

While on duty after midnight I saw Lieutenant Sears approaching. He was halted, advanced, and permitted to enter the room, where the sleeping men were awakened to sign the payroll. I was called in to sign it five minutes before being relieved. We were not paid, just saw the amount due us. Possibly the lieutenant's real object was to see if our post maintained a guard.

After his departure we were too wide awake to sleep, so we argued about Great Britain and her relations with America. It was 0300 when all talk ceased and each side—unconvinced—fell asleep.

Though our dugout was a strong position, it had no barbed wire around it. During the day we put up five strands, making a circular tangle that would temporarily check any assaulting force. By overlapping the ends an entrance was made at the path to the village.

We were now issued our rations, so no longer had to leave our comfortable quarters to eat. Last night, upon opening three boxes of rifle ammunition, we found two were Bolo dumdums—soft copper tips. To fight the enemy with his own, some slipped a few clips into their cartridge belts. I took a clip for a souvenir.

Mail was distributed. A letter from Mother arrived exactly a month after it was written.

When the enemy evacuated Bolshie Ozerki in April, he left via the road leading southward to Shelaxa. His retreat was precipitous and large quantities of ammunition were strewn in the forest. Many one-pound shells were eagerly picked up for souvenirs; this was the size we frequently saw bursting about the Allied plane as it daily scouted over Bolshie Ozerki when we were at the 18th Verst Pole in March.

When Corporal Baker asked if I'd like a couple for souvenirs, I said, "Yes, but not enough to risk cleaning them." He cleaned two for me. These shells were manufactured in America and shipped to the czarist or Kerensky governments for use against the Huns, but with the overthrow of these regimes they fell into the hands of the Bolsheviki, who used them against us.

After we occupied Bolshie Ozerki, fatigue parties began clearing the forest of these explosives. They were collected into two piles and destroyed in great explosions. From our dugout I saw the columns of black smoke rise above the forest.

During the afternoon, while scuffling with one of the men, I struck my right knee against a sharp corner of the stove, tearing my trousers and breaking the skin. I walked to a British Red Cross station, where my knee was examined and dressed by a medical officer who also gave me a bottle of liniment. My return walk took me past the strong point. Though not completed, much had been accomplished since our squad had provided logs. The evening was cool and quiet. I enjoyed being away from the confinement of the dugout and found it a splendid opportunity for undisturbed reflection.

At 2100 it was snowing hard, but ceased before 2315, when I relieved the guard. The large, beautiful moon shone brightly. Lieutenant Sears, while making his rounds as Officer of the Day, told me we would go directly from Bolshie Ozerki to the boat taking us from Russia, and that we would be permitted to take our souvenirs.

I got up early and, heedless of the cold, cloudy day, washed the one suit of underwear I had with me. Water came from a shell hole. In expectation of an inspection we cleaned our mess kits and other equipment. At noon we enjoyed a good meal of pancakes.

An E Company patrol sent southward yesterday—Saturday, 17 May—returned to report a force of the enemy posted at the 37th Verst. Their position was approximately eighteen to twenty versts due west of our force on the Railroad Front. So far as I was concerned that was satisfactory, providing they neither came our way nor started anything till after we boarded the homeward-bound boat.

Though we had been in this semi-Arctic land nearly nine months, its marvels had not ceased. To the list of phenomena, such as the Arctic twilight, the sun barely visible on the horizon, and rapid melting of the deep snow, was now added another that could not be duplicated in southern Michigan. At 2315 on 18 May, when I stepped outside to relieve Leemaster, I found him giving less attention to the possibility of a Bolo surprise than to a small YMCA pocket Testament. Though it was very light, it had not occurred to me that one could read at that hour, much less a volume of such small print.

Quite surprised, I asked if he could actually see to read. "Yes," Leemaster said, handing me the book, which I easily read.

Remarkable as this was, I overlooked, till interviewed by a Charlotte editor, that more remarkable than that the Testament *could* be read at that hour is the fact that it *was* read.

Soon after relieving the guard, Lieutenant Sears approached the dugout and, though he was easily recognizable, I meticulously halted and advanced him. His mission was as foolish as any I had heard during the campaign. He inquired if any men wished to volunteer for another six months of duty in north Russia. This created great amusement. He appreciated our humor and laughed heartily when asked the same question—and he replied *"No!"*

At midnight on Monday, 19 May, a resplendent full moon broke into view as it cleared the uneven line of treetops. It flooded the clearing with a mellow light, indescribably beautiful and almost as light as day. And daylight came early, for the sun rose at 0225. What a contrast were these short, balmy nights to those of the dark, gloomy fall and the long, cold, snow-bound winter.

Throughout my shift of guard duty ending at 0030, countless birds passed overhead on their way to more northerly latitudes. Their happy songs and calls buoyed my war-weary spirit. Mingled with these was the chorus of many village dogs. Reverting to the habits of their wild forebears they barked, yelped, and howled for hours each night. Though long-drawn-out and mournful, I enjoyed it. Just as Stony Castle recalls the bugle school, Bolshie Ozerki always brings to mind those midnight vigils and the chorus of plaintively howling dogs.

Due to the whim of a restless cook we were awakened for breakfast at the ridiculous hour of 0415.

We stood venereal inspection and no one of our group was found diseased. Then, we were informed we would leave Bolshie Ozerki on Wednesday.

Chapter 15
Farewell, Bolos!
21 May to 1 June 1919

It was a cool Wednesday forenoon when we made up our blanket rolls and prepared to leave THE HOME OF THE WETS. This name, expressing the anti-Prohibition attitude of all our group except myself, was printed in capital letters above our blockhouse door. While we were there it had been so dry that even good drinking water was difficult to obtain.

At 1420 we were relieved by a small force of English Royal Yorks. Leaving our comfortable quarters of the past ten days, we hurried to join the rest of E Company assembling in the village street. At 1530 we took up the hike to Obozerskaya; a gladsome moment, for every step was nearer home and those dear to us.

The roads were dry and hard. The long hike was fast and hot. At the 9th Verst we halted, unslung our packs, and rested. Beside the road and scattered amidst the pines was a small outpost of the British Slavic Legion, guarding the long, narrow bridge we'd just crossed.

This was a sorely needed rest; many, including myself, were footsore and lame. For nearly three weeks we had done no marching and so constantly worn our shoes that our feet soon heated and blistered. Many quickly exhausted the water in their canteens. Cigarette fiends with their smoke-parched throats suffered most. I drank sparingly and better stood the ordeal.

The aroma of boiling coffee and cigarette smoke soon filled the air. Voices rang merrily as men called to one another, chatting with friends they had not seen for weeks. Mingled with our conversations were the gutturals of the stolid Russians.

A young woman droshky driver halted opposite us and wept bitterly. I was told she was compelled to leave her child and drive the droshky, and was worried lest she be forced to sleep with British officers upon reaching Obozerskaya. I was revolted by a system so cruel and inconsiderate of the rights of others. The woman was well built, of good appearance, and dressed in crude clothes of coarse material with a colored cloth headdress and soft felt boots.

Refreshed with hot coffee and doughnuts, we resumed the hike, arriving at Obozerskaya a half hour before midnight. It was so light that marching after sundown presented no difficulty.

During our stay of less than three days in Obozerskaya we were quartered in one of the new American-constructed billets near the railroad. The main part of the town lay on the opposite side of the tracks. In spite of marching 23 versts I did not sleep well, as the room was hot and stuffy.

We were told that our souvenirs, if divested of explosives, could be packed for transportation. My two one-pound shells—filled with rifle ammunition—and the rifling band were wrapped in a linen crash towel, tied with heavy cord, and marked with indelible pencil. My letters from home were in a small tin box. All were placed in one of the two large wooden boxes privates and NCOs were permitted. Lieutenant Sears, in charge of arrangements, kidded me about the letters. I laughingly attempted to convince him they were from my mother. I carried bullets, shrapnel balls, and foreign coins in a small tobacco sack.

With our fighting concluded, I thought military drill was superfluous, but our company was marched to a large field near the Allied aerodrome and drilled. If anyone suspected we lacked proficiency, the morning's performance confirmed it.

Other companies were on the field and the afternoon ended with two reviews. The first was a preliminary, by Major Nichols; the second, by Brig. Gen. Wilds P. Richardson, USA, and Brig. Gen. A. J. Turner, the British officer in command of the Railroad Sector. General Turner addressed the troops and bestowed decorations on two men of I Company.

Near the eastern edge of the clearing were wooden crosses marking the graves of our dead. Among these were the first three Americans killed fighting the Bolsheviki. These I Company men were killed on 16 September 1918.

In Obozerskaya we were partially refitted for the homeward voyage. I was issued a new overseas cap. We were ordered to clean our equipment, so before leaving the drill field I washed my pack.

We entrained about 1915 Sunday. Four of our squad, including the corporal and myself, occupied the front compartment of this Russian Pullman car. Heretofore we had traveled to and from Obozerskaya in boxcars. Now, on our last train ride in Russia—as veterans of the World War—we traveled in luxury à la Russky. Though the coach was divided into compartments, it was possible to traverse its length. Above each of the two seats facing each other was a board three feet by six feet and hinged so that it could be dropped as a shelf. These and the two long seats constituted the upper and lower berths of our sleeper.

In the evening I heard a number of revolver shots. Our officers were celebrating. One was our tall, red-faced company commander, Lieutenant Baker, who, as he said, "had been for six months as sober as a Philadelphia judge and now I'm going to enjoy myself." He staggered about, firing his .45 revolver into the forest.

In the morning his Italian dogrobber, Joe Ross, entered our compartment and emptied the shells on the floor at my feet. I snapped up two as souvenirs of Lieutenant Baker's spree.

At 2330 our spark-sputtering, wood-burning engine pulled out of Obozerskaya. Soon we were speeding through the pine-clad land and away from the Bolo front. How fortunate most of us had been. This was the scene of many desperate experiences—experiences I little valued or appreciated then. Now, for the last time, we rode northward over the Archangel-Vologda Railroad.

It was still light and I stretched out on my bunk to watch the scenery. Occasionally a small clearing or vacant cabin was seen, or the rare appearance of a village. Here and there was a rippling brook. A forest fire! Bright flame showed through the dense smoke. Finally, I fell into a fitful sleep as the train jolted and rattled through the night. Little did it matter that my bed was hard and my rest broken, for I was homeward bound.

Early in the morning of 26 May our train stopped and we detrained at Bakaritza. After stacking arms on a section of the covered wharf area, those not assigned guard duty were dismissed with orders not to leave the premises. While breakfast was being prepared I whetted my appetite by pacing my beat for an hour. Corporals Murphy and McIntyre sang happily as they lounged near the rifles.

Bakaritza was still a busy place. In the river or along the wharfs were many seagoing craft, including five British ships: *Bonaventure, Katyan, Stephen, Czar,* and *Czaritsa;* a large Red Cross vessel (hospital ship), a French cruiser, and the cruiser USS *Des Moines.*

In formation we marched to the quay, where E Company boarded two small river tugs and began a ride of twenty versts down the calm Dvina River; one of my most enjoyable experiences of the war. Nature was in her best springtime mood. On the opposite shore was Smolny, where we first touched Russian soil. Soon we were passing Archangel with its long, colorful waterfront, massive stone warehouses and public buildings, and large cathedrals with gilded minarets. Farther north was an occasional flour mill, resembling a Dutch windmill.

Small villages with quaint log houses and fire towers were passed. Men and women working in the fields waved at us, and we heartily returned these farewell salutes. River craft of various types were met. Large, low-lying wooded islands were passed. We were a happy group and indulged in considerable cheering, particularly when the second tug increased speed, then caught up with and soon passed us. Seated in the bow, I viewed these scenes that I was too ill to watch when we entered Russia in September.

About noon we reached Economia, forever remembered as the port of embarkation for home of the famous American North Russian Expeditionary Force. This small port, situated on a corner of a large, silt-formed island in the delta of the Dvina, had been selected for an embarkation camp. As various units of the 339th were withdrawn from their respective fronts, they were assembled here, deloused, stripped of their Russian equipment, and prepared for the homeward voyage.

Early in April, B and C companies were relieved at Toulgas and Kurgomen. K Company left Kholmogori late in May. G, L, M, I, and E companies—in the order named—were withdrawn from the Railroad Front also in May. Some of these units arrived in Economia ahead of us, others followed. This was a logistic and administrative problem efficiently accomplished with widely separated forces, without advantage to the enemy.

F Company, the last to get into action during the fall, safely withdrew across the treacherous ice of the Volga River on 19 April, and on 5 June—after our departure from Russia—had the distinction of being the last unit of the regiment to be withdrawn to Archangel.

Getting off the tugs at Economia's dirty quay, we marched a short distance to a small camp located between the residential section of town and an outlet of the river to the west. We were quartered in white canvas tents—tents oppressively hot when the sun shone, as it did on our arrival. These were equipped with floorboards, and like those in camps Mills and Stoney Castle, the sides could be raised for ventilation. A squad was assigned to each tent.

Our yard was covered with chips and sawdust. A few rods farther back from the river were the hewn-pine houses of the Russians. Nearby was a YMCA, where books, magazines, and writing materials were available. Near the river was a bathhouse. Except for a small section of the village where I did guard duty, I knew little about the place, for I was content to remain in camp or at the Y.

On Tuesday, 27 May, we were required to stand reveille. In the evening we were assembled in company formation for retreat. This routine continued to the end of our military service, plus more regulations than at or behind the lines. Officers were punctiliously saluted; formalities of guard duty were closely observed; neatness of dress and appearance was strictly required. In general, discipline resembled that at Camp Custer.

Many E Company men, including Leemaster and me, were ill with severe diarrhea—resembling the symptoms of cholera—possibly due to drinking polluted water in Bakaritza the previous morning. About to board the homeward-bound vessel, and ill! Instead of reporting to the infirmary, I swallowed some Pacal Balm and awaited the outcome. Though in no condition to work, I did enough to allay suspicion. Those reporting for medical attention were confined to the infirmary and many were not released until after our ship departed. At least one soldier reported merely to escape the day's fatigue detail, and barely got away in time to board the ship.

Leemaster, so ill that he was unnaturally white, spent three days in the infirmary; but anxious to see his wife and nine-month-old daughter—whom he had never seen—he convinced the doctors that he was in condition to leave Russia and returned to our squad the day the ship docked in Economia. Corporal Jim Sanders and Aaron Leventhal, both of Charlotte, Michigan, and many others, were less fortunate. They came out of Russia on a large British Red Cross (hospital) ship and did not reach the United States until August—about a month later than the rest of E Company.

May twenty-eighth—the anniversary of our arrival in Camp Custer. In the forenoon it rained and even snowed. Though not recovered from my sickness, I was much better and worked with the fatigue detail raking up pine chips, shoveling them into baskets, and carrying them to the river.

In front of their houses, idly watching us put their dirty street and front yard into a state of sanitation heretofore unknown, stood ten or twelve curious, unkempt, heavy-featured, sandy-whiskered Russian men and boys in old, ill-fitting clothes. Smarting under the task of cleaning up their dirt, I itched to express my opinion of their brand of patriotism, which permitted foreign soldiers to fight for their country, then clean it. One grinned at me as I worked. Making some caustic remarks profanely punctuated I shouldered my rake like a rifle, took it off my shoulder, handed it toward him, and said, "Take it and fight for your damned old country!"

When I repeated the act he understood my meaning and assumed an unpleasant expression. My comrades were amused, saying, "That's right, Carey. . . . You tell him! . . . You've got the education."

We were given another shot that made my arm sore and swollen.

During our stay in Economia the meals, particularly those at noon, were frequently unappetizing "slum" or "corn willie." Today, instead of getting the noon issue, I remained in my tent and ate a can of salmon, the despised "goldfish" of army culinary. Having the afternoon off, I went to the YMCA.

Economia, Russia, 28 May 1919

Dear Folks,

You see from the above that I'm out of the interior and am not far from the White Sea. Better still, we weren't put here by the Bolos.

*Their great boast about running us into the sea didn't materialize
and all of their efforts to gain any points recently left them in worse
shape than before they started. It isn't particularly healthy for them to
get within range of our fire.*

*You may be thankful, as I am, that we have finished fighting. We
have not been here long, and I take it that our stay won't be more
than a few days. I hope to get a cablegram on its way tonight. We
don't expect to go directly to the States, though of course, that would
best satisfy me.*

*Yesterday we were deloused and cleaned up. During the two
months at the front I was far more fortunate than at the Kodish
Front last winter, for this time I found only four of those fiendish
crawlers on me. These were full grown, old enough to know better,
and consequently executed.*

*Do you realize it was a year ago today that I left home for Camp
Custer? It has been a great year, but I would rather not have experienced it. However, I'm mighty thankful that so far all has gone well
with me. It looks as though a full year will have passed before I see
you after last leaving home.*

*Best wishes to you, Mother, for the thirtieth (her birthday), and
many more of them. It is two days away, But I won't forget then.*

With much love, Donald

After breakfast on this clear, cold day we lined up in front of our
tents for venereal, lice, and teeth inspection. Our squad passed.

Then we marched to a warehouse and turned in our Russian rifles—our most cherished relics of the campaign—the rifles we'd
done our fighting with. While in moments of ill humor we made remarks to the contrary, every soldier desired—and deserved—to take
his rifle home as a souvenir of the war. As for mine, though it was
not the one issued in England, it was prized as a rifle captured from
the Bolos at Kodish.

A competitive parade was held to determine which company of
the 339th should be in the Memorial Day parade in Archangel when
units of the Allied forces marched to the cemetery to pay homage
to our fallen comrades-in-arms. It was fitting that M Company, who
fought and won the outstanding engagement of the North Russian

Campaign, should be selected for this honor. When I considered the long, tiresome march as a member of a funeral detail in September, I did not envy their winning first place.

Today it was noised about camp that the English, quite indignant because we were being withdrawn, had created some disturbance in Archangel and insulted our flag. It is reasonable to suspect our English allies are incensed by our government leaving them to finish a side issue of the war that either should never have been begun or should have been pushed to a successful conclusion.

I felt the war we had been inducted to fight was over. Despite English plans and policies, we should have been recalled after signing the Armistice. The British, even with large reinforcements, were soon unable to cope with an enemy whose successes on other Russian battlefronts made it possible to devote more troops to the Archangel area, so they abandoned the struggle before the close of the year. (General Ironside, RA, departed Archangel on 27 September 1919.)

My last guard duty on Russian soil was a beat on a boardwalk extending around a block or so of the village. A special order was to halt everyone after 2300. It was almost as light as day during my shift from 2300 to 0100 and all objects, including Sam Browne–belted officers, could be clearly identified at considerable distance. I permitted a number of officers to pass with a mere exchange of salutes. I tried that on Second Lieutenant Broer, the Officer of the Day. He wanted to know why I had not halted him.

"It's so light that I regarded it as unnecessary."

Without a trace of irritation he told me I should have halted and advanced him, and that regardless of the light I should observe the formalities of guard duty. After repeating the general orders, I presented arms; he saluted and departed.

Later, an officer was about to cross my beat fully a half block ahead of me. He was evidently in a hurry. My "Halt!" brought him to an abrupt stop. After being advanced, he inquired if I had to do this.

"Yes, sir. It's an order I have just been bawled out by the Officer of the Day for disregarding." I was amused to hear him swear as he disgustedly made some remark before returning my salute and going on his way. Still later I saw a soldier cut across the street to avoid me. I let him pass unchallenged. He, too, was a private.

Friday, Decoration Day. This is Mother's birthday. Early in the morning M Company left by boat to parade in Archangel. With many officers attending the ceremonies the camp was unusually quiet.

On Saturday, units of our regiment in Economia stood a rigid morning inspection. Some were certain that this inspection was preparatory to embarking. It did not matter that no ships had been seen or reported. Corporal Naugzemis believed we would march directly aboard a vessel. Remembering his physical anguish while crossing the Atlantic, he crammed his pockets and cartridge belt with cigarettes in anticipation of the homeward voyage. I was positive we would not leave immediately, so planned to take a bath and get into clean clothes in the afternoon. With the dirty collar of my shirt turned outside my blouse collar, as I had never before worn it, I stood inspection.

Lieutenant Baker had not been seen about camp. He was now on the job. While standing at ease he gave his beloved doughboys the once-over. As he approached, the first sergeant called us to attention. Scarcely looking at the sergeant, he came to me and immediately espied my dirty collar. In a low voice biting with sarcasm, he said, "Is this the only shirt you have?"

Stiffly at attention, I replied, "No, sir."

"Where is the other?"

"In my barracks bag, sir."

"Is it clean?" he snapped.

"Yes, sir."

"Then why haven't you got it on? You look like a damned John Bolo!"

Without expecting a reply—which I had no intention of making—he passed along the line. Almost furious enough to run him through with a bayonet, I cursed him through my teeth—as soon as I considered it safe. Then it struck me as humorous and I had difficulty in keeping from laughing aloud.

The lieutenant reached our cigarette-loaded corporal and curried him down. In due time we were dismissed. Just before reaching our tent, Miller called out, "Well, Carey, you and the corporal were the only ones in our squad to get bawled out."

My none-too-polite reply was another compliment for the lieutenant to the effect that no one was getting as much fun out of it as I.

I got my hair cut, took a bath, and changed clothes—as I had planned. At 1500 we were inspected for venereal disease and lice. In spite of having been deloused, I picked off a cootie during the day. Leemaster, still weak but appearing much better, returned from the infirmary and was welcomed by our squad.

"The *Czar* is coming!"

The news quickly spread. The Y was soon deserted and we eagerly watched the ship enter port. With its large hull, two masts, two stacks, many lifeboats, sailors on deck, and name in large letters shining in the sunlight, it was an imposing sight as it slowly and majestically glided by our camp and moored at the quay about 2015. In August, at Newcastle-on-Tyne, this ship, loaded with Italian troops, lay alongside our transport, the *Nagoya,* and traveled with us as far as Murmansk.

June first was my last Sunday in Russia and I spent the morning doing fatigue duty. Before noon we carried our barracks bags to the dock to be loaded into the hold of the *Czar.*

Late in the evening—when I least expected to be disturbed, and was about to turn in—I was ordered to serve on the ration detail. I freely expressed my idea of this as four of us with a two-wheeled cart made our way over a rough route along the riverbank to the dock. For some time we waited for the arrival of our rations, brought by tug from Archangel. After carting them to the company kitchen we were dismissed.

While with the ration detail I saw a large quarter of beef or horse meat on the dirty planks of the quay. It was a putrid green and a swarm of large blue flies hovered about. No doubt it was for some company of our regiment. The sight caused me to abstain from meat while we remained in Economia. How much like it, or even worse, had I already consumed?

Chapter 16
Good-Bye, Mother Russia!
2 June to 10 June 1919

Soon after breakfast on Monday, 2 June, we rolled our heavy packs and marched to the field where all units of the 339th Infantry in Economia were inspected and reviewed by many senior military and civilian functionaries. This was the only assembly of our regiment in nearly its entirety while in north Russia. In full dress and heavy marching order, without rifles, we found maneuvering and parading in the hot sun unpleasant.

The various companies were in parallel lines behind each other. E Company was well to the rear and far from the reviewing stand. After a long wait we were snapped to attention and Maj. Gen. Edmund Ironside—the British officer in supreme command of the Allied Expeditionary Forces in North Russia—accompanied by a small group of officers, passed through our ranks.

Though I had seen him before, I took a good look at this remarkable officer as he passed an arm's length in front of me. Fully six feet four inches in height, he was a man of powerful physique, keen intellect, and unusual personality. His courageous countenance and excellent features combined with blue eyes and clear, ruddy complexion were fairly handsome. His military bearing was dignified and without a trace of arrogance. Ironside looked us over and, so far as I know, said nothing. He was the officer of highest rank that it was my privilege to see during the war.

While the inspection addresses were made I could hear so little that I soon lost interest. It was said that our ranking American officer was so intoxicated that he was unable to make a coherent speech and broke down and cried. From what I saw I am certain that something unusual occurred.

At noon we passed in review. To maintain our position in the parade, we were obliged to double-time just before passing the reviewing stand where generals Ironside and Richardson, and the Russian governor-general of the northern district of Archangel, stood. Sweating and hungry, we hurried—after dismissal—to our tents to dispose of our equipment before running to get in line for chow.

After dinner we again assembled and in heavy marching order hiked to the wharf, where other units were gathering. Marching alphabetically in single file the men of E Company mounted the gangplank to the deck of HMT *Czar*. Photographers, their cameras situated to catch a profile view of our column with the *Czar* in the background, snapped or reeled off film.

At 1400 and near the head of E Company, I boarded the *Czar*. We had been on Russian soil nine months, lacking two days. The men, though in high spirits, were quiet and orderly. Our embarkation was accomplished quickly and without confusion. Natives watched us with a stolidity that would have puzzled a psychologist.

Upon reaching the deck we were led below and assigned a section in the bow furnished with canvas hammocks. I slept next to the left side of the bow. The ship was clean. I sat on deck visiting, joking, and speculating while viewing the log village and its surroundings. The nauseating stench of the old *Northumberland* was conspicuously absent. Food was the best I ate since leaving Camp Custer. For supper we were given sardines, bread and butter, applesauce, and tea.

Tuesday, 3 June, dawned clear and soon became hot. We were up early. About 0800 the nearby landscape appeared to be slowly gliding past and I realized the *Czar* was moving. We headed north along the deep, dark waters of one of the estuaries of the majestic Dvina River. We were glad to leave. I was elated, but like other soldiers, repressed all outward indications.

Five ships were in our convoy: an icebreaker; a large British Red Cross (hospital) ship; the transport *Stephen,* and another of the same type. The *Stephen* was loaded with French troops. France was also withdrawing her troops. In no particular formation, the ships were strung out at irregular intervals for a considerable distance.

During the day we passed the USS *Des Moines*. The sailors and our troops enthusiastically waved and noisily exchanged greetings. We entered the White Sea and remained in it until the following forenoon. As we steamed north it became colder. By late afternoon this raw chilliness, so pronounced on deck, penetrated the hold, making it uncomfortably cold. After supper I saw the cause of this sudden lowering of the temperature: We were in a large ice pack. For forty miles we followed the icebreaker at reduced speed. Irregular-shaped chunks of varying sizes, broken here and there by narrow, winding lanes, was a beautiful and novel sight, compensating for the delay. The icebreaker steadily plowed its way through with our transport in its wake. All night as I lay in my swinging hammock I heard ice bumping and grating against the ship's side.

Morning found us still in the ice pack. It was even colder than last evening. During this and the following day, while on deck, where we spent most of our time, we found our overcoats—rummaged from our barracks bags—none too warm. Even the compulsory forenoon exercise was an appreciated stimulant of warmth. Of special interest to me were eight seals swimming among the chunks of ice or resting on them. Had not their black coats sharply contrasted with the ice they would have escaped notice. I was disappointed not to see a polar bear.

During the forenoon we cleared the ice. The icebreaker turned back. Later, the *Stephen,* possibly to pick up troops in Kola, turned south and the Red Cross ship turned north.

As we neared the Arctic we were treated to a snowstorm. The sea became rough and the ship's movement made many men sick. I felt light-headed.

All day I could see the snow-mottled coast of the Kola Peninsula and northeastern Norway. Our route was nearer the Norwegian coast than last August and I saw Cape North.

During the forenoon we encountered a Norwegian fishing fleet. Dozens of small smacks, most with their sails furled, bobbed like corks on the restless sea. The fishermen, usually two, three, or four to a boat, ceased work to wave and watch us pass. Wild ducks and seagulls were in flight or riding the waves. A school of porpoise accompanied the transport and leaped in graceful arcs.

In the afternoon I looked over some sheet music on the *Czar*'s piano. Among the pieces were "Beautiful Ohio," a song I'd never
heard, and "I'm Forever Blowing Bubbles." I was to hear both many
times after returning home.

A list of fifty-nine first class privates was posted. Since October I
had been accorded this slight increase in pay. Some of my friends
were disappointed not to be promoted.

On 6 June we were required to sign the payroll, a procedure that
had been in abeyance since 19 August when we were in Camp Stoney
Castle, England. Mine amounted to $199.74 for six months service.
I did not collect this hard-earned pay as I still carried an adequate
amount of cash.

The sea became rougher in the afternoon and worse during the
night. The ship rocked uncomfortably. Sleeping in our swaying
hammocks saved many from seasickness.

The *Czar* stopped about 0500 Sunday. Immediately everyone was
astir. On deck I learned that we were in Lerwick, Shetland Islands.
The small town was comprised of gray weathered stone buildings
with tiny, narrow windows and steep roofs.

For breakfast we were given bread, bacon, oatmeal, and a boiled
egg. Though probably from cold storage, the egg was a real delicacy,
as I had had none since leaving Camp Mills nearly eleven months
earlier.

I spent most of the day on deck. Our presence created no particular interest and a Sabbathlike stillness pervaded Lerwick. Except
at the entrance, land surrounded the circular harbor, sloping back
into the hills forming a vast bowl. The natural fastness of the harbor
and its location between the Atlantic and the North Sea were factors
making it, during the war, an important naval base—particularly for
submarines.

A few sheep and cattle grazed on the rocky slopes. Though it was
the native land of the Shetland pony, none was seen. The neat, green
fields were enclosed with well-constructed stone fences. Except for
grass—affording scant pasturage—not a tree or shrub was to be seen.
I had no desire to live in such a barren region.

Late midafternoon Major Nichols and the *Czar*'s captain left with
our mail in a small boat. We lay at anchor for twelve hours, joined

by the Red Cross ship we'd last seen Wednesday forenoon. Shortly after the two officers returned we departed at 1700. The Red Cross ship preceded us.

Many pleasure boats sailed among the islands. The men and women heartily waved at us. On a tug I noted the name *Ambitious*. After assisting DePue in writing his neglected diary, I took to my hammock as a relief from the ship's disagreeable rolling.

It is humiliating to admit that my geographical knowledge was so deficient that it was years before I learned this group of about one hundred islands constitutes the northernmost county of Scotland, and Lerwick, the county seat, was on Mainland, the largest island. Lerwick is about 223 miles west of Bergen, Norway.

We were in the Irish Sea when I went on deck at 0500, 10 June. Gleaming in the sunlight, through the early morning haze, were a number of villages along Ireland's low coast. I was thrilled to see my paternal grandmother's native land.

For the first time since leaving the Dvina River the sun's warmth was not chilled by a breeze off the Arctic or the North Atlantic. We were nearly surrounded by land. Scarcely a wave ruffled the sea's surface, the quietest of this three-thousand-mile journey. Most of the day was spent going through the Irish Sea. The hills of England or Wales could be seen far to the east.

For the third time in five days we were lined up for venereal inspection. Those afflicted could not long escape the customary punishment of reduction in rank or loss of pay. I doubt if there were any cases. The examinations were tedious.

In the afternoon we were called on to furnish our permanent address for an E Company booklet entitled "Lest We Forget" and dedicated to 2d Lt. James F. O'Brien, wounded at Kodish. Sergeants Rogers, Untener, and Rawlings were appointed to prepare it. Published after our return to civilian life, each man was sent a copy.

On this last night at sea many of us, including DePue and me, deserted our hammocks in the stuffy hold and slept on deck. Though it was cool, we made our bunks on the leeward side and put in a comfortable night.

Chapter 17
Brest, France

11 June to 20 June 1919

Our last day at sea was bright and somewhat warmer. Land was not in sight when I got up, but the coast of Brittany came into view during the forenoon.

When we sailed from Hoboken in July 1918, we expected, after a brief period in England, to cross to France and help "make the world safe for democracy." Now at last, though we were too late to "put the Hun on the run," we would set foot in the great French republic that for four long, soul-trying years heroically bore the brunt of the world's most desperate struggle.

The coast was high-bluffed. Heavily foliaged trees lined its crest. Shortly after noon we anchored in the harbor of Brest. This port was world-famous for the debarkation and embarkation of the American Expeditionary Force that turned the war in favor of the Allies.

White masonry houses were surrounded by trees and shrubs. Small, hedged fields with thriving crops were a pleasing sight. Gracefully poised above the bluffs and tethered by ropes was a small "sausage"-type dirigible.

In the harbor were numerous vessels ranging from rowboats to battleships. There were at least seven American battleships and cruisers, plus two transports. The *Imperator,* a three-stacker crowded with khaki-clad veterans about to return to the United States, was the largest vessel I'd seen. The *George Washington* awaited President Wilson's readiness to return home.

My interest centered chiefly on the nearest ship, the USS *Missouri,* which was about to leave Brest. A half dozen motorboats with flags flying and bands playing paraded around the battleship. This continued for an hour or more, then a small group of officers boarded the ship and formalities were exchanged before a formation of blue-jackets. To my disappointment we were ordered into the hold as the *Missouri* got under way. From a crowded porthole I caught a partial view as she steamed by.

In the afternoon a large flat-bottomed barge came alongside and disembarkation began. Late in the afternoon E Company was transported to a pier, and I stepped on French soil.

Then began an extremely hot and exhausting march of at least three miles in company formation. Though without rifles, we had heavy packs, carried our overcoats, and wore O.D. blouses and heavy woolen underwear. The forepart of our hike was up a grade along a seemingly interminable winding road. In less than nine days we had come from the Arctic and were unused to such heat. An occasional rest was necessary. I marched along doggedly, paying little attention to the strange French scenes, intent only upon reaching our destination—wherever it was. Finally, in a narrow cobblestone street walled by closely adjoining buildings, we were halted and permitted to rest. With the sun beating on us and the heat reflecting from the white walls it was almost unendurable. A few, including Corporal Naugzemis, were overcome and toppled to the ground.

We resumed our march. The overlong upgrade ended. Long lines of Negro fatigue parties passed, coming from work or going out on night duty. Marching in columns of fours, they wore blue or rust-colored denims. Their good nature was highly contagious. I saw more Negroes than I had during my twenty-six years. I thought a goodly portion of Alabama's Black Belt had been set down near Brest.

At Camp Pontanezen each squad was assigned a tent equipped with a small stove—at no time did we have a fire—and eight steel bunks. The camp was large, and near our quarters were tents occupied by other units of the 339th. In other sections were units that had served in France.

We soon marched to the mess area for supper. On high steel dining tables in a warehouselike mess hall was the debris of a unit that had eaten earlier. Crusts of white bread, partially eaten or untouched baked potatoes, pickles, and other food covered these tables, where we stood to eat the best meal we had been offered in months. This was American food palatably cooked and seasoned. Seldom since leaving the States had we so keenly relished a meal as we did this first one at Camp Pontanezen.

The wastefulness we saw here was not characteristic of us in north Russia, where our tables were cleaned to the last crumb. Now we realized how negligent the authorities had been. More than one voiced my own pathetic remark, "Oh, if we'd only had this in north Russia!" (Brigadier General Smedley D. Butler, USMC, winner of two Medals of Honor, had been detailed to organize and make fit this vital camp and, as always, did an outstanding job. See Butler's biography, *Old Gimlet Eye,* by Lowell Thomas.)

Unaccustomed to a real bunk, I put in a restless night. But I was not assigned fatigue duty for tardiness at reveille, as were a number of my comrades who failed to get up on time. Except for a brief period of fatigue duty in the afternoon, I remained near our quarters reading and writing a dozen postcards showing scenes of Brest. While in Russia I was told that censorship had been lifted. Yet at least two of these cards sent to relatives were censored by Lieutenant Sears.

Feeding of the troops was well organized. We were required to go as a company unit for our meals and were always led by a sergeant— usually First Sergeant Comstock, who assembled us early. For breakfast we had bread, bacon, coffee, mush, and syrup. For dinner, bread, baked potatoes, beef, gravy, and coffee. For supper, bread, beans, spaghetti, pickles, jam, and coffee. So different from our own winter diet of bully beef, M&V, dried grass, and hardtack. Though bread and coffee were items with each meal, there were many types of bread and these varied from day to day.

If one was not satisfied with this menu, additional luxuries such as fruit, candy, and chocolate could be obtained from the Salvation Army located in a large building beside the mess area. There, tobacco, toilet articles, handkerchiefs, writing materials, and practically everything a soldier desired and needed was available.

The policy of permitting those not able to pay to help themselves made the Salvation Army exceptionally popular. Probably few were unscrupulous enough to take advantage of this. Similar organizations—the YMCA in particular—not operating on this policy were objects of scorn. Never did I hear anything but praise for the Salvation Army. DePue put it strikingly when he said, "The Salvation Army is the only army I'll ever join again!" Considering our attitude toward the army, this was the supreme compliment.

After midday chow we were taken to the delousing station for much needed baths and were inspected for venereal diseases. This was the first of a series of preparations for the homeward voyage. While we were bathing, our clothes were steamed to exterminate nits and cooties.

We were issued U.S. Army rifles and bayonets; a convenient method of returning them to the States. Then too, upon reaching home, what of the glamour of the conquering heroes without them? Executing the manual of arms with these, after nine months use of the Russian model, was at first embarrassingly awkward. With the long, ungainly piece we'd used in the far north we had developed a technique ridiculously *à la Russky* with a sprinkling of the Enfield manner—something characteristic of the Polar Bears and incapable of duplication. I never regained my proficiency in handling the American rifle. Instead of standing retreat we cleaned the Cosmoline from our rifles. We gladly turned in our heavy woolens for an issue of light underwear.

Soon after arriving we placed claims against our debtors. Ex-sergeant Frank Marten was compelled to make restitution. My four English pounds was settled for fifty-seven French francs.

We were lined up for another venereal and lice inspection. At least two of our company not rid of cooties had their armpits and pubic area shaved. Though the infernal itching was ever present I was confident I was rid of them. However, just before the rubber-gloved medico with his wooden spatula and group of officers approached me I raised my undershirt to my nipples for a preliminary check and found a full-grown cootie crawling across my chest. With a quick sweep of my hand I canceled his passage to America and saved myself the special shave. This was the last of the crawlers that for five months kept me in torment. For months after reaching home I was afflicted with that disagreeable itching sensation. (For the remainder of his life Carey would itch and scratch after entering a chicken coop or other building where lice might be present.)

After supper, while the sun was yet high, an excellent photograph of E Company was taken with a large panoramic camera. We were arranged in a series of concentric arcs. The 187 privates and corporals were placed in three double lines. With Lieutenant Baker, the company commander, and his officers—except Lieutenant Broer—seated in front and flanked by seven sergeants on a side, the group of 205 men was complete. All wore blouses and overseas caps. Lieutenant Baker wore the French *Legion of Honor* and the *croix de guerre* medals won in Russia.

As members of our squad returned in late afternoon, our tent became the scene of its usual noise and activity. Then McCarthy staggered in with considerable lack of grace. He was loquacious, his actions ridiculous, and he became the butt of crude jokes and coarse remarks.

Later, battalion inspection was inopportune for McCarthy, and unusual in both the hour and day, being the only inspection I participated in on a Sunday. Utterly immune to our advice to stay in the tent, he persisted in taking his place in our squad. First Sergeant Comstock was apprised of his condition. Efforts to induce him to return to the tent were in vain.

McCarthy vaguely realized his blunders almost as soon as he made them. He nearly struck a comrade when shouldering his rifle. He staggered and stumbled, invariably executing the commands incorrectly. Everyone was out of step except Mac. Once the entire company was headed in the wrong direction. I smiled to see him marching alone at one side of the company. Leemaster, at my side, was in paroxysms of suppressed laughter. The lieutenant recognized the symptoms and with a half-smothered remark had Mac hauled out of the ranks for an interview. If Lieutenant Baker tried to shield Mac, as I think he did, it proved impossible under the eyes of his superiors. Mac was promptly arrested and escorted to the guardhouse, where he did fatigue duty until the day before we sailed.

Monday forenoon we had an inspection—our last here—and suffered a hot march. We were issued new service stripes, and before nightfall many, including myself, had them sewed on. During the day I replaced the worn YMCA pocket Testament I read and carried most of the time since leaving the States.

A letter received this afternoon from Mother dated 27 May revealed mail service between home and France was little, if any, better than that with Russia.

Passes to visit Brest for the remainder of the day were issued about noon on 19 June. Few failed to take this opportunity. No doubt I was foolish not to go. On the advice of the first sergeant I secured my pass solely as an immunity from duty.

After dinner our barracks bags were brought in by trucks and dumped on the drill field, making it possible to secure necessities for the homeward voyage. While the trucks waited we hastily ransacked our well-packed bags. What confusion! I changed breeches. Others did likewise. Men stripped off their shirts and got into clean ones. After getting my hair cut I was ready for our departure.

Arrival of our service records, compiled by the company clerk and approved at regimental headquarters, was evidence we were to leave soon. Those having foreign money converted it into American currency. I had only a few francs. Leventhal, who had gambled or sold cigarettes, had large Russian notes amounting to thousands or tens of thousands of rubles.

I saw more French soldiers in Russia than in their native land, but the memory of one remains vivid. He was one of those unnamed heroes whose bravery and sacrifice helped defeat the enemy. I frequently saw him standing beside a post as we went to and from our meals. A lonely figure, tall and erect, neatly dressed in a light blue uniform and stiff officers' cap, he would have attracted attention anywhere. He was especially conspicuous, having lost both arms at the shoulder. Men generously tossed coins at his feet. Slipping his right foot from a low shoe, he picked them from the mud, gave them a dexterous flip with his toes, and invariably dropped them into a French army mess can suspended by a cord about his neck. We were most fortunate. With such a handicap, what charm had life?

When well-intentioned individuals attempt to mitigate the actions of ruthless Germany in precipitating this hellish war, I think of him and of my comrades who fell in north Russia, and entertain naught but reproach for the system and the nation that created such conditions.

As we stood in the rain and mud on our way to dinner I beheld another type—a young man in civilian dress. Not physically handicapped, he pursued a despicable trade. Furtively approaching us, he displayed packets of obscene pictures for sale.

A sergeant told me we would leave camp tomorrow, so I completed preparations by taking a bath. I retired happy. This was my last night in Camp Pontanezen.

Chapter 18
Homeward Bound Aboard USS *Von Steuben*
21 June to 29 June 1919

Saturday morning dawned clear and cool. Nature had saved this lovely day with bright sky beautifully decked with billowy silver clouds for our embarkation for the finest land on the face of a magnificent, though war-torn, globe.

During the forenoon, after thoroughly policing up our area, we rolled our heavy packs. Roll was called and Lieutenant Baker—properly leaving nothing to chance—lined us up to practice "the gangplank movement." An imitation gangplank was provided and we practiced boarding a number of times.

We were instructed to keep absolutely quiet on the way to the ship, not even to wave, and regardless of our attitude toward the country, its people, and their customs, to say and do nothing offensive till our vessel left port. This he emphasized. Some organization, he told us, had been recalled from their ship because of a disparaging remark or failure to comply with these instructions.

Roll call revealed that Corporal Damagalski, of Detroit, was missing. Search and inquiry failed to locate him. Many believed he was AWOL on a drunken spree. Lieutenant Baker swore and said, "This is one hell of a time to get drunk!"

On the way to the wharf the lieutenant made inquiries at two likely looking places, but Damagalski's disappearance remained a mystery.

After dinner we fell in with rifles and heavy packs, then marched to the docks where we had landed. A few civilians, including girls, were seen, but there was no demonstration for us. At the dock the Red Cross distributed cigarettes and other items. As we passed in single file through a narrow gateway we were checked off by an officer who called out our first names and middle initials; we responded with our surname. To his "Donald E.," I replied, "Carey." Thereupon we boarded a boat taking us to the USS *Von Steuben*. Aboard, we were led to deck D2; a hot, stuffy place equipped with individual steel bunks. Other units of the regiment were already aboard.

We were soon given two boat drills in case of fire or other disaster. At suppertime we were led below to a large mess hall where swinging tables hung from the ceiling. Standing beside these we ate a good meal of wieners, sauerkraut, potatoes, bread, and tea. Unlike the army's unsanitary system, clean, hot dishwater was provided for washing our mess kits.

After chow the ship's band assembled forward and treated us to an excellent concert. Scarcely a day passed without the band's contributing to making the voyage pleasant.

Prior to the war, the *Von Steuben* was the *Kronprinz Wilhelm*, owned and operated by the North German Lloyd Steamship Line. The outbreak of war in 1914 found the *Kronprinz Wilhelm* on the American side of the Atlantic. With Allied warships patrolling the coast she was likely to remain in port. After weeks of preparations, she slipped away from the Hoboken docks one night and began her career as a raider.

Over a month elapsed before she was sighted in West Indian waters coaling the German warship *Kaileuke*. On 26 September 1914 she sank the British steamer *Indian Prince*. A month later she destroyed the British *Bellivue* and the French *Montageh*. Unheard of for weeks at a time, she continued her depredations until by 12 April 1915 she had sunk sixteen vessels.

Pursued by warships off the coast of Virginia, she put in at Newport News for safety. Six of her officers and a like number of enlisted men escaped inland, later fleeing the country in the steam yacht *Eclipse,* which was claimed sunk by the cruiser HMS *Sydney* on 20 October 1915. To prevent her from again slipping out to sea in violation of international law, she was interned by the U.S. government on 4 May 1916.

On 4 February 1917, the day after President Wilson broke off diplomatic relations with Germany, the *Kronprinz Wilhelm* was seized by the United States. Her machinery and boiler rooms had been sabotaged by the German crew.

Fitted out as a U.S. Navy auxiliary cruiser and troop transport, her name was changed to *Von Steuben,* after the famous drillmaster of the Revolution who served the American cause. The repairing and remodeling continued into the fall of 1917. Five- and three-inch guns were mounted, and depth-charge racks were rigged on her stern.

Refitted, coaled, and with a coat of camouflage, she was ready for sea. Troops, nurses, hospital and aviation corpsmen, and trucks were taken aboard in Philadelphia before sailing to New York.

Von Steuben sailed from New York on 31 October 1917, forming up with a convoy before proceeding to Brest, France. Less than a day from port a U-boat's torpedo missed her bow by about two hundred feet. On the return trip she was only thirty miles from Halifax, Nova Scotia—to load coal—when one-tenth of that city was destroyed and 1,654 lives lost on 6 December 1917 by the explosion of a French munitions ship. After rendering assistance, she returned to Philadelphia, having experienced one of the roughest crossings in her history.

Von Steuben made nine trips to and from Brest before the Armistice. On her sixth voyage she carried the famous Naval Battery that did such effective work with their large naval rifles mounted on railway cars; on her eighth she carried the Thirteenth Regiment of Marines, commanded by Col. Smedley D. Butler, USMC.

After the Armistice the *Von Steuben* underwent remodeling as a transport to bring troops home. This was the finest, best-equipped, and fastest of the four ships I traveled on while in the service, and the only United States naval vessel I boarded. She was a four-stacker of 15,000 gross tons, 637 feet long with a beam of 66 feet, and propelled by twin screws. Her complement was 43 officers and 975 enlisted men.

On our homeward voyage, according to a paper published aboard, she carried 2,945 passengers. Among these were units of the 339th Infantry: 46 officers and 1,496 men. Except for 50 prisoners, the rest of the troops were casual units from France. Among the prisoners were Pvt. Harry Jones of E Company, whose attempted suicide resulted in the death of Cpl. Martin Campbell, and the demented chap who killed an English officer and set fire to the Smolny guardhouse.

On 22 June *Von Steuben* steamed out of Brest. The sea was calm. My elation knew no bounds until I was detailed to move heavy boxes in the hold. For a dollar I purchased six souvenir folders and sent them to relatives and friends. DePue bought a sixty-four-page booklet entitled "History of the *Von Steuben* and the Part She Played in the Great War."

For the next three days I was off duty. The lovely weather continued. Viewing the fascinating sea was far more pleasant than remaining in the hold. I never tired of watching its moods.

Of particular interest were the ship's numerous guns. The breeches with their delicate mechanisms were usually covered with close-fitting canvas jackets. But I saw them as they were cleaned and greased by the gun crews.

While I was on deck before breakfast we overtook and passed the USS *Montana*. Excepting a venereal inspection, nothing interfered with my leisure. Two schools of happy porpoise cut graceful arcs as they frolicked in the water. In the evening we met another transport headed for Europe.

I mailed a card to my parents and they received it on 2 July, postmarked "U.S. Navy, 25 June 1919." It arrived with my mail from France; evidence that *Von Steuben* carried our mail from Camp Pontanezen.

Thirteen men of our company were made privates first class. After signing the payroll I stepped to a table where Lieutenant Baker and an assistant were seated, and stated my surname. The lieutenant looked up and pleasantly said, "Donald E." Without doubt he knew the full name of every man in his command.

While in Camp Pontanezen we frequently saw troops wearing bright colored insignia, such as a red CD for the Custer Division; a red arrow for the Arrow Division; and a rainbow for the famous Rainbow Division. The colors and ornamental designs appealed to me. On our last day in camp we were given a badge representing a polar bear on ice. It could not be recognized without an explanation. I was disappointed. Many were contemptuous. Selected as the best of many competitive designs on paper, it fell far short on cloth and was soon discarded.

We were now issued our official regimental insignia: a white NR on a diamond-shaped field of dark blue and worn on the upper left shoulder of our blouse. It gave a distinctive air to our uniforms, already decorated with service stripes, and in some cases wound stripes. I took pride in wearing this sign of service in the far-flung battle lines of north Russia. Before mounting guard I turned in my steel helmet to be painted and got my insignia sewed on by the company tailor.

The monotony of my guard duty from 0900 to 1100 was relieved by watching the sailors' Saturday inspection in their neat white uniforms. I could barely suppress a smile at their difficulty in forming up in two lines, which were ridiculously far from straight. Our outfit in its crudest days did it quicker and better. We met a battleship and a one-stacker as I came off guard.

My white-painted helmet was returned with RUSSIA neatly printed in blue capital letters across its crown.

German delegates signed the Treaty of Versailles on the fifth anniversary of the assassination at Sarajevo that precipitated the war. Isolated, except by wireless, we received the glad tidings and paid fitting homage. About 1600 a battery of two one-pound guns at the stern fired a salute of twenty-one guns. Sailors eagerly seized the shell casings as souvenirs. Two flags were hoisted and the band played.

Beautiful whitecaps in ceaseless motion covered the dark blue water on Sunday, 29 June. The ship rolled and pitched. Some hurried to the rail. I became light-headed and felt mean. Probably the Negro troops suffered most. I went into the hold where they lay about listlessly. Their faces, usually jovial and animated, registered indifference and commiseration. None were singing. Few were talking.

Among the three civilians aboard was the famous American sculptor Lorado Taft, whom I saw standing by the rail on the upper deck reserved for officers. The morning breeze was cool and he wore a dark overcoat; it contrasted unfavorably with our uniforms.

We were subjected to another venereal and vermin inspection.
Late in the evening we approached American waters. Our enthusiasm was high and there was much activity. As our ship glided silently
in the dark, I sat on deck with DePue and Ottney. The sea breeze
was too cool for comfort as we talked and viewed the thousands of
lights along the south shore of Long Island.

The *Von Steuben* dropped anchor at about 2300. We turned in for
our last night aboard a ship (29 June 1919).

Chapter 19
Home—At Last!
30 June to 7 July 1919

We were up early on Monday, 30 June, to watch our ship dock. All eagerly viewed the harbor scenes. Everywhere there was an air of expectancy, as one might see among children at Christmas. Joy and anticipation showed on every face. Men were jubilant.

I was disappointed to be one of a small detail to clean our quarters. It was accomplished in haste. We were recalled to finish what we had slighted. I reached the weather deck in time to see the Statue of Liberty come into view at 0830. The men cheered, yelled, waved their hats, hugged each other, slapped one another on the back, and danced for joy. It was the supreme moment—the climax of our military career. At no other time did I see such emotions. There were faint indications of it when we captured Kodish. To all, this was a great moment. With suppressed emotion and little outward expression of my happiness, I viewed with delight the Statue of Liberty, its surroundings, and the demonstration aboard.

Among the various craft in the harbor was a flag-bedecked launch filled with a band and a delegation of Detroit people to welcome Detroit's Own. We were greeted with music and considerable cheering and waving as the boat circled the *Von Steuben*. Among the pieces played was "JaDa," a recently published fox-trot that I first heard aboard the *Czar* while bound for France. The delegation was a welcome sight; their ovation, gratifying. The ceremony reminded me of the farewell given the American battleship at Brest.

Passing the Statue of Liberty, the *Von Steuben* slowly proceeded up the Lower Hudson River and docked at Pier 3, Hoboken, New Jersey. About 1100 E Company, in heavy marching order, disembarked. How good it was to again be in America. None but a home-returning soldier could fully realize it.

We marched aboard a ferry and went upstream. Coming off the ferry we were met by representatives of the YMCA, Knights of Columbus, Salvation Army, and Jewish Welfare Board. These men gave us useful articles and provided stamped postal cards. I received a khaki handkerchief marked in one corner *K of C;* from each of the others, a postal card. These I hastily filled in and addressed to my parents. There was doubt as to where we were going. I filled one out, "Going to Camp Mills," and the two others, "Going to Camp Merritt." Through the Salvation Army I sent Father a brief telegram that reached him 5 July.

We were given coffee, biscuits, apples, chocolate, pie, and ice cream. Such delicacies, scarcely seen for more than a year, had become luxuries.

Finally, ordered to fall in, we marched to a train that took us to Dumont in northeastern New Jersey. Detraining, we marched along a dirt road to Camp Merritt. Though the route was short it seemed long, for the day was hot and we were in heavy marching order. As the road turned slightly, from my position at the right of the column I had an excellent view of the outfit ascending a slight incline beyond the turn. It was the most beautiful marching I saw during the war. The company was in column of fours and every movement, whether shoulder, leg, or arm, was in perfect cadence. The white-painted steel helmets attached to the middle of our heavy packs were conspicuous, and moving in perfect unison emphasized the precision of our marching.

Reaching Camp Merritt about 1400, we were assigned to a wartime barracks similar to those at Camp Custer. Practically deserted, the place was quiet and dull. However, we appreciated its shade trees and the ice cream that could be purchased at a nearby canteen. We were soon taken to a delousing station, inspected, ordered to bathe, then moved to another barracks.

Not knowing when we might be called out, many of us did not unroll our packs and slept uncomfortably on steel cots without blankets. We did not undress and used our blouses as a cover.

Late in the afternoon a newspaper correspondent came into camp. Corporal Naugzemis, knowing I kept a diary, brought him to see me. He expressed a keen desire to obtain my record. I refused. He asked about our experiences and was particularly interested in our reactions rather than in the fighting. We talked freely concerning everything except criticism of our officers. A couple men stated that some officers were intoxicated in action. I declined to say anything, except praise for Major Nichols, whom everyone agreed was upright, efficient, and competent.

Detroit Free Press 1 July 1919
339TH TROOPS BARELY AVOID DRIFTING MINE

Veterans also pass through 80 miles of dangerous ice while making trip from North Russia to French Port.

1,119 Wolverines come with detachment of 1,540 reaching U.S.

Soldiers will arrive in city for big celebration July 4; Men bring back first white helmets ever seen in U.S.

After breakfast we returned to the barracks, where other E Company men were unpacking the large boxes filled with souvenirs of the war. I arrived just in time; my one-pound shells and box of letters were in view. I mailed them to my parents. Troops who had not been in Russia endeavored to buy the one-pound shells for as much as ten dollars apiece. Corporal Hahn's were stolen.

Considerable excitement was created just before dusk by the order for all Camp Grant, Camp Taylor, and Camp Sherman men to fall out with full equipment. Men inducted at these camps had been sent to Camp Custer and assigned to E Company. They were now returning to their home area camps. We all turned out to bid them farewell.

From my squad Corporal Naugzemis and privates first class Noone and Waterstreet left. Amid much sincere handshaking, clever remarks, hilarity, and best wishes they left for camps near Chicago, Louisville, and Chillicothe.

July second passed languidly. At dusk we were still in camp. Faith that we would leave neared the breaking point. At last the welcome order to move was received. Falling out in heavy marching order, we left the barracks at 2215 and proceeded to Dumont, then boarded a long passenger train that pulled out about 2245. Despite the cramped quarters many men tried to sleep. Some gambled much of the night.

About 0745 we stopped at Syracuse, New York, Cpl. James Catellani's hometown. His mother and sister were at the depot and he got off to greet them, reboarding at 0800 when we departed.

Occasionally I saw the Erie Canal, various rivers and lakes, mountains, farms, and villages; all absorbing my interest. Crossing the Niagara River into Niagara, Ontario, we entered Canada about 1500. At Windsor our train stopped and an electric engine was connected to take us through the great tunnel under the Detroit River.

At 2045 (3 July 1919) we emerged in Detroit. I was out of Russia, off foreign soil, and in the city, state, and country of my nativity. Guards were posted around the train. Leaving rifles and packs on our seats, we quickly detrained and were fed supper by the Red Cross.

I was among the last to be fed. At the impatient insistence of Ottney, DePue, and Hahn, I hurried to catch up with them. As we walked up the middle of the dirt street Father casually, but suddenly and unexpectedly, appeared. This was so unanticipated that I could scarcely accept its reality. We greeted each other with a handshake and a kiss. Having been separated for nearly a year, each felt the occasion with emotion. Then he shook hands with my comrades, whom he had met in 1918 at Camp Custer.

From former neighbors my people learned that my name was on the list of men landing at Hoboken. So Father and Mother drove his Dodge to Charlotte, where Mother remained with her sister, and Father took the morning train to Detroit. After booking a hotel, he waited near where we were to be fed.

We were temporarily released from army restrictions. Rumor had it that we were to depend upon the hospitality of Detroit's citizens. My apprehensions vanished when I learned Father had a room for us at the Norton Hotel. After some wait we were taken to the hotel in an auto driven by a civilian—one of many men who volunteered these considerate acts.

In our room we swapped experiences and I was assured that all was well with Mother. I was denouncing in my account of the past year's events. Though tired, I found it difficult to rest in a real bed.

July fourth, 1919, dawned propitiously. A lovely morning of a cloudless day that became hot. A glorious Fourth of July, and how glorious it was for our uniformed men, bronzed by the hardships of a cold winter of Arctic warfare. Though weary of marching and tired of parades, we were glad to be back—back to be feted and to bask in the warmth of the city's gratitude and admiration. And how glorious it was for Detroit. Her regiment, the 339th—Detroit's Own—was back from a long campaign on foreign soil; back to receive the hospitable welcome of a gracious city, a happy state, and a grateful nation.

I anticipated this day with great pleasure. Accordingly I got up about 0530. We enjoyed a light breakfast of hash and eggs. Then Father went to the city hall, to be taken by the reception committee to Belle Isle.

After being shaved at a barber shop near the new Michigan Central Depot, I joined the men of my outfit assembling with other companies in the large area in front of the depot.

Soon a neatly uniformed civilian band arrived. The tall bandmaster, carrying a shiny baton and wearing a tall shako that accentuated his height, was most conspicuous. Led by the band, we marched with belts, rifles, blouses, and sheathed bayonets to a ferry that took us to Belle Isle. I enjoyed this short ride on the Detroit River, but somewhat resented having my path strewn with flowers by girls when we set foot on the isle. Our systematic disembarkation was immediately converted into a parade along a winding road lined with thousands of civilians.

That was followed by a tedious inspection, where medals and decorations were conferred on a few men whose daring and bravery had been notable. Standing at attention in the sweltering sun while dressed in woolen blouses was an ordeal. I saw four men fall to the ground.

The ceremony finally ended. We were dismissed with orders to appear at the depot in the morning. I found Father, who, rather than endure the oppressive heat to see the parade and inspection, had rested in one of the tents provided for the comfort of guests. I was disappointed.

While we were talking, a slender, dark-complexioned man of perhaps forty-five years and of medium height appeared and inquired if I knew a certain soldier. In a happy mood I said, "I know everyone in E Company and he's not in our outfit." I was about to turn to Father, when he asked if I knew Lloyd Robinson. Scrutinizing him closely, I finally recognized Mother's adopted brother. Uncle Lloyd had changed greatly in the thirteen years since last seeing him. Father enjoyed a good laugh at my expense.

Then I learned how Father, too, had been surprised. Lloyd had seen my name in the list of those returning to Detroit, and believing Father would meet me, searched the registers of Detroit hotels and located Father in the last one. When Father returned from breakfast Lloyd approached and shook hands, but not until he laughed did Father recognize him.

No feature of our reception by the people of Detroit, who did everything possible for us, was more satisfying to me than the excellent fried chicken dinner on Belle Isle. It was the first chicken I had eaten in nearly a year. I indulged in a second ample helping.

Then Father, Lloyd, and I joined a large crowd, chiefly civilians, assembled in front of the casino to hear an address by Sen. Hiram Johnson of California. If, as reputed, his vigorous efforts were responsible for getting us out of Russia, and the western camp troops withdrawn from Siberia, it was appropriate that he be the speaker of the day. The address was neither long nor inspiring. I would rather have seen President Wilson.

Late in the afternoon we left Belle Isle, boarded a streetcar, and located a restaurant; guests had not been fed. Lloyd left us and Father and I returned to the Norton Hotel, where we obtained better quarters. I turned over to Father most of my money and souvenirs. I took a bath in a real bathtub, the first I'd been in since entering the army.

We got up at 0530 and after breakfast went to the new Michigan Central Depot, where Lloyd joined us. We bade Father good-bye as he took the 0800 train for Charlotte. Soon Lloyd left and I boarded our troop train, which pulled out about 1000.

Though many of the men were from Detroit, they were obliged to return to Camp Custer for their discharges. Some members of E Company missed this train and took the next one without punishment.

We arrived at Camp Custer about 1400. Assigned to barracks, we made ourselves at home. This was not the hurly-burly camp we lived in a year ago. Now there was a listless atmosphere, which left time for homesickness. The glamour of war was gone.

In the afternoon I was detailed to work in the "discharge mill." I was assigned a pen-pushing task writing discharges for soldiers about to sever their connection with Uncle Sam's greatest "no man's army." This consisted of filling out a form with the discharge on one side and the enlistment record on the other.

Taking a seat behind one of a series of long tables placed end to end, and with a large group, I went to work filling in the blank forms for a lengthy line of eager men waiting with their service records.

Sunday, 6 July 1919, was hot and clear. I wrote discharges all day. "U. of M., Jr. Lit., (name), Negro, etc." Thus in three lines did I make one of the briefest records of any single day while in the army.

For those of us in the discharge mill there was little opportunity to loaf. Regardless of the day, Uncle Sam was anxious to return his many soldiers to civilian life and the pursuit of peace.

On Monday the seventh I returned to the discharge mill. Finishing the work, I was released during the forenoon. A chap from another company wrote my discharge and I wrote his. Then I presented it to Lieutenant Baker and Major Nichols for signing.

No meal except breakfast.

We waited in line to be paid. Lack of funds held us up until late afternoon. It was said that a car was sent to Kalamazoo for money. Battle Creek is nearer and more plausible. At 2045 I was paid $299.39.

I was addressed as Mr. Carey. It sounded strange. It took a moment to realize that though in uniform, I was a civilian. Nevertheless, I was still under army authority for another twenty-four hours.

Having turned in my equipment Saturday afternoon, I had only my barracks bag. I was one of the last, if not the last, of the E Company privates to leave. Upon leaving the barracks I shook hands and bid farewell to 1st Sgt. George E. Comstock. I did not see him again until 30 May—Memorial Day—1930 (at military burial services for Polar Bears returned from Russia).

I started to walk to Battle Creek and was overtaken by a young couple, and with two other ex-soldiers was given a ride. I induced the couple to take me to the Grand Trunk Depot and paid him a dollar—at his protest.

My train left Battle Creek about 2210 and arrived in Charlotte at 2250. At the Michigan Central Depot I telephoned Father, telling him, "I'm a free man!" then talked with Mother for the first time in over a year.

Father's car was at the farm, so Max came after me. While waiting I enjoyed some ice cream.

At 0020 (8 July 1919) I arrived at home and greeted the folks— Mother in particular, as I had seen Dad in Detroit. I had been away one year and six hours to the minute.

Though tired, we visited until late and retired about 0145—after conducting a cootie inspection. Father said it was just my imagination. I slept on the floor.

At the time I would have happily sold the whole experience for fifty cents. Now it couldn't be bought for ten thousand dollars.

It was a great experience.

Editor's Note:
Numerous men and officers of the ANREF were recognized for their courageous service in north Russia, including twenty-three who won the *Distinguished Service Cross,* the United States' second highest award for extraordinary heroism.

Foreign decorations, in addition to decorations previously noted, awarded to officers most closely associated with E Company, 339th Infantry, for their conduct of the entire campaign:
Col. George E. Stewart, 339th Infantry, *French Legion of Honor.*
Maj. J. Brooks Nichols, 339th Infantry, *French Legion of Honor.*
Maj. J. Brooks Nichols, 339th Infantry, *French croix de guerre.*
Maj. J. Brooks Nichols, 339th Infantry, *British Distinguished Service Order.*

Maj. J. Brooks Nichols, 339th Infantry, *Russian St. Vladimir with Swords and Ribbons.*

Maj. Michael J. Donoghue. 339th Infantry, *Russian St. Vladimir with Swords and Ribbons.*

Conclusion

***Detroit Free Press* 1 July 1919**

New York, June 30—Describing the record of the 339th, Major J. Brooks Nichols, commander, gave out the following statement today:

"The American troops left the United States July 22, 1918, and arrived in Liverpool August 4, 1918. They were detached from the 85th Division and encamped at Stoney Castle, England. They left Newcastle August 26, and arrived at Archangel September 4, 1918.

"On leaving England no one seemed to have any definite idea as to just why American troops were being sent to North Russia, but soldiers do not ask questions, and the information finally leaked out, from what source no one seems to know, that the mission of the North Russian expedition was as follows:

"First, to guard war material and supplies at Archangel, sold by the Allies to the old Imperial government of Russia.

"Second, to prevent the Germans from coming through Finland and South Russia and establishing a submarine base on the White Sea or on the Murmansk coast.

"Third, to assist the Russians in re-establishing the eastern front and in reorganizing their own army, thus diverting some of the Germans' attention from the western front.

"One battalion of Royal Scots and another of French Colonial troops had arrived about a month before. On their coming the Bolsheviki fled, after looting the town, taking with them everything of value they could carry.

"All the military stores that were supposed to be there, which were to be guarded by the American troops, had vanished. The city had the appearance of having been gone through thoroughly by a large gang of professional burglars. All the boats, the railroad rolling stock, ammunition, guns, food supplies, hardware, etc., which could possibly be dragged away, were gone.

"The Scots and French, assisted by about sixty sailors from the USS *Olympia,* then at Murmansk, lost no time in pursuing the Bolsheviki and, though the Allies succeeded in pushing them back about 100 miles from Archangel, it was not without severe losses, so, when the American troops arrived, it might be said that there were two fronts, one on the Dvina River and the other on the Archangel-Vologda railroad, both thinly held by a handful of troops who had been fighting for a month without relief, who were worn out, tired, and without power to continue further or to hold without reinforcements.

"Archangel is the greatest lumber port in the world. In peace times it boasted of from 50,000 to 75,000 inhabitants. When the American troops arrived, it was flooded with 75,000 refugees. Business had ceased. There was no food except fish and fish products. Ten pounds of sugar or a sack of flour would buy a silver fox worth $5,000 in the United States, but the question was where to get the sugar or flour.

"The people were virtually starving. There was no coin money. Paper money of all varieties and makes, from imperial prints and Kerensky issues to the provincial paper of Archangel, was plentiful, but it would buy nothing, for there was nothing to buy. A ruble was worth about ten cents. There was no work of any kind going on, and all the people had to do was walk the streets and figure out some new way to revolt.

"The country surrounding Archangel is one vast forest and swamp—swamp of the variety that sucked up those lost legions of Russia in the early days of the great war. Except along the streams, the country is sparsely settled. Here and there one finds a small clearing inhabited by a few wood cutters or trappers and perhaps a few peasants. It is indeed a forest primeval, with untapped treasures beyond the dream of man.

"Immediately after the Bolsheviki departed from Archangel a provincial government was set up, virtually the same as under the Kerensky regime. A few days after the Americans arrived this Provincial government was kidnapped by a Russian colonel named Chaplan (Grigori E. Chaplan, an ex-Imperial Russian Navy captain), taken aboard a boat and shipped out into the White Sea. By this coup Chaplan hoped to place in power some of his friends. David R. Francis, the American ambassador, interposed in words both strong and full of meaning and forced Chaplan to return the 'government.'

"Meantime the streetcar employees had struck in protest against the kidnapping and at once the Americans were operating the car system as if they had been there all their lives. When the 'government' was returned the strikers went back to work.

"This government endeavored to co-operate with the Allies. There seemed to be an impression among some who had been in Russia that the mere sight of Allied troops, with food, would cause the Russians to scramble wildly in a rush to arms against the Bolsheviki who, it was stated, were being urged on by German propagandists. Such evidently had been the report to the Allied supreme command in France.

"But the Russians did not rush to arms; there was no scramble. There wasn't even a flurry.

"The English had sent up probably 500 or more officers and as many noncoms to organize this vast Russian army that was to spring to arms at the sight of the Allies and didn't spring. The feelers of the pulse of Russia merely had made another bad guess.

"The truth is that the average Russian was pretty well fed up on fighting. He'd been through the war on the eastern front and a couple revolutions thrown in, and he couldn't see where he had benefited materially and he wasn't exactly what you would call enthusiastic.

"Also a great many of the people were either Bolsheviki at heart or enthused with Bolshevist tendencies.

"This new-found freedom was something they couldn't understand. What they wanted was enough grub to live on and no work to do. They also had a misgiving as to just why the Allies were in Russia.

"About halfway to Archangel from Newcastle, an influenza epidemic began in the American forces. Thirty to fifty men in each company were seriously ill. The men were taken to (British) hospitals and in some instances had to sleep on bare floors with insufficient blankets. About 70 died the first two weeks in September.

"In England, all American rifles and automatics had been taken away and the Americans armed with Russian rifles, which the boys said would 'shoot around a corner.' These rifles were far inferior to the American or English Enfields, and the men had little confidence in them; they jammed and broke and were inaccurate. Each man had shot this rifle just ten times on the range in England when he arrived in Russia. The Americans had no automatic arms, no grenades, no trench mortars, no one-pounders, nothing with which to fight except the Russian rifle.

"With this equipment and weakened by influenza, the American troops were sent out to fight, not with a month's training, or a week's rest, or even a day's respite, but loaded directly from the boats into boxcars and tugs and shipped to the front.

"Many of these boys had been drafted in the middle of June, 1918, and had spent one month of their short army careers on the high seas. The third battalion, first to debark, was immediately sent to the railroad front. Within a few days two companies were detached and ordered to the left flank, where they established the Kodish front on the Petrograd road. The first battalion was sent down the Dvina River and was divided at Bereznik, a portion advancing further down the Dvina, the other part moving south on the Vega River.

"H Company was sent to Onega, and a portion of G Company to Pinega. Thus six fronts were established, forming a semicircle around Archangel, with a circumference of about 500 miles and a radius of from 120 to 300 miles.

"Besides the Americans, there were on these fronts, Russians, French, Polish, British, and Canadian troops in small numbers. The total on all the fronts in North Russia then did not exceed 8,000, with possibly 2,000 more at the bases and in the service of supply. In October, 2,000 British reinforcements arrived.

"Up to the Armistice, the operations may be summarized as consisting of a general advance on all fronts from 20 to 75 miles, the ground gained being held on nearly all fronts. The signing of the Armistice meant nothing to the Yanks fighting in North Russia. No word came from France or the United States defining the position of their forces in Russia. There was no Armistice celebration.

"Arctic winter, biting snow and cold swooped over the land. It was useless to try and proceed without aid, and the policy became to hold what had been taken until reinforcements should come and to get troops under some kind of shelter to combat the rigors of the climate.

"The Bolsheviki had asserted that when winter came on they would drive the Allies into the White Sea. And they might have carried off their boast. They made several efforts.

"To shorten the lines, the Allies planned a general offensive on the Onega railroad and the Seletskoe fronts December 31, 1918. On December 30, some Russians who were on the railroad front deserted to the 'Bolos' and gave away the entire plans.

"Before zero hour the next morning, the Bolo was pounding the fronts with everything he had and after a few costly advances, it was decided to call off the attack. Shortly after the first of the year the enemy got reinforcements and concentrated them on the Vega front whose outposts were about 20 versts south of Shenkursk.

"About April 1, the Bolo began a general offensive attacking both the railroad front south of Obozerskaya and on the new front which had been established just east of Bolshie Ozerki. The main effort was on the Bolshie Ozerki front, where M Company bore the brunt of four day's fighting.

"Though at times surrounded and cut off, they finally succeeded in beating back the Bolsheviki. The attacks on the railway front and on the position east of Obozerskaya having also failed, the Bolo began gradually to withdraw from Bolshie Oz-erki, which he finally evacuated.

"Having been defeated on all fronts, the Bolo seemed content to take it easy and the Americans were in no engagements after May 1, 1919."

New York Times 1 July 1919

339TH SAY MUTINY CHARGE IS FALSE. OFFICERS AND MEN RETURNING FROM ARCHANGEL ASSERT INCIDENT WAS EXAGGERATED.

The 339th Infantry, one company of which was reported to have mutinied in Archangel in April as a result of the Red propaganda, returned yesterday on the transport *Von Steuben*, and its officers and enlisted men were unanimous in branding the charge as unfounded, although they admitted there had been much dissatisfaction in the ranks. They said it was true that the enlisted men had demanded from their officers the reason for being kept in northern Russia, but maintained they had a right to do so. One enlisted man summed it up thus:

"If Senator Hiram Johnson and others can ask such questions in the Senate, why shouldn't we, the ones involved, ask them. And we did, and that is all there is to it."

Major J. Brooks Nichols of Detroit, Mich., commander of the 46 officers and 1,495 members of the regiment who returned on the *Von Steuben*, said the incident which inspired the report that there had been a mutiny had been exaggerated. "I have heard more bunk about this alleged mutiny than could be written in a dozen books," he said. "The incident which gave rise to the rumors was a misunderstanding between a sergeant and one of the privates. The men of the 339th are the best disciplined and the most courageous of any outfit I know, and all any officer could desire."

Major Nichols declared that conditions in northern Russia were chaotic, and no one could prophesy the future. The better classes were hoping that the Bolsheviki would eventually hang themselves if given enough rope.

Captain H. G. Winslow of I Company said he was very anxious to clear up the stigma which his command received by the reports of the mutiny. He said: "There was positively no mutiny.

Statements which my boys had read in newspapers received from the United States caused them to question their officers as to the reason they were being held in Russia. The feeling that nobody knew just why we were there spread among the men. Then Colonel Stewart explained at length to them that what we came there for originally could be summed up in four points. These four reasons, he said, were: First, to guard the huge stores of war materials and supplies at Archangel which had been sold by the Allies to the old Russian Government; second, to prevent the Germans from coming through Finland and South Russia and establishing submarine bases on the White Sea and Murmansk coast; third, to assist the Russians in re-establishing the eastern front and reorganizing their own army, thus diverting some of the attention of the Germans from the western front; fourth, to assist the Czechoslovaks.

"The argument between the Sergeant and the private, which started the mutiny story, was a trivial incident. The noncommissioned officer ordered a Polish boy to load a truck. Because of his lack of knowledge of the English language, the boy refused to obey the orders which had been given to him. Later, after the order had been explained to him by officers of the company, the soldier readily loaded the truck. That was the nearest to a mutiny that we had.

"Captain Winslow said that the men of the 339th were amused by the report that they had served in Siberia. Where they did serve, he said, was at Archangel, protecting the Vologda Railroad, in the northern Russia district. He said the weather was intensely cold, and no one could blame the soldiers for complaining, as they frequently experienced days when the thermometer registered 50 degrees below zero. Food conditions were not exactly satisfactory, he said.

The 339th went to Archangel in September from Newcastle, England. When they arrived at their destination they found that the Bolsheviki forces had fled, leaving the inhabitants virtually starving to death, according to officers of the contingent. They said they set up a provisional government along the lines of Kerensky's. The returning soldiers were loud in their praise of the YMCA and Red Cross. "We do not know what the "Y" has been doing on other fronts," one officer said, "but they certainly did treat us right. The YMCA also won a place in our hearts when they erected a Hostess House for us."

Detroit Free Press 2 July 1919
UNANIMOUSLY ACCEPT INVITATION TO JOIN THE AMERICAN LEGION
Returned Archangel Battlers of 339th Infantry Announce "Open Warfare Against Reds in the United States."

Camp Merritt, July 1—"Detroit's Own" today launched open warfare against bolshevism in the United States.

Having had plenty of experience with the Russian type of Reds, these veterans of the 339th Infantry have decided to join the American Legion en masse, for the sole purpose of delivering a knockout to the Bolshevists here.

Major J. Brooks Nichols says that on the voyage across from Brest he explained to all the Archangel veterans, by platoons, that one of the platforms of the American Legion was to stamp out bolshevism in America. They vociferously informed him that they wanted to join the legion.

Upon learning the extent to which Bolshevist propaganda had spread in their own country, several members of I Company, which was wrongly branded as a mutinous unit, said they were ready to take up arms against the enemy at home if necessary.

Upon learning the extent to which they had been advertised in this country as mutinous soldiers, members of I Company today were furious, particularly Private John Petrowskas, of 385 Thirty-third Street, Detroit, who identified himself as the man who misunderstood an order issued by Sergeant Whitney McQuire, of 319 Selden Avenue, Detroit, March 30, when the alleged mutiny was reported to have taken place.

Detroit Free Press 4 July 1919
HERE ARE THE TALES THE BOYS OF THE 339TH TELL
Home from Tsardom!
Thursday night he ceased to be a figure marching on for

endless versts in blinding snow, the silent figure in the daily cable from Archangel. Russia can have its Tolstoy and vodka. He'll take the Saturday Evening Post and 2 percent.

Behind him was the land of hairy students and Kerensky and isms and Sviatogor and ice over boot-tops and Rasputin and cigarettes at five bucks a pack.

Here are some of the things the doughboys of the 339th infantry did and said and saw, as they told them in the tumultuous train-shed:

The patrol was out. Twenty miles away was the nearest town, Shenkursk. A hundred yards away unfriendly eyes slanted along rifle barrels. It was a little before midnight when a lieutenant arrived where Corporal Max Troutner was on post.

They damned war together.

"What would you do in case of attack?" It was the lieutenant's question. Troutner's everlasting humor was one cause of Company A's sustained high morale.

Troutner looked out into the shadows. "I'd holler, 'Corporal of the guard'—just twice, once here and once in Shenkursk."

The lieutenant, chuckling, started to go.

"Just tell the boys," Troutner said, in parting, "when you go back, not to shoot if they see a cloud of snow coming down the middle of the road, for I'll be in the center of it."

Frank Gray, private, of Fair Haven (Michigan), was talking. He hadn't seen an electric light from October to March.

"What else was missing that you were accustomed to?" a Red Cross woman asked.

"Smoke. We didn't see anything that made smoke outside of cannon. If there was anything running by steam, we never got a glimpse of it.

"And them Russians ain't got no pride. I'm telling you. They can fight, yes, but when a man and his wife is coming down the road and there's a load to carry the woman is carrying it."

I Company was credited with a mutiny some time ago. I Company says: "We kicked like hell, but we didn't mutiny."

Here's the story they tell:

"The men complained for a long time because they did not understand why there was fighting in Russia when the war was over. Late last March I Company was ordered to entrain at Archangel for the front. When the top sergeant transmitted the instructions to the men in barracks they refused to don their packs.

"Why in hell are we here?" somebody roared.

The "top kick," not being any favored visitor at general headquarters, couldn't answer. He sent for Captain Winslow, in command of the second train to reach the city Thursday night. Winslow, in turn, passed the buck to Colonel Stewart.

It was morning. Stewart lined the men up.

"What is it, boys?" he asked.

Some unidentified man in the ranks spoke up.

"What are we fighting for anyhow, Colonel?"

"Well, the United States hasn't declared war, so I guess you're fighting to save your own lives."

The colonel asked if there was anything else. There wasn't. I Company strapped on its packs and went forward. And it stayed four days, being subjected to a fair pounding. Within 48 hours the company fought off a superior force outnumbering them seven to one.

There is no attempt on the part of the officers to deny that the men were highly dissatisfied because they had to fight in Russia.

Men of G Company were authority for the statement that artillery shells made in Detroit had been used against them by the Bolsheviki forces. Empty shell cases were offered as proof.

Tribute to the fighting power of the Bolshevists was unstinting and unqualified.

A Company testified to the courage of the foe in strong terms. At one time, according to the men of the 339th, in a battle of four days and five nights the Bolshevists drove ahead across a clear space in three feet of snow in spite of artillery and

Browning gun fire that swept them in the face, and they straightened and held their line.

Private Geren, of E Company, and the Russian schoolteacher he won as a bride, were left behind at Brest. Army authorities promised them passage on another boat than that on which the 339th sailed.

In all, seven members of the 339th found heartmates in northern Russia.

There was an idea the 339th might appear emaciated, but they are hard looking, fit and bronzed from the rigors of winter winds as they trooped off the trains with "Russia" lettered in blue on their white helmets.

"Is the war over?" "When did it end?" they shouted.

Some musical anathemas were directed at the tobacco furnished in Russia. They mostly got British product. One made was stamped "Prize Medal." It was like waterlogged rope.

"An' then," said a solemn-faced buck private, "they began to send us some that were not made by purveyors to the king, and, boy, you can't imagine what those were like!"

Afterword

Major J. Brooks Nichols told the homeward-bound men of the 339th Infantry that one of the platforms of the American Legion was to stamp out bolshevism in the United States. Having witnessed the effects of bolshevism in Russia, many members of the 339th joined the American Legion. Carey remained a proud legionnaire throughout his life.

In September 1920 Donald Carey married Mildred Granger. Instead of "staying down on the farm"—as he daydreamed while in Russia—he resumed his teaching career in the fall of 1921 and soon became a school superintendent. Finally, Carey achieved that dream in 1936, when the family moved to their recently purchased farm near Vermontville, Michigan.

It is not known how many of the Polar Bears marched on Washington, DC, with the Bonus Expeditionary Force (Bonus Army) in the summer of 1932. The bonus law of 1924 had awarded all veterans a certificate payable in 1945. Due to the depression, these unemployed veterans could not wait, and the bonus was paid during the mid-thirties. Carey used his bonus to buy farm equipment.

When the ANREF departed north Russia in 1919 they brought with them more than a hundred of their comrades' bodies. Bodies of 121 soldiers remained buried on land retaken by the Bolsheviks. After prolonged diplomatic negotiations, and financed by the Michigan Legislature and, finally, a $70,000 congressional appropriation, the Veterans of Foreign Wars was permitted to enter Russia as a pri-

vate agency in August 1929. During a three-month search in cemeteries, forests, swamps, and the front yards of peasant homes*,
eighty-six bodies were recovered. Eleven were buried in Europe at
the request of relatives. On 28 November 1929 the SS *President Roosevelt* arrived in Hoboken, New Jersey, with seventy-five bodies;
twenty-six remain unidentified. Some were interred in Arlington and
other national cemeteries. A special train conveying the remaining
bodies to Detroit was honored along the route.

On Memorial Day, 1930, fifty of the Polar Bears were buried with
full military honors at White Chapel Memorial Cemetery, Troy,
Michigan (near Detroit). These were the last Polar Bears to come
home. An impressive white stone monument of a polar bear—with
teeth bared and guarding a fallen cross topped with a helmet—dom-
inates their portion of the cemetery.

World War I—the Great War—failed to "end all wars." The Carey's
only child, Neil, born 1922, served in the enlisted and officer ranks
of the U.S. Navy throughout World War II and the Korean War. A
grandson served with the U.S. Army in Vietnam.

Donald E. Carey died of a heart attack on 23 April 1945—exactly
five years after his son joined the U.S. Navy.

*The searchers reported that the Russian homes were still vermin in-
fested.